THE COMPLETE GUIDE TO
LIVING TOGETHER

Tobe Aleksander is a writer and broadcaster on consumer issues. A professional adviser, she has worked with the Citizens Advice Bureau (CAB). She also teaches negotiation, assertiveness and communication skills. Her first book, *The Assertive Consumer – An Everyday Survival Guide to Your Rights at Home, Work and in the High Street*, was published in 1990. Tobe lives in London with her lawyer husband and their three cats.

The Complete Guide to Living Together

Tobe Aleksander

HEADLINE

To Nicholas, for his continued love,
respect and support

First published in 1992
by HEADLINE BOOK PUBLISHING PLC

10 9 8 7 6 5 4 3 2 1

ISBN 0 7472 3739 5

Phototypeset by Intype, London

Printed and bound in Great Britain by
Harper Collins Manufacturing, Glasgow

HEADLINE BOOK PUBLISHING PLC
Headline House, 79 Great Titchfield Street, London W1P 7FN

CONTENTS

How to Use This Book

Modern relationships are on the move. Gone are the days when a couple got engaged, wed and then, more often than not, stayed married until death did them part. Cohabitation, single parenting and divorce are all part of the 1990s culture. Unfortunately, tradition, custom and the law have not always caught up.

This book deals with the unromantic side of relationships – your legal rights, money, a roof over your head. Like any book concerned with legalities, it looks to the future – what if things *don't* work out?

This book is designed to be dipped into in a hurry when you need an immediate response to a specific question. Or it can be read at leisure from cover to cover to get the complete relationship picture.

To help you find answers quickly the book is arranged in six parts. One of these is a skills section and two are intended for reference. Since relationships are rarely clear cut, you may need to look at more than one part of the book to understand your position fully.

Part One: Communicate Effectively looks at people skills. Part One aims to help you make your relationships and dealings with other people more productive . . . and cut down on lawyers' bills!

Part Two: Everyday Legal and Financial Basics is for reference. It explains the essentials and demystifies the technical jargon of everyday life, from owning your home and investing your money to understanding tax and making a will. There are also chapters on how the legal profession works, where to find a solicitor and how you can get help if you can't afford to pay for advice.

Part Two is not intended as a bed-time read! Refer back to it to find out, or refresh your memory, about the meaning of the legal and financial terms used in other parts of the book.

Parts Three and Four deal with the nuts and bolts of partnerships. There are separate sections for cohabitees and married couples.

Part Three: Getting Together is about starting a relationship – what the law says, the formalities, your home and your money. It explodes the popular myths about the rights of cohabitees and if you're thinking about getting married, it gives you all your wedding options.

Part Four: Breaking Up looks at how to go about ending a relationship as well as the legal and financial consequences. There is also a chapter on what happens when one partner dies.

If you're just starting out, breaking up is probably the last thing on your mind, but read Part Four in any case. Much of what happens when you end a relationship depends on what you did when you began.

Part Five: Parents and Children is for anyone, parent or not, who cares for kids or is contemplating caring for them. It tells you about your responsibilities and highlights the different rights of married and unmarried parents.

Part Six: Useful Addresses is again for reference. It gives you details of all the organisations mentioned in the book. You'll also find the addresses of other organisations which may be able to offer specialist information or additional support.

IF YOU LIVE IN SCOTLAND OR NORTHERN IRELAND

The information in this book is based on the law in England and Wales. If you live in Scotland or Northern Ireland you will find certain differences in the law and common practices. The principal differences are outlined at the back of the book but you should always check with a local advice agency or lawyer to find out detailed information.

PRICES AND LIMITS QUOTED IN THIS BOOK

Where prices or limits have been quoted you should check the current amount before taking any action since they are always liable to change.

PART ONE:
Communicate Effectively

CHAPTER 1

The Two-Way Process

What on earth have communication skills to do with the legal and financial ins and outs of relationships?

Well, if the fine details of the statute books are going to be of any practical use to you, you'll need to know how to put them into action. That means making decisions, expressing how you feel, negotiating with your partner, talking to professionals. In other words, communicating!

The penalty for failing to communicate effectively is likely to be a catalogue of misunderstandings, resentment, frustration, undue stress – and vast lawyers' bills. Whether you're getting together or breaking apart, you might as well maximise the positive aspects of the experience. And if you can't enjoy it, then at least take away the angst and just get on with the job.

This chapter isn't meant as the ultimate guide to becoming an assertive, confident communicator. It simply presents ways to improve your communication skills and enable you to make your relationships and dealings with other people more satisfying and more productive.

Effective communication is a two-way process. It involves each person having the confidence to put across their ideas and feelings assertively. It means really being able to listen to what others are saying. Good communicators learn to confront difficult situations and understand the process of negotiation.

These skills are important for everyday life. They're not optional extras to be employed just when the going gets tough. Drawing up a cohabitation contract in a loving but still new relationship can be just as difficult as working your way through a divorce after ten years of marriage. The point is to deal with the browbeating in a constructive way and use your energy positively.

This section looks at four key skills:

- Listening
- Acting assertively
- Confronting difficult situations
- Negotiating

Don't view them in isolation. Any situation will require you to use at least two skills.

HOW TO LISTEN

Have you ever been in conversation with someone and found yourself shouting at them in exasperation, 'You're not *listening* to me!'?

They then tell you that they heard everything you just said and proceed to repeat back to you your exact words.

Unconvinced, you cry, 'Maybe, you *heard* everything I said, but you're still not *listening* to me!'

There it is in a nutshell – the gigantic gulf between being heard and being listened to.

How does it feel when you have a conversation with someone but don't believe they're listening to you? Frustrating? Lonely? It probably doesn't do a lot for your self-esteem either.

The big problem is that we spend a great deal of time hearing what other people say and failing to listen properly. And when we do listen, we tend to forget most of what we've heard. We're all too busy waiting to get in our own penny's worth or simply daydreaming about something completely different.

Listening is an art; it's part of the communication process. By listening properly to someone else talk you can make them feel more comfortable about putting across their point of view, you'll be able to understand more clearly what they've said and your response, if it's needed, will be appropriate.

There are three ways that you can help yourself to listen.

Listen with your whole body, not just your ears!

If you've ever addressed a group of people, you'll know how disconcerting it is if no one's looking at you because they're all reading their papers, looking out of the window or twiddling their ear lobes. The same applies if you're having a conversation with just one other person. If they're distracted, you know you're not getting your message across.

Make sure your body indicates you're ready to listen.

- Don't hunch yourself up or cross your arms protectively. Lean forward, keen to hear what they have to say.
- Keep in eye contact. Eyes are amazing things which tell you a lot about someone's interest and desire – or not – to listen. Try having a conversation with someone wearing reflective sunglasses – you'll find out just how unnerving it is. You'll also learn a lot about the mood and inner feelings of the speaker by watching them.
- Cut out other distractions such as a TV or radio.

Listen to help others to talk

How many times have you sensed your partner or perhaps a colleague is out of sorts? They haven't said anything but you can tell from the way they're behaving that something's up. What do you do about it? Perhaps you tell them to snap out of their mood or try to reassure them and say, 'Cheer up!' Either way they probably clam up even more. So how do you get them to open up?

- Describe their behaviour: *You look a bit under the weather* or *Your face is beaming today*.
- Invite them to talk: *Want to talk about it?* or encourage them to keep talking: *Please go on* or *I'm interested in what you're saying*.
- Keep quiet and give the other person a chance to decide whether they want to talk or what they want to say.
- Keep listening with your eyes and the rest of your body. Aim simply to 'open the door' and encourage the other person to

talk. Don't then proceed to drag them through the open door by nagging them to speak to you.

- There are other ways to indicate verbally that you are willing to listen. The most common one is 'mm-hmm'. But there are many brief responses you can use to prompt the speaker: *go on; oh?; right; I see; yes; really; then?*
- It's also useful to ask the odd question. You can ask closed questions like *Do you enjoy your job?* which tend to elicit a straight yes or no response. Or you can ask more productive open-ended questions such as *What do you enjoy about your job?*
- Whatever you do, once the speaker gets going it's best simply to shut up and listen.

Good listening means responding

This *doesn't* mean you throw in any old jibe. Nor does it mean taking over the conversation so that instead of listening to your companion talk about the open heart surgery they've just had, they end up listening to you go on about what happened when you had stitches in your cut finger.

A good listener can respond to the talker by helping to sum up, very concisely, what they've said or the feelings they have expressed; they don't judge the other person.

There are a number of positive ways of responding to show you've understood and accepted what the other person has said.

- You can summarise in a few words what the other person has said. For example:

Cathy is talking to her colleague, Jan, about whether she should continue her career or start a family.

    Cathy: I'm in a real dilemma. I don't know whether I should try and get pregnant right now. Neil isn't sure either. I love my job . . . it's really challenging, I'm getting ahead and what's more it's well paid. At the same time, I really want to have a child and be a full-time mother.

    Jan: So you feel you're being pulled both ways. You enjoy your job but motherhood is equally appealing.

    Cathy: Yes.

A simple nod from the talker is usually enough to tell you you've got it right. It's just like double-checking train times when you call a station for information. It saves any misunderstandings later on.

– In the same way you can summarise what the other person is feeling. For example:

Brian: Everything's such fun. I've been enjoying life since I met Sally. The only downer is, she's been posted out of town for three months. I feel so lonely.

Alison, his sister, picks up the words, 'fun', 'enjoying' and 'lonely' and responds: Sounds as if even though you're having a good time, things are a bit down just at the moment.

You can also help the talker to focus on what they've been saying. For example:

Alistair embarks on a very long rambling story. He doesn't know what to do. His marriage is on the rocks and he's fallen in love with another woman. After talking all evening, Alistair finishes in a confused and dejected heap. With the pub landlord calling out 'last orders', his friend, Roger, helps him focus on his dilemma.

Roger: You think your marriage is over for good but you don't know how or when to get out of it. You want to move in with Jenny and get on with your life. But at the same time you're worried about your wife and your kids. You said that whatever happens, your priority is to make sure they're well provided for.

You can help the talker see the wood for the trees and move the conversation on. The danger is that if you don't, the talker will simply continue round in circles until it's time to go home – or go to bed.

HOW TO BE ASSERTIVE

Assertion is not about being a domineering, self-opinionated lout pushing people around. Neither is it about quivering and mumbling like a frightened mouse and letting others walk all over you.

Being assertive means having the confidence to deal with all sorts of people and situations effectively, from a demanding child to a manipulative parent or aggressive colleague. Assertive people feel comfortable stating their views and making demands but are also aware of other people's needs and feelings.

How assertive are you?
Take this everyday situation.

You've had a hard day at the office. You come home tired, hungry, with a thumping headache and you've got some work to complete before tomorrow morning. You walk through the front door to discover your partner has got back early and is lazing on the sofa. The TV is on full volume, there are dirty pots and pans piled up in the kitchen sink, a load of clothes waiting to be washed and no sign of dinner.

How would you react? Would you:

(a) Throw your bags down, turn off the TV and yell at your partner, 'Can't you see I've had a lousy day and I've got a headache? You live like an animal. You're selfish and you're a mess. I don't know why I bother living with you.' (Stomp out.)

(b) Complain and grumble inwardly and feel thoroughly put upon but get on and clear up the mess, subtly banging the pans about.

(c) Behave somewhere between (a) and (b), smile but silently vow to wash your partner's purple, non-colourfast socks with their favourite white shirt.

In their own way, (a), (b) and (c) are all very non-assertive reactions: (a) is very aggressive, thumping and shouting; (b) plays the passive little martyr; manipulative (c) can be pleasant on the surface but will no doubt find the means to get their own back.

In the short term these might be ways of dealing with a difficult situation. In the long run they achieve very little. They serve only to feed resentment and do nothing to solve underlying tensions.

How, then, would an assertive person approach the same situation? They might come in and say:

I've had a lousy day and I've work to complete by tomorrow. I've got a thumping headache, please turn the TV right down. (Thanks.) I'm really fed up that you got home early and haven't cleared up. I need to eat and get on with my work. If you wash up, I'll put the clothes in the machine and we'll make dinner together.

This exchange highlights some of the key assertion skills: making demands; offering criticism and finding practical solutions.

Sound assertive

Use the first person, I, when you speak. So instead of saying, 'It's cold in here', try, *I feel cold.* In the same way avoid using phrases like 'people believe' or 'one believes' when what you actually mean is, I believe.

Learn to express your own feelings. When you think about it, it doesn't seem entirely reasonable to come through the door at the end of the day and say, 'Can't you see I've got a headache?' We spend a lot of our lives participating in a very sophisticated guessing game called 'Try and work out what's the matter with me'. This is a big time-waster and the root of a good deal of misunderstanding. Try saying, *I feel very angry / happy / comfortable / let down / appreciated / frustrated when . . .*

Learn to make demands and state opinions assertively. There are three easy steps.

1. Decide what you want to say.
2. Say it.
3. Stick to it and repeat it if necessary.

Don't be put off by people making irrelevant comments, like, 'I can't help you, I wasn't here yesterday.' Simply repeat your request. And ignore the guilt-tripping, 'You're holding everyone up' or 'But you're the only one who can do it' and stick by what you've said.

Don't get led into arguments. You know the kind, where one person starts out by making an ordinary statement to someone else and ten minutes later they're both blaming each other for the downfall of the universe. If you get baited, just repeat your original statement.

Keith discovers to his horror that he's just shrunk Jane's silk blouse in the wash. He apologises to Jane.

Keith: Look, I'm sorry, I put your silk blouse into the washing machine and it's shrunk. I'll buy you another one.

Jane hits the roof: You imbecile. Only you could be that stupid. That's absolutely typical of you, you can't do anything right . . .

Now at this point, Keith can either help fuel the start of World War Three by retorting with similar name-calling or he can just repeat what he first said. He decides to do the latter and eventually Jane simmers down and comes round.

Listen to other people and acknowledge what they've said. Keith might have responded to Jane's outburst with:

Yes, I agree it was a stupid thing to do. I can see you're upset but it was an accident. I'll buy you another blouse.

Look assertive
Neither shuffling and mumbling nor thumping and shouting are assertive ways to behave. You need to be open, direct and ensure that your voice, your gestures and manner are appropriate to what you have to say.

- Sit or stand up straight and avoid any nervous habits like hair twisting, nose picking or ear lobe scratching.
- Look at people when you talk to them (see page 5).
- Smile if you're happy. Don't smile if you're not.

- Make sure the distance between you is appropriate. There's no point in trying to have a meaningful conversation with your deaf aunt if you're standing across the other side of the room.

HANDLING CRITICISM

Criticism, like confrontation, is one of those things people tend to skirt around. As children we get bombarded with criticism from parents, teachers and peers and much of it is downright unpleasant. Kids get labelled as 'stupid' or 'clumsy', teased for being slow at games or spotty as teenagers. Small wonder, then, that by adulthood, we don't know how to give or accept criticism – even the nice things, like compliments.

Criticism can be good or bad. Even when it involves picking someone up for shoddy work or a poorly completed job, there's no reason why it should be destructive and it certainly shouldn't dent a person's confidence.

Since criticism often involves some sort of confrontation, have a look over the advice on pages 13–17.

Giving criticism
Think through what you're going to say. Write yourself a script if necessary.

- Don't beat about the bush. Get straight to the point.
- Be constructive. Compliment the person on something they've done well. Describe what is actually wrong.
- Don't label the person, label their behaviour.
- Find out if there's a reason for the problem.
- Be specific about what you want done in the future.

Karen has just started working as Celia's secretary. For the first two months she came in promptly at 9 a.m. but over the last week she hasn't been getting in until 9.30 a.m. This holds Celia up and she's concerned about it, so she decides to tackle Karen.

Celia: I want to talk to you about the time you arrive in the office. I really appreciated you arriving promptly at 9 a.m. because it meant I could get on with my heavy workload. However, recently you've not got here until 9.30 a.m. Is there any reason for this?

Karen says that she oversleeps.

So Celia continues: I feel very frustrated when you arrive late because it holds me up. Please will you be here at 9 a.m. sharp so we can work as effectively as before.

Receiving criticism

There's no point in getting uptight about every ounce of criticism you receive – some of it might be justified. You need to consider whether the criticism is valid, in which case you ought to acknowledge it; invalid and needs refuting, or simply a nasty put-down which should be ignored.

Taking the Karen and Celia scenario, how could Karen have handled it if Celia had criticised her in a non-assertive way?

Celia: Karen, you're late again. This really is extremely inconsiderate. You strike me as a thoroughly lazy, incompetent young woman. How on earth are we supposed to get on if you can't be bothered to turn up for work on time?

Karen: Yes, I'm late again this week. I'm sorry, I overslept. I realise that I'm holding you up and apologise. But I don't think your comments that I'm lazy or incompetent are justified. I've stayed late whenever you've asked me to and completed work quickly. Only last week, you said how pleased you were. Once again, I'm sorry for being late and I'll make sure I'm on time tomorrow.

Deal with criticism square on. Don't pass the buck or put the blame on someone else.

BEING ANGRY AND ASSERTIVE

Don't be afraid of expressing anger. There's nothing worse than bottling it up and making your insides curl or unleashing anger on an innocent partner. You can deal with anger assertively.

- Acknowledge how you feel.
- Keep your anger in perspective. You might feel like tearing the world apart but consider the root of your anger.
- Imagine an 'Anger Ladder'.

Going to blow a fuse!

Infuriated

Incensed

Indignant

Cross

Impatient

Displeased

Think where you on on the ladder. Are your feelings and behaviour appropriate to the situation? Have you room to manoeuvre if you become angrier?
- Consider whether you are really angry or whether in truth what you are feeling is frustration, resentment or hurt.

HOW TO CONFRONT

Confrontation has a bad name. It's something very many people go to great lengths to avoid, spend hours worrying about and, ultimately, do rather badly.

There are different sorts of confrontation, and not all of them are inherently unpleasant. There are the ones that don't look too promising, like giving someone the sack or confronting a belligerent builder who's botched up your double-glazing. Then there are others, that should in theory gladden your heart, but seem to cause the same disquiet – situations like meeting your prospective in-laws for the first time or throwing a party.

The pre-confrontation condition is well documented: devious avoidance techniques, sweaty palms, thumping heart, horrendous nightmares, furious rehearsing of your opening line. Confrontation is a fact of life. There really is no getting away from it. Avoiding it is just as stressful as tackling it head on. But it needn't be an awful experience. Properly managed confrontation can be just as fruitful as any other encounter.

The confrontation gameplan

You know it's confrontation because you get that pre-confrontation feeling. How, then, do you master those feelings to enable you to get on with the job in hand?

Here's a straightforward three-point plan.

1. The skeleton

What exactly is this confrontation all about? In other words, take away the nightmares and the palpitations and what have you got?

Fred is a quaking, shaking mass of nerves. He won't actually admit it to himself but he can't sleep and he can't eat and he'd give a million dollars to be anywhere but Little Glossop this Saturday afternoon. Why?

Well, when Fred stops thinking about Houdini techniques for a moment, it dawns on him that all that's happening this weekend is he's going to meet his fiancée Sandra's parents for the first time and everyone's a bit nervous about it – not least of all, Sandra's parents.

But that's not enough. The skeleton needs some fleshing out. What are the monsters that are looming?

Fred makes a list of his imaginary beasts. It includes: the fact that Sandra's dad is old-fashioned and Fred hasn't exactly asked his permission to marry his daughter; Sandra's dad might not like Fred; he might refuse to let Sandra marry him; Sandra's mum's a dab hand with cream cakes but cream makes Fred sick: what happens if he refuses to eat Sandra's mum's cake; what happens if he doesn't?

2. Imagine the worst

Like Fred, you probably dwell on all the awful things that *could* happen in the confrontation and let them fester. Get them out of your system. Look at your list of 'monsters' and ask yourself, 'What's the worst that could happen?'

Fred imagines the worst that could happen is for Sandra's dad to take an instant dislike to him and throw him out of the house. Or if he refused her mum's cakes, she would try and force-feed him and he'd be sick.

You then need to ask yourself, 'Will the worst *really* happen?'

Fred has a more rational think. He decides that Sandra's dad would be highly unlikely to throw him out of the house, but he might be just merely civil to him. He also doesn't really believe that Sandra's mum would actually force-feed him, although she might be a bit hurt he refused her cakes.

3. Write yourself a survival script
By now you know exactly what the confrontation is about, you've explored your worst nightmares and brought them nearer to reality and you should also have come to grips with the people you're confronting. What makes them tick? How are they looking forward to this meeting?

By writing yourself a survival script you can plan ahead for the meeting, imagine how you're going to deal with the situation and practise the words you're going to use.

The script needs to have four elements:

- where and when the confrontation takes place;
- something about the other person or people;
- what you're going to say;
- how the other person might react and what you're going to do about it.

Fred's script looks something like this.

Setting the scene: meeting Sandra's parents, George and Mildred, for the first time, at their home in Little Glossop this Saturday.

15

The players (based on what Sandra has told me): George, old-fashioned, concerned that his daughter marries the right sort of man, could be put out that I haven't asked his permission. Mildred, wants to create the right impression, proud of her baking, can be easily offended. Sandra, nervous, wants me to like her parents and vice versa. Me, want them to like me and approve.

Since Fred's in for an entire afternoon of Sandra's parents he doesn't want to script the whole of tea-time, that would be ridiculous. However, two situations are preying on his mind, so he scripts those.

Fred knows George expects him to ask his permission to marry Sandra so Fred thinks about two scenarios. He decides either to catch George alone, or if necessary to respond to any veiled comments.

'George, I imagine you would have preferred us to talk to you in advance about our intention to get married, but it just wasn't possible. I hope that you approve of our engagement and we have your support.'

Fred also decides that if George then complains, he will simply apologise and reiterate his hope that George and Mildred will support their engagement.

The second scenario is to do with Mildred and her cream cakes.

'Thanks very much, Mildred, but I must refuse. It looks wonderful but cream makes me ill. Perhaps I could have another jam tart.' (Fred's pretty sure there'll be plenty else to eat!)

If she continues to press him, Fred decides to be assertive and stick to his first response. He decides that he'll simply put up with Mildred's sulks.

Having written his script, Fred goes over it carefully and then rehearses what he intends to say. The result is that when he does meet Sandra's parents he feels much more confident about dealing with any awkward situations. He handles George well and since he's generally feeling confident he doesn't make the awful gaffes he was dreading, like not knowing what to say, or spilling strawberry jam down his tie.

The point about getting the 'monsters' out in the open and scripting the situation is that you familiarise yourself with it in advance. You anticipate any difficult moments and have a ready-made means of handling them. What's more, if you feel more confident, the situation will seem less of a confrontation.

HOW TO NEGOTIATE

Negotiations aren't just about world leaders sitting round tables in obscure parts of the globe thrashing out international issues in the full glare of the television cameras. We all do it, every day. We negotiate our place in bus and check-out queues, parents negotiate homework times with their children, workers negotiate job priorities with their bosses, spouses and partners negotiate their relationships. Parents introduce the negotiation process to their children in baby-hood. The *one more mouthful of spinach and then you can have a banana* syndrome is essentially one which we carry into our adult lives.

So there's nothing superpowerish about negotiation – it's really a very ordinary everyday happening. World leader or humble citizen, the important thing is to make the negotiation process productive.

What is negotiation?
It's really very basic. The parties start out with a common goal such as, let's delegate the cleaning chores, or let's agree on a financial separation. Then, a bit like a tennis game, the ideas, suggestions, acceptances and rejections go back and forth, over the net. The game finishes when all the issues for discussion have been 'served' and agreed or compromised upon. Ideally both players should leave the court with a friendly handshake and a sense that play was fair. If necessary, the players can call in an independent umpire to settle their differences.

However, to play the negotiation process successfully, you need to know the principles and some of the rules!

THE COMPLETE GUIDE TO LIVING TOGETHER

The rules

Negotiation, in this context, is *not* about scoring points. If you set out to get 'one over' on your partner, you'll defeat the whole purpose of productive negotiation. You may well 'win' your case in the short term, but you'll also find in the long run it probably won't work out.

Achieving all your own objectives is all very well, but since your partner's objectives may not be the same as yours, it rather leaves them out in the cold. People who walk away from the negotiation table with nothing are likely to feel frustrated and resentful and may decide to put a spoke in your early gotten gains.

There are two main guiding principles to negotiating:

– you need to aim to reach a fair compromise;
– you need to ensure that whatever you agree on will actually work.

A fair compromise: means that the end result recognises the needs of everyone involved in the negotiation process. This isn't solely about physical requirements such as money or possessions but emotional needs like reassurance and support. A fair compromise suggests that not everyone gets exactly what they were after but that on balance each person is satisfied with their lot. Negotiation, like most other things in life, is a matter of give and take.
Compromises must work: there's little sense in coming up with grand agreements that won't work. You must make sure that whatever you decide will be practically possible. You need to be realistic, to think ahead and consider the solution from every angle.

Katy and Mick lived in a pigsty. Their grimy, untidy flat was a source of constant arguments between them. However, they were both busy people and getting the cleaning done was an issue.

They sat down to decide how to resolve things. After much debate, Katy suggested that they each took responsibility for cleaning the flat on alternate weeks.

The whole plan turned out to be a farce. Katy went off on a business

*trip for ten days and Mick insisted she make up her turn when she got
back. But Katy didn't see why she should since she hadn't been around
to make the place dirty. Besides, Mick was never satisfied with the way
Katy cleared up. They rowed and sulked for about three days. Their
compromise wasn't workable. In the end they decided both to contribute
towards the cost of employing a cleaner.*

Putting it into action

There are five stages to the negotiation process.

1. Setting your common goal

This is usually pretty straightforward: it's the reason why you're
having the discussion in the first place. Your perspectives may be
different but you should share a common goal. If you don't, you're
going to be negotiating along two parallel lines and may not find a
meeting point – which will be a waste of time.

*Helen and Jane are concerned about John's elderly mother Violet. She's
eighty-five and physically quite frail. Up to now she's lived on her own
but the increasingly frequent calls for help are becoming a strain on
Helen and John. They decide that they must now find a more appropriate
way to care for Violet.*

2. Establishing individual objectives

What do you want to achieve out of the negotiation process? What
are your particular needs? What is your 'bottom line', the point
beyond which things become non-negotiable?

*Helen is very fond of her mother-in-law but feels John should take the
strain of deciding what happens to Violet. She has a full-time job and
she and John also have two teenage sons at home. Ideally she'd like
Violet to go into a residential home. Helen is reluctant to have Violet
come to stay with them and would only agree to it as a last resort.*

*John wants his mother to come and live with him. He knows that
would place an additional strain on the family but thinks Helen might
be persuaded to give up her job. John's very much against the idea of*

his mother going into an old people's home.

3. Brainstorm your options and find out the facts

Brainstorming is basically creative thinking where you put down on paper every idea that floats into your mind. Some of them may be plain daft, others might prove to be a real winner. It's a game best played by two or more people. The point is not to censor any thoughts, just let them all flow out, and when you can't think of any more, *then* go back over them and weed out the crazy ones.

Once you've gone through the brainstorming process you will still need to find out your facts before you can be sure your proposals will work. How much do things cost, how long will it take, what about necessary paperwork, who else do you need to involve? There are all sorts of considerations to practical plans.

Helen and John each brainstorm the issue individually, Helen with her work colleagues, John with his brother. Between them, these are some of the ideas they come up with.

Violet could remain in her own home with a companion or with a home help and meals on wheels; she could go into a residential home; she could live with Helen and John; Helen could give up her job to look after her; they could get extra help in their own home; they could send Violet on a world cruise with a nurse; John could give up his job; their teenage sons could look after their gran as a school project.

Helen and John talked over their ideas informally and decided they needed some more information. It was all very well making decisions about Violet, but what did she want for herself, and what about their sons? They also needed to know the cost of hiring a companion or paying residential home fees. When they had some more facts, they agreed to sit down and sort things out.

Brainstorming can be done with your partner as part of the decision-making process. Or you can brainstorm and factfind alone or with someone other than the person with whom you are negotiating. This way, by the time you come to sit round the table, you will have in mind one or two sensible, workable proposals.

4. Making decisions

You need somewhere appropriate to carry out your discussions. An intimate restaurant is probably not the most suitable place to come to an agreement about your divorce or a crowded shop-floor the ideal spot to ask for a pay rise. The setting should be businesslike, even if it is round your kitchen table, and there shouldn't be other distractions like ringing telephones or screaming children.

It's at this stage that the negotiations start in earnest, especially if you've undertaken stages two and three alone.

Helen and John had always found it relatively easy to talk to one another but they were both aware that this was a particularly difficult subject. They decided to drive out into the countryside away from the kids and the house so that they would have somewhere quiet and private to talk.

John said he was very anxious about his mother and that he felt very strongly that she should spend the last years of her life amongst her family. He didn't want her vegetating in an old people's home.

Helen agreed that she too was worried about his mother and that she should continue to lead a stimulating and dignified life. She also told John that she was worried about the effect any changes might have on their own family and particularly any additional burdens she might have to take on.

They discussed all the feasible options they had. Violet resented the idea of going into a home. Full-time companions were expensive and the home help and meals on wheels service inadequate. Violet simply couldn't remain in her own home. John pushed hard for his mother to come and live with them. Helen rejected totally the idea that she gave up her job.

Gradually they found common ground. They both agreed that it wasn't in Violet's best interests to go into a home. John accepted Helen's reluctance to have her live with them but Helen realised there was very little choice. However, John agreed it would be unfair for Helen to stop working and to take on the job of looking after his mother. Since their sons had shown no particular interest one way or another, Helen and John reached a compromise.

Violet would come to live with them. Helen would continue working but not do any overtime. They would have a daytime companion for

Violet and she would spend holidays in a residential home, so that Helen and John could get away. John agreed to help Helen more with shopping and preparing meals and to encourage their sons to do so too. Finally, they both agreed that they would review the situation in a year, or before that if Violet's condition deteriorated.

5. Tying up the ends

This means putting into practice what you've agreed. In Helen and John's case this meant finding a companion and moving his mother into their home.

Whatever the result of your negotiation, it's well worth deciding how you will monitor the decision you've made to make sure that it's been carried out and that it's working. Helen and John put a timescale on their agreement.

Negotiation: the do's and don'ts

Do
- Leave each person's self-esteem intact. Negotiation is not a battle: there is no victor and no vanquished.
- Outline your concerns and priorities.
- Listen to the other person.
- Seek the opinions of other people who matter: children, new partners, family members.
- Be realistic, compromise.

Don't
- Be excessive or abrasive in your demands and alienate your partner; this only leads to retaliation.
- Manipulate or guilt-trip the other person.
- Be too passive and give up everything; you'll only resent it later.
- Trade in your kids, your affections or sex.

PART TWO:
Everyday Financial and Legal Basics

The following chapters are intended for reference. They look at everyday legal and financial dealings, like investing money, buying a home or making a will and explain the basic principles behind the jargon.

The information contained in these pages is very general. To find out your rights and responsibilities in specific circumstances like moving in with someone, or getting divorced, you should refer to the appropriate chapters later in the book.

CHAPTER 2
Money Matters: Borrowing

CREDIT

In a consumer-hungry world there are two ways to pay: cash or credit. Cash is simple enough, it's a straightforward matter of sufficient coins and notes, but credit? A mortgage for a new home, Visa card for the holiday or HP for a colour TV, it's all credit. How much it ultimately costs you depends on how wisely you use it.

WHERE TO GET CREDIT

Banks
Banks, and increasingly building societies, offer a wide range of credit facilities including credit cards and mortgages.

Bank overdrafts
Unless you have some kind of automatic overdraft facility you must get permission from your bank manager to overdraw on your account. The amount by which you can then overdraw will be up to an agreed sum for a specified period of time.

As you pay money into your account, so the loan is repaid. Interest is calculated on a day-to-day basis and the manager can insist that you repay the loan in full at any time.

Bank loans
There are usually two types of bank loan:

- *Ordinary loans* for a specific purpose approved by the manager

which are available only to bank customers. A variable rate of interest is charged, usually higher than for overdrafts.
- *Personal loans* which are available to customers and non-customers alike. Loans are usually for up to three years although they can be extended. The interest rate is fixed.

Credit cards
There are three broad types of credit cards:

- bank credit cards;
- charge cards;
- store cards, which might be credit or charge cards.

Bank credit cards
Although traditionally there have been only two bank credit schemes operating in the UK it is misleading simply to talk about 'Visa cards' or 'Access cards'. They are offered by many different institutions and not necessarily under the same terms and conditions.

A bank credit card bills you each month and, subject to a minimum payment, you pay off as much or as little as you like. Usually if you pay in full within twenty-five days no interest is charged. But even if you are one day late you may find yourself paying interest from the date you made the purchase with your card.

Charge cards
Charge card holders pay a joining fee plus a yearly fee. Unlike bank credit cards there is no credit limit but you must pay off the account in full each month.

Store cards
Essentially there are three kinds of accounts:

- *Option accounts* which are similar to bank credit cards but are often more costly.
- *Monthly accounts* which operate like charge cards except that the card is usually free.

- *Budget accounts* where you pay a regular monthly sum and can borrow a multiple of your monthly payment.

NOTE: If you lose your credit or charge cards you must report their loss immediately. Normally you won't be charged for any purchases made on your stolen card *after* you've reported its loss. You may incur a charge of £50 for items purchased on your stolen card *before* you report its loss.

Hire purchase
HP is usually offered by individual shops and can be one of the more expensive ways of getting credit. Interest is usually at a fixed rate throughout the agreement. You pay for the goods in instalments and you legally own them only when you have paid the last instalment.

You cannot sell the goods until they are legally yours. Once you've paid one-third of the total amount payable, the owner (usually a finance company) cannot reclaim the goods without a court order.

If you find you cannot keep up with the repayments you can end the agreement by paying at least half of the total amount payable (unless the agreement says otherwise) and returning the goods.

Credit from shops
Shops and chain stores often offer credit sales. These are similar to HP agreements except that the goods belong to you immediately. You normally pay a deposit and then weekly or monthly instalments over a fairly short period – perhaps six months or a year. Interest is usually fixed throughout the agreement, although it can vary.

A shop or dealer may also arrange a *finance company personal loan* for you if you are buying an expensive item like a car. If you are offered this type of loan, shop around to see if you can get a better deal elsewhere.

Mail order credit is offered by the big catalogue companies. Agents will collect your repayments or you can send them by post. Keep a clear record of any money you send through the post in case a dispute arises.

Moneylenders

Moneylenders often make loans where no one else will. They tend to be extremely expensive and can be less than scrupulous in recovering any unpaid debts. Anyone who stops you in the street or calls uninvited at your home offering you a loan is committing an offence. Most moneylenders need a licence, so contact your local Trading Standards Department if you have doubts.

Pawnbrokers

Pawnbrokers have thrown off their somewhat seedy image and are back on the high street. For small, very short-term loans, pawnbrokers may be useful but they tend to be expensive.

If you pawn anything, the pawnbroker must give you a receipt in the proper form headed, 'Notice to Debtor'. Read this carefully because it tells you what your rights are in reclaiming your pawned articles. If you cannot pay the full amount by the agreed date, you will have to pay regular interest to prevent your goods from being sold.

Credit unions

The number of such unions is increasing. They operate like a club with members making regular savings to form a central fund. Out of this members then get low-cost loans.

CREDIT JARGON

Fixed and variable interest rates

Almost all credit deals will include an extra charge or 'interest'. This can be either fixed or variable.

- *Fixed rates* mean that there will be one standard rate of interest throughout the life of the credit agreement.
- *Variable rates* mean that the charge could go up or down depending on the state of the financial markets. You take a bit of a gamble because you could be paying a lot more – or a lot less – in the long term.

APR: annual percentage rate of charge

Before you commit yourself to a credit agreement you need to shop around to find the best deal. Because the arrangements for repaying credit, the length of the loan and other factors such as a deposit or insurance vary so greatly, it would be difficult for the average consumer to work out exactly how much any one deal would cost them. APR enables you to compare the cost of the various types of credit on offer without having to do a whole lot of complicated sums.

The APR is a standard way of quoting the total amount for credit and it represents the complete cost of borrowing the money calculated as a yearly percentage. However, one word of caution. Some lenders are becoming unscrupulous about the way they quote the APR so always check that it includes all possible costs such as insurance or a deposit to ensure that you compare like with like.

Secured loans

When you borrow money, usually large amounts, you may well be asked to give your house or car as 'security'. Unless you can be sure of meeting your repayments or you take out insurance, avoid secured loans. If you default on the repayments, whatever you have given as security will be sold, not necessarily at the best price, in order to raise money to repay the loan.

LOANS: WHO'S RESPONSIBLE?

If you take out a loan and yours is the only name on the agreement, then you alone are responsible for making the repayments. If two or more people sign an agreement then they become *jointly and severally liable*. This means that if the debt remains unpaid the lender will sue every one of you in order to see that the debt is paid.

If you use credit to buy something for someone else, paying for it remains your responsibility.

Guarantors

When you ask for a loan, the lender might express some concerns about your ability to meet the repayments and may ask you for a *guarantor*. This means someone who will guarantee the repayments if you default.

If you're asked to be a guarantor, do not accept lightly. It's not just a question of putting your name on a piece of paper for formality's sake. If the person for whom you are acting as guarantor fails to make the repayment, then it'll be over to you to pay up.

MORTGAGES

Banks and building societies, as well as a growing range of other financial institutions, offer to lend money on a mortgage to buy property. They will lend money according to your income, typically two to three times your salary. Repayments can last up to thirty years depending on your age. Interest rates are likely to vary during the term of your mortgage, perhaps by as much as six or seven per cent.

Your home will be used as security, so if you default on the repayments the lender may proceed to repossess it (see above) so that it can be sold to repay the loan.

There are three basic types of mortgage on offer.

Repayment mortgages

Your monthly payment goes to pay off both the capital you have borrowed and the interest which has accrued on it. To start with your money will be going largely to pay off the interest. Most institutions insist that you take out an additional life insurance policy so that the repayment is covered if you die.

Endowment mortgages

Part of your monthly repayment pays off the interest on the money you've borrowed and the rest is paid to an insurance company for the premium on an endowment policy. The policy is designed to pay off the mortgage at the end of the term and in some cases give you an extra lump sum. There is built-in life insurance so that the loan is automatically repaid if any of the borrowers die.

Pension mortgages

These are similar to endowment mortgages in that you make a monthly interest payment on your mortgage plus a premium payment to an approved pension scheme. Upon retirement you will get a cash sum to pay off the remainder of the mortgage plus a small pension for the rest of your life. Most lenders will insist that you take out additional life insurance.

In addition lenders may offer *low-start mortgages* where you pay a lower interest rate or a discounted rate for the first year or so followed by a higher or normal rate for the rest of the term of the loan.

NOTE: Before you commit yourself, seek the advice of an *independent* financial adviser to find out which type of mortgage would be most advantageous to you.

DEALING WITH DEBT

Debt is one of the fastest-growing consumer problems. A single incident such as illness, redundancy or marriage break-up can make all the difference between making ends meet and facing an upward spiral of debts. If you find yourself confronting financial difficulties, it's vital that you act quickly before the brown envelopes pile up and creditors start knocking on your door.

1. Make a list of *all* your financial commitments and outstanding bills. Don't be tempted to skip over an unpaid gas or telephone bill. Putting everything down on paper may look frightening but it will also make the situation more manageable.
2. Contact each one of your creditors. You must make them aware of your situation and reassure them that you intend to settle your debts. (If you don't tell them you're facing financial

problems, can you blame them for assuming you just don't want to pay their bill?) A telephone call followed by a letter acknowledging the outstanding bill and explaining your position and your intention to put forward an offer to settle will be sufficient at this point.

Your priority need not always be your largest creditor. Credit card companies for example cannot take any immediate action against you, except perhaps to cancel your card. Gas, electricity and telephone companies, on the other hand, can cut you off and make a substantial charge to reconnect you when you do finally pay up.

3. See your mortgage lender. Even if you are only one month in arrears, if your income has been severely reduced, tell them about your new financial situation. Many mortgage lenders will extend your mortgage by six months (which means that you make extra repayments at the end of the mortgage period).

    Before you stop making contributions to any pension or savings plan, get independent advice and check whether you are covered by an insurance scheme.

4. Make out a weekly budget, excluding all your current debts and your mortgage if you've managed to defer it. Subtract your outgoings from your income and whatever you have left can be divided up amongst your creditors. Don't despair if there is virtually nothing left in the kitty. If you can rethink your weekly outgoings, then do so.

5. Write to each creditor with an offer to settle the debt – even if it is only a few pence a week. You will need to explain your financial situation in detail and enclose a copy of your weekly budget. If you owe money to a credit company, ask them to freeze the interest on your account.

6. Once a company has agreed to your accept your proposals, you must keep up with the repayments. If you find yourself with further financial problems, write to them again.

Since debt is on the increase, you will probably find your creditors more sympathetic than you might have imagined. Provided you keep them up to date, many will be happy to negotiate a realistic repayment.

For further information and advice contact your local Citizens Advice Bureau (CAB) or Money Advice Centre.

CHAPTER 3

Money Matters: Investments

Investing money is not simply about piggy banks, shares and tax-efficient savings accounts. Pensions and life insurance schemes are also forms of making an investment. Opportunities for financial investment are increasing all the time. As schemes become more complex, the consumer is left the more bewildered.

Make sure your money works for you:

- always read the small print;
- watch out for any charges and take them into account;
- review your investments regularly.

Before you make any substantial or long-term commitment, *always* seek the advice of an independent, reputable financial adviser.

MONEY MAKING MONEY

Aside from pensions and life insurance schemes there are essentially two ways to invest your hard-won cash. You can either invest in companies or you can invest in savings accounts.

Where you decide to put your money will depend on your circumstances. The amount of money you have available will often determine the type of scheme or account you can or should invest in. Many schemes specify a minimum initial investment and with others it is not worthwhile to invest, say, less than £1,000. There is also often a ceiling on the maximum amount you can invest.

You also need to think about how long you can afford to lock your money away for; some schemes penalise you for taking out the money before the end of a specified term. Do you need instant access to your cash? You also need to assess the risk value – the more you stand to gain through your investment, the more you stand to lose. Don't put your rainy day fund into a long-term, high-risk scheme!

Whatever your investment, remember that unless you opt for one of the tax-free schemes, your savings will attract tax. To minimise your tax liabilities, get expert advice.

INVESTING IN SAVINGS ACCOUNTS

After the shoebox under the bed, building society savings accounts are perhaps the simplest and most common form of financial investment. However, the range of accounts available can be quite daunting.

An alternative to the bank or building society is one of the many government schemes now on offer. As these accounts tend to be safer than the ones described under 'Investing in Companies', the returns are comparatively less substantial.

Banks and building societies
The well-known high street names offer a wide range of savings accounts. Some offer instant access, which is useful for a rainy day fund; others give a higher return on your investment but you may have to give three or more months' notice to withdraw cash without suffering a penalty.

The banks and building societies also offer *TESSAs – Tax-Exempt Special Savings Accounts*. The interest you gain is tax-free providing you keep your account for five years and make only certain limited withdrawals. There is a ceiling on the maximum amount you can invest.

Government schemes
The Post Office provides a number of savings opportunities from an ordinary savings account to *National Savings Certificates* and capital bonds.

You can also buy *British Government stocks* or *gilts*. Gilts pay a fixed income each year and, like shares, their value can fluctuate.

35

Gilts often form part of a unit trust to add stability to the portfolio (see below).

INVESTING IN COMPANIES

You can invest in companies directly either by buying shares or through a *Personal Equity Plan* (PEP). Or you can invest indirectly by means of collective investment schemes such as *unit trusts* and *investment trusts*.

Investing directly

Buying shares
When you buy shares you become part-owner of a company. There are different types of shares, the main one being *ordinary shares* which give you a dividend, a share in the business profits, and usually a vote at shareholders' meetings.

The value of your shares will depend on how well the company performs and the general state of the market.

Because dealing charges (the amount you pay a broker to buy and sell your shares) can be high, it's not worth investing small sums. For the same reason investment in shares tends to be more long term.

Personal Equity Plan (PEP)
This is a special scheme which enables you to put money into the stock market without having to pay tax on your income or gains. You either leave all the investment decisions to a plan manager or you make the decisions yourself.

Although some PEPs are set up only to invest in shares, others invest in unit trusts or a combination of the two.

There is a limit on how much you can invest each year. As long as you're a tax-payer, a PEP may be worth considering, although once again it's not for people looking for a quick kill.

Investing indirectly

Unit trusts and investment trusts

In a *unit trust* you pool your money with other investors to buy shares in a range of companies. The pooled fund of money is divided into equal portions or units and is looked after by trustees (usually a bank). Hence the name, unit trusts.

As an individual investor you can't determine exactly which companies to buy into; that decision is left to the fund manager. However, you can specify the type of companies you want to invest in. Ethical funds won't invest in, for example, the tobacco industry.

An *investment trust* is a company which in turn invests in other companies. If you buy a share in an investment trust, your dividends and the value of your share will depend on the success of the investments made by the investment trust company.

Investing in unit and investment trusts means you don't have to worry about picking a *portfolio* (range of investments) from the myriad of shares on offer. You simply have to pick successful trusts!

PENSIONS

There are three sources of pensions:

- the state;
- your employer;
- private provision you make for yourself.

The state pension

State provision consists of the basic state pension and the *State Earnings Related Pension Scheme, SERPS* (and its predecessor, the Graduated Pension). Both of these are paid through National Insurance Contributions made by you and your employer.

You will automatically pay into SERPS unless you contribute to an employer's pension scheme which is contracted out of SERPS, or you are self-employed or you decide to make your own arrangements.

For younger people SERPS may have limited benefits by the time they reach retirement, so it could be worth looking around for alternative provision. Get an expert to do the sums before you decide to contract out.

The Employer's Pension

Your employer may invite you to join a company pension scheme. This could operate in one of two ways: as a *final salary* scheme or a *money purchase* scheme which works in a similar way to a PPP (see below). In the final salary scheme your pension is calculated by looking at your final pensionable pay and the number of years you've paid into the scheme.

There are also two ways to boost your employer's pension.

- *Additional Voluntary Contributions: AVCs* are a safe, low-cost method of boosting your pension but the benefits may be limited by the company scheme. All employer's schemes must offer AVC provision.
- *Free-Standing Additional Voluntary Contributions: FSACVs* are money purchase plans that enable you to choose the level of investment risk and range of benefits. There will be some costs for setting up and running the plan.

Personal Pension Plans (PPPs)

These are available to workers who are self-employed or not in an employer's pension scheme. If you are part of an employer's scheme then you can only use PPPs to receive transfers from past employers' schemes or to contract out of SERPS.

PPPs work on the *money purchase* principle, which means that the contributions you make are invested to build up a fund.

When you retire you take up to twenty-five per cent of your fund as a tax-free lump sum and the remaining has to be used to provide your pension by buying an *annuity* from a life assurance company.

An annuity is an investment which pays out a pension for the lifetime of the person holding the annuity. It can also be used to provide a widow or widower's pension and other benefits.

INSURANCE

Insurance is about protecting yourself against the unexpected: theft, floods, accidents. You can insure almost everything – your home, your health, your car, your possessions, your life (see page 40).

What's important is to ensure you have the right type of insurance and that it adequately meets your needs.

Getting the right cover

Insurance policies look much the same – what they actually offer depends on the small print – so read it thoroughly. Whatever you decide to insure and whatever you decide to insure it against, the same basic rules apply.

- Make sure you have sufficient cover – the total amount of the insurance – to ensure that you can replace the item or get emergency treatment. Don't underestimate the cost. If appropriate get a valuation, for example for a piece of jewellery.
- Shop around for a suitable policy or ask a broker to do it for you. Compare the terms of different policies and the cost of the *premiums* – the amount you pay for the policy.
- Check out any *exclusion clauses* to see what's not covered.
- Make sure you review your policy each year, even if it is index-linked, to ensure you have adequate cover.

House insurance

Owning your own house means that you will usually be responsible for two kinds of insurance: building insurance and contents insurance. If you rent property then you only need to be concerned about the latter.

Buildings insurance

This is about insuring the actual bricks and mortar of your home. If you live in a leasehold property then it's usually the freeholder's responsibility to arrange the buildings insurance, but don't rely on this – check first.

Buildings should be insured for their full rebuilding costs and not what you would normally expect to sell them for. Most insurance companies will provide you with a guide.

Contents insurance
This covers your furniture, carpets, domestic appliances, clothes and other belongings. Many policies specify an upper limit on the value of any single item insured and you may have to list more expensive belongings separately.

You'll also need to decide whether you want a new for old policy where the insurance company provides the full cost of replacing the damaged or stolen item.

Or you can opt for a policy which takes into account wear and tear and will give you a reduced amount towards replacing the goods. These policies obviously cost less than new for old ones.

If you have expensive items such as an engagement ring or camera which you take out of your home, then you should consider insuring them separately.

Car insurance
Car insurance comes in three packages.

- *Fully Comprehensive* covers you for any loss or damage someone else causes to your car or you cause yourself or you cause to someone else or their property. It also covers you for theft or damage to the contents of your car.
- *Third Party Fire and Theft* covers you for any damage you do to someone else or their property, in other words a third party, and gives you limited cover for your own car.
- *Third Party* is the cheapest kind of car insurance and only covers you for the damage you do to someone else or their property. By law you must have at least third party insurance.

Life insurance
Centuries ago when the insurance industry was still in its embryonic stage it was possible to insure anything – or anyone, such as a public

figurehead. The Life Assurances Act of 1774 put a stop to that and from then on, if you wanted to insure someone else's life you had to prove you had an *insurable interest*.

Everyone is regarded as having an interest in their own life and therefore you can take out life assurance or insurance against accidents or ill health. Husbands and wives are also deemed to have an insurable interest in each other's lives but cohabitees are not (see page 102).

The amount of benefit payable must be directly related to the amount of the loss the person taking out the policy is likely to sustain.

In order to take out insurance on someone else's life you have to show that you will lose financially if the person whose life you have insured dies.

What type of insurance?
There are two types of insurance:

- *term insurance* which you take out as protection;
- *endowment* policies which you take out as an investment.

Term insurance means that the policy will only pay out if you die before a specified age. This means that you may never get any of your money back. As a result, term insurance is usually very cheap.

Endowment insurance means that the policy will pay out when you reach a specified age or if you die before then.

CHAPTER 4
Tax

Tax is a highly complex and specialist subject. Tax rules, rates and exemptions change annually in the government budget. This book makes no pretensions to offer expert tax advice and you should always seek the counsel of a qualified person to gain up-to-date information and find out how best to handle your personal tax affairs.

Below you will find an outline of the key principles and rules behind the main forms of tax today. In addition, most of the following chapters contain a series of tax notes as a guide to the relevant tax points.

The Inland Revenue produces an excellent set of free, non-technical leaflets explaining how the different types of tax affect you.

The three most common forms of tax paid by individuals are:

- income tax;
- capital gains tax;
- inheritance tax.

The other kind of tax which you're probably familiar with is Stamp Duty which is paid when you buy a new home.

INCOME TAX

Income tax (IT) is simply a tax on your income. Taxable income includes: wages or income from employment; income from savings such as building society accounts, shares and other investments and certain state benefits such as statutory sick pay and statutory maternity pay.

However, there are other sources of income which do not attract tax. These include: the vast majority of state benefits; most maintenance payments and tax-free savings schemes such as TESSAs (see page 35).

The amount of tax you have to pay will depend on your financial circumstances; your age; your marital status, your gender and whether or not you have children.

You do not have to pay tax on all your income. Everyone has tax allowances which are amounts of income which are exempt from tax. In addition there are tax reliefs which work in the same way but apply to certain outgoings you may have, for example if you take out a loan to buy a property.

Tax allowances
The main types of tax allowance are:

- The *personal allowance* which is given automatically to everyone, male or female, married or single. The amount you will get will depend on your age.
- The *married couple's allowance* which is given to a married man living with his wife. Once again there are different levels of allowance depending on your age.
- The *additional personal allowance* which is mainly for unmarried parents.

There are also a *widow's bereavement allowance* and a *blind person's allowance*.

Tax reliefs
There are a number of different types of tax reliefs. These are the most common ones:

- *Mortgage Interest Relief at Source (MIRAS)* can be claimed if you have taken out a loan to buy your only or your main home. Most people get their tax relief through the MIRAS system. If your mortgage lender does not use this system you may have

to claim this relief direct from your tax office.
- You may be able to claim tax relief to buy or improve property which you rent out to tenants, or to buy a car or other machinery that you need for your job.
- Some maintenance payments are entitled to tax relief.

Deeds of covenant made out to charities also attract tax relief as do certain types of life insurance and pension schemes.

How is tax calculated?
In its simplest form, all your taxable income for the year is added up. Your tax allowances and reliefs are then deducted from the total amount of your taxable income. What's left is what you're taxed on.

The rate at which you will be taxed will depend on the level of your taxable income after you've made the appropriate deductions. Most people pay basic rate tax. If your taxable income is higher than the upper limit allowed for this, then you will pay higher rate tax on the surplus.

If you want to do the calculation yourself, remember that much of your taxable income will already have had tax deducted from it. Most wages are paid under *PAYE (Pay As You Earn)* (see below). This means that your employer will have deducted tax by the time you get your salary cheque. The same applies to most building society and bank accounts and other investments, which will all deduct tax at basic rate.

The tax year runs from 6 April until 5 April the following year.

You must tell your tax office of any changes in your circumstances, for example if you get married or divorced or your partner dies.

If you think that your tax office has made an error in calculating the amount of tax you have to pay, you should write to them immediately to point out the error. If you don't take any action within thirty days of receiving your tax assessment, you may lose your rights to challenge the tax office's calculation.

CAPITAL GAINS TAX

Capital gains tax (CGT) is paid whenever you dispose of an asset. The asset could be a house, or some land, money or shares. The disposal doesn't have to be in the form of a sale, it could be a gift from one person to another.

However, not every sale or gift of an asset attracts CGT.

- Everyone has a CGT limit, called the annual allowance, up to which amount they are able to make a capital gain without being taxed. The rate is set annually by the government.
- There is no CGT payable on gifts between spouses.
- If you sell your main home there is no CGT payable.

In addition, in some cases, for example gifts of land, payment of CGT can be postponed until the person receiving the gift in turn disposes of it. To take advantage of this, both the giver and the receiver will have to sign a special hold-over agreement.

How is CGT calculated?

If you sell an asset for a greater price than you paid for it, then CGT is paid on the difference or your 'gain'.

- If you're giving the asset as a gift, then you work out its market value and deduct from that the price you paid for it originally.
- If you inherited rather than bought the asset in the first place, then you deduct the market value of the asset at the time you acquired it.
- Don't despair if you acquired your asset many moons ago. If it came into your possession before 31 March 1982, then its acquisition value is calculated as its market value in the spring of 1982.
- Having established the amount of your 'gain', you can then deduct from it any expenses you incurred in either buying or selling the asset. In the case of a house this might include estate agent's fees and conveyancing costs on both the purchase and the sale.

45

 – You can also deduct an indexation allowance which takes account of the effect of inflation.

These deductions could substantially reduce any gain and might take it below the level at which CGT becomes payable. Your final capital gain, if any, is added on to your total taxable income for the year and taxed altogether at the appropriate rate.

INHERITANCE TAX

Inheritance tax (IHT) is a tax on gifts. Despite its name, IHT can arise on gifts you make during your lifetime as well as those that you make after your death. Although it's normally the donor who pays the tax bill on IHT, in certain cases the beneficiary will be liable.

As with other forms of tax, IHT has a large nil rate band below which you do not have to pay tax.

Lifetime gifts
Most lifetime gifts are not subject to IHT. There are a number of reasons for this:

 – Lifetime gifts between spouses do not attract IHT.
 – Most outright gifts are what are known as *Potentially Exempt Transfers (PETs)*. For the gift to be a PET, the donor cannot retain any benefit in it. For example, if you make someone a gift of your house, you cannot then continue to live in it. As long as the donor doesn't die within seven years of making the gift, it remains free of IHT.
 – There are also a multitude of other exemptions which mean that you may avoid paying IHT.

IHT after your death
When you die, you will be treated as though you have given away everything you own. Your estate (see page 72) will be subject to IHT. In addition, your estate will also be liable to pay IHT on any

46

taxable gifts or PETs which you made within seven years of your death.

As with lifetime gifts, property left to a spouse will not be liable to IHT.

PAYE (PAY AS YOU EARN)

Most employees pay tax through PAYE. Each year the Inland Revenue works out your PAYE code according to your individual circumstances. You will be sent a copy of their calculations as a *Notice of Coding*. If you think it's incorrect, you should let them know by return post.

Once your employer has your PAYE code they can deduct the right amount of tax from your earnings. However, the system is far from perfect. If the code is wrong or your circumstances have changed, you may have too much, or too little deducted.

If your situation changes, notify the tax office. Don't wait for a tax return, you could wait for ever!

National insurance

In addition to paying income tax, workers, both employees and the self-employed, must also pay National Insurance Contributions (NIC).

If you are employed, your employer will deduct Class 1 contributions directly from your pay.

If you are self-employed you must pay both Class 2 contributions which are at a flat weekly rate and Class 4 contributions which are assessed as a percentage of your business profits.

CHAPTER 5

Taking Legal Advice

The legal profession is divided into two groups of lawyers: solicitors and barristers. Your first legal port of call will invariably be a solicitor. Firms of solicitors vary widely. A sole practitioner, an inner city practice specialising in legal aid work and a multi-partner city firm will all operate differently.

Solicitors

In any average high street firm the structure will be much the same. At the bottom are the trainee solicitors, who although they will probably have passed all their law exams, still have to spend two years in a law firm before they are fully qualified. They will work with more senior solicitors but may be assigned to your case, under supervision, if it is a minor matter.

Then there are the main body of the firm's solicitors who will have a wide range of experience and expertise. Working alongside them may be legal executives who, although they are not fully qualified lawyers, may be very experienced in certain types of cases.

Finally, there are the firm's partners. Commensurate with their position they will charge you more for their services. The nature of your case will dictate the number and seniority of lawyers assigned to it.

Barristers

Barristers, the ones who appear in wigs and gowns, are a very different breed. They have more of a specialist consultant role within the profession. You won't find one in your local high street as they are closeted in sets of offices, or chambers, in London and some of the major provincial cities. If it is necessary your solicitor will find a barrister appropriate to your case. It is the barrister who more often than not will stand up before the court and represent you, although of course your solicitor will be present throughout.

HOW TO FIND THE RIGHT SOLICITOR

Most high street solicitors handle a wide range of everyday issues including conveyancing, wills, divorce and so on. So which one do you choose? There are two guiding principles:

- Does the solicitor regularly deal with cases similar to yours?
- Do you think you could have a good working relationship?

Where to look
Solicitors are now allowed to advertise their services but many of their clients still come through personal recommendation.

- Ask your family, friends and colleagues. Bear in mind, though, that a solicitor who was first rate on a house transaction may not be the most sympathetic in a divorce case.
- Look for advertisements in your local paper or Yellow Pages.
- Visit your local library or advice centre which should have a list of all the solicitors in the area.
- Go through a copy of the *Regional Directory of Solicitors* which is published by the Law Society. The directory, which is kept by Citizens Advice Bureaux (CABs), law centres, advice centres and libraries, lists not only the names and addresses of all the solicitors in your area but also gives details of the kind of work they do, whether they offer Fixed Fee Interviews or the Legal Aid and Advice Scheme and if they speak any languages other than English.
- If you have a particularly complex case, perhaps involving immigration law, you might want to contact one of the specialist agencies (see Part Five) who may be able to recommend solicitors with a good track record.
- To find a good matrimonial lawyer in your area contact the Solicitors' Family Law Association. The association sets out a

code of practice for its members and those practising family law. The code emphasises that the role of the solicitor should be to help clients reconcile their differences and avoid making the case a contest with winners and losers. The aim is to resolve the case in the most reasonable amount of time with the least disruption to the family.

What to look for

You won't know for sure whether you made the right choice until your case is finally closed. However there are some safeguards.

- In particular areas of the law – for example immigration – certain practices are renowned for their expertise. Other firms have a reputation for a sympathetic approach to abuse or divorce cases or can guarantee a woman solicitor. Your local CAB or advice centre may be able to point you in the right direction or look in the *Regional Directory of Solicitors*.
- To 'test the water' you could make an initial visit to the solicitor under the Fixed Fee Interview scheme (see below) but do remember your solicitor is unlikely to be able to offer you much advice in half an hour.
- Although you can change solicitors if you are unhappy about the way they are dealing with your case (see page 57), such action is generally viewed negatively in the profession. Taking up where someone else left off can be messy. If you have doubts then either discuss them assertively (see page 56) or make the change right at the beginning. If you act the professional client the relationship can be very successful.

SOLICITORS' CHARGES

Before you instruct a solicitor and ask them to act for you, you must find out what it will cost you. The Law Society requires solicitors to:

- Give you the best idea they can of the costs involved when you instruct them.
- Consider whether you are eligible for Legal Aid and Assistance.
- Confirm in writing any agreed fee, what it covers and whether it includes VAT and disbursements (other costs the solicitor might incur on your behalf, e.g. court fees or Stamp Duty paid to the Inland Revenue).
- Tell you how the fee will be calculated, for example as an hourly rate, a percentage of the value of the transaction or some other agreed method, if no fee has been agreed.
- Confirm any estimate in writing. The final bill should not vary substantially from the original estimate unless you have been informed in writing of any changes.
- Tell you at appropriate stages throughout the case, regardless of whether you are legally aided, what costs you may be liable for. For example, even if you win your case you may not get all your legal costs met by the 'other side'.

In addition they should also tell you who will be handling your case and who you should go to within the firm if you have a complaint.

The Fixed Fee Interview
This is quite different from the Legal Aid and Advice Schemes. The Fixed Fee Interview is open to everyone and is not means-tested. It means that you get a half an hour interview with a solicitor for a flat fee, currently £5. Not all solicitors' firms offer the scheme.

The advantages are that you get an idea of whether your case is worth pursuing and you have the opportunity to meet the solicitor on a working basis. The drawback is that thirty minutes isn't very long and may not be enough time to explain and assess your case fully.

Always prepare carefully and thoroughly for the meeting: time is precious. And a word of caution. Make absolutely certain that the solicitor understands you have come to consult them under the Fixed Fee Interview. You don't want any unpleasant surprise bills!

FINANCIAL HELP TOWARDS LEGAL COSTS

If you need legal help from a solicitor or barrister and you cannot afford to pay for it, you may qualify for financial assistance under the Legal Aid and Advice Schemes.

There are three basic types of scheme available. *Legal Advice – The Green Form Scheme* is for non-court work and includes uncontested divorce. *Civil Legal Aid* continues where the Green Form Scheme stops and is for people involved in a court case. Both these schemes are publicly funded and are administered by the Legal Aid Board. The third scheme, *Criminal Legal Aid*, is for people facing a charge for a criminal offence and this is administered by the courts.

The Green Form Scheme

The Green Form Scheme, so called because the application form is green, is a means-tested scheme. If you qualify it will cover you for initial advice and assistance from a solicitor. This might include advice at a first interview, preparing divorce or other papers and writing a few letters.

There is an upper limit on the cost of the work a solicitor can complete under the scheme, but the scheme may be extended so that the solicitor can undertake more work for you.

Do you qualify for help?

Your advice centre or solicitor will be able to tell you whether you qualify and help you complete the necessary forms. The calculation is based on two things: *disposable income* and *capital*. There is an upper ceiling on both and you must have less than the specified limits to qualify. Legal aid is then awarded on a sliding scale according to your financial situation. You may not have to pay anything at all. If you are in receipt of state benefits you will only be means-tested on your capital.

Your *disposable income* is your weekly income less deductions for tax, national insurance and 'fixed amounts' – set deductions for dependent spouses and children according to their age.

Your *capital* is all your capital resources excluding your home and its contents, the tools of your trade and personal effects. It also excludes the sum of capital (if any) over which you have sought legal advice. For example, if your partner has made a claim against you for a particular amount of money, then that amount would be ignored.

If you are in any doubt about whether you are eligible for help, always work your way through the calculation. People with quite substantial gross incomes but with hefty outgoings can still qualify.

Assistance By Way of Representation (ABWOR)
This covers the cost of a solicitor preparing your case and representing you in most civil cases such as separation and maintenance proceedings in the Magistrates Court. To apply for ABWOR you will need to complete another form in addition to the Green Form. Assessment is very similar to the Green Form.

Civil Legal Aid
Civil Legal Aid is means-tested in much the same way as the Green Form Scheme, the difference being that your solicitor can do more complex – and therefore more expensive – work.

Legal aid cannot affect the quality of work a solicitor undertakes on your behalf. You should expect, and receive, exactly the same service as if you were paying privately. Bearing this in mind, you should also expect to work with your solicitor in the same way as if you were paying for their time yourself (see page 54).

If you qualify will legal aid be granted automatically?
The decision to grant legal aid is made by your local legal aid office. Your solicitor will help complete the forms for you. This is particularly important if the costs involved are likely to be high or the case complex.

Legal aid will not be granted automatically even if you meet the financial requirements. You will not get help if the assessment officer decides that your case is of no public interest or stands every chance of failing before it even gets to court.

NOTE: If your financial situation changes, for example you remarry, your entitlement to legal aid may well be affected. You should always inform your solicitor of any changes.

The statutory charge

Even if you are granted legal aid, the Legal Aid Board is entitled to claw back some or all of your legal costs if you are successful in your case and gain or regain money or property or win compensation. This is known as the *statutory charge*. However, the first few thousand pounds of any 'gain' is ignored. Ask your solicitor what, if anything, you will have to pay if you win your case.

ARE YOU READY FOR A SOLICITOR?

Solicitors are expensive. Their job is to assess the legal implications of your case, guide you through the complexities of the legal system and represent your best interests before the law. If you use them as counsellors, companions, punch bags upon which to vent your frustrations or shoulders to cry on, you will pay for the privilege. And you probably won't get the best advice either.

Before you call your lawyer, consider if it's a lawyer you actually need to talk to, or whether a counsellor or friend would be a better listener and provide more appropriate advice.

By the time you reach the solicitor's door, you should be crystal clear about exactly why you are consulting them. The solicitor's office is not the place to discuss your failing relationship and whether separation would solve the problems. It is the place to instruct a professional to begin divorce proceedings and consider the legal and financial implications of breaking up your relationship.

WORKING WITH YOUR SOLICITOR

Remember two things when you consult a solicitor. One: time is money. Two: communicate the facts clearly. To do this you need to be succinct and organised.

- Go prepared to your first meeting with the solicitor. Collect together all the relevant documents you have: letters, marriage or birth certificates, bills, diary dates of telephone calls, eyewitness statements. If you can, photocopy them and put them into files.
- Make a list of everything that has happened to do with the case and set down the information in the order in which it occurred. This will save you a great deal of time – and ultimately money – later. It will also help you channel your thoughts and make it easier to communicate clearly with the solicitor. If you are unsure of certain facts, or need to check out information then this is the time to do it.
- Be on time for all your appointments, even if the solicitor keeps you waiting – and they can do. If you can't make an appointment, telephone in advance.
- Establish how much the solicitor is going to charge you (see page 50).
- Communicate the facts of your case clearly and briefly, providing documents where appropriate. Don't be tempted to waffle.
- Find out what the solicitor is going to do for you. If they start talking in jargon and you don't understand what they are saying, then ask them to stop and explain in plain everyday language. You are paying for their service and have every right to understand what they are doing on your behalf.
- If the solicitor offers to write to or telephone someone about your case, establish when they expect to receive a reply. Many clients believe their solicitors are too slow in getting answers or action on their case. Unfortunately, lawyers often need to deal with large bureaucratic organisations or government bodies or with solicitors on the 'other side' who may not consider it in their client's best interests to respond speedily. It may be weeks rather than days before your solicitor contacts you again. If you think the delay is excessive or they have taken more time than they originally said they would, then chivy them up.
- Avoid making unnecessary calls or writing superfluous, long letters to your solicitor; they will all add to your final bill.

– If you have an important piece of new information connected to your case, then tell your solicitor immediately. Withholding information may make you both look complete fools in the long run, not to mention upset your case.

DEALING WITH PROBLEMS

There may be all sorts of reasons why you feel unhappy with the way your solicitor is dealing with your case. Problems do arise, and it's worth considering what might have caused them. The solicitor may have misunderstood part of your instructions: perhaps you didn't put over all the facts clearly; they might be completely over-worked and because your case doesn't have an immediate deadline, it has gone to the bottom of the pile. Your expectations about what your legal adviser can do for you are perhaps unrealistic.

NOTE: If there is a problem you *must* talk it over with the solicitor immediately.

– Arrange to see or speak to your solicitor. If you already have an appointment planned, set aside time to discuss the way the case is being handled. You could start off by saying: *I realise you are extremely busy and time is money but I'd like to raise a few points that concern me about the way you are handling my case.*
– Be positive. Highlight something that you think has been dealt with well. *I appreciated the way you listened to me at our first meeting and also the way you immediately returned my initial calls.*
– Spell out specifically what you think is wrong. *In the last fort-night I have telephoned your offices and left messages on six occasions but none of my calls has been returned. In addition I haven't received copies of the correspondence you agreed to send me. I am very concerned that my case is not receiving your full and prompt attention.*
– Be specific about the changes you want. *I would like you to answer my calls within twenty-four hours or else let me know when*

it would be convenient to speak. I would also like copies of all the letters you have sent so far and to receive copies of any future letters as they are written.

- Listen to the explanation the solicitor gives. If you think it is unsatisfactory, say so and reiterate your request. On the other hand, there may simply have been a breakdown in communications and your discussion will probably have done much to put matters right.
- Clients are often told, 'not to worry' or 'the matter's in hand'. You might want to consider responding: *I'm delighted that everything is in hand. However, I am still very concerned about the outcome of this case and therefore in the future* . . . (and state your request again).
- The more specific you are about what you consider wrong with the way the solicitor is handling your case and what you would like done about it, the more likely you are to cement a better working relationship and avoid time-consuming argumentative discussions.

WHEN THINGS DON'T WORK OUT

It may just be that you don't 'get on' with your solicitor. If a frank discussion about the way you feel your case is being handled proves fruitless and a chat with the senior partner fails to resolve the problem, then changing your solicitor may seem the sensible option.

If your criticisms and concerns are serious, you need also to consider whether your lawyer was guilty of professional misconduct or negligence (see below).

Changing solicitors

You must first find a solicitor who will agree to take on your case. Ensure that you tell them that you previously instructed someone else.

Write to your original solicitor stating that you have decided to withdraw your instructions to them and ask them to forward all your papers to your new solicitor. They may not be prepared to do this until you have settled all their outstanding fees.

If you were granted legal aid and wish to change solicitors, you will need to check this with the Legal Aid Board before you take any action.

Professional misconduct

The majority of complaints about solicitors are to do with professional misconduct. The Law Society considers professional misconduct includes: persistent delay in answering your letters or inquiries – or not answering them at all; delay in dealing with your case; failing to keep proper accounts of money held on your behalf; acting for others involved in the same case as you, where your interests conflict; overcharging and dishonesty. They also include 'shoddy work' which means work that is substandard and which may have caused you inconvenience or distress.

If you think that your solicitor has been guilty of professional misconduct, discuss the matter first with the most senior partner in the law firm which is handling your case. If you cannot resolve the problem by talking it through, you will need to complain to the Solicitors Complaints Bureau. This is a separate organisation set up by the Law Society to investigate complaints against solicitors.

Write to the bureau giving the following information:

- the name and address of the law firm;
- the name of the solicitor handling your case;
- the kind of matter your solicitor was dealing with;
- your complaint;
- whether you object to the bureau sending a copy of your letter to the solicitor.

Do not send any documents at this stage. The bureau will write and ask you for further information if they think it necessary.

If the bureau decides that your solicitor has breached the rules of professional conduct then it will either deal with the solicitor itself or refer the matter to the Solicitors Disciplinary Tribunal. If appropriate it will then strike the solicitor from the Roll of Solicitors, suspend them from practice or fine them.

Neither the bureau nor the tribunal can pay you any compensation. However, in cases of shoddy work the bureau can order your solicitor to: reduce the bill; rectify mistakes or take any other necessary action.

Negligence

If you consider your solicitor has made a serious mistake which has cost you money or resulted in some other loss, then you may be entitled to claim compensation. There are a number of actions open to you, although they are not necessarily exclusive.

- Find another solicitor to take on your case against the first solicitor. If you encounter difficulties contact the Solicitors Complaints Bureau and ask to be put in touch with the *Negligence Panel Scheme*. This is a panel of senior solicitors in your area who will give you free advice about your negligence case.
- Take advantage of the Law Society's Arbitration Scheme which means you avoid the complications and expense of going to court.
- Take your case to court. Most negligence cases are settled 'out of court', before you actually get to court. You should not embark on this option without the advice of a lawyer.

Overcharging

If you think your solicitor's bill is too high, discuss the matter with them first. They may well reduce it if your arguments are valid. If you are not satisfied with the response, you can have the bill examined.

- For non-contentious cases – those that don't involve going to court – insist that your solicitor applies to the Law Society for a *remuneration certificate*. The Law Society appoints a panel of lawyers who examine the disputed bill, the work that was undertaken and your comments. They then issue a remuneration certificate stating whether they consider the bill is fair

and if not by how much it should be reduced. They have no authority to increase the bill. The service is free.
- If the case was contentious then it is up to the courts to assess the bill and decide whether it is right. This is known as having the bill *taxed*. Your solicitor or the Law Society will explain how the procedure works.

NOTE: If you want to challenge your bill you must do so immediately as strict time limits are in force.

Complaints against barristers

You should first register an official complaint with the barrister's Head of Chambers (the most senior barrister at that office or chambers).

If you get no satisfaction you can write to the Bar Council. You will need to give the following information:

- the name of the barrister and their professional address;
- the name of the solicitor who employed the barrister;
- a detailed statement of your complaint.

The Bar Council has limited powers. They can reprimand members and in extreme cases suspend or disbar barristers. Even if your complaint is upheld, they cannot offer you any compensation.

On the whole it is extremely difficult to take legal action against a barrister for negligence.

WHERE ELSE TO GET LEGAL ADVICE

Law centres

A local law centre will be staffed by qualified lawyers and their advice is usually free. However, there may not be one in your area and unfortunately many are severely understaffed so opening hours and appointments may be restricted.

Citizens Advice Bureaux

The CAB has a comprehensive network of centres throughout the country. In addition there are other advice centres run by local authorities. Most of these will be able to give free information and help on a wide range of issues. Although many are very experienced the quality of advice does vary and you may well be referred on for specialist help. Advisers are unlikely to be qualified lawyers and the majority are often volunteers. Again, financial cuts mean opening hours are becoming increasingly restricted and it may be extremely difficult in some areas to obtain advice over the phone.

Campaigning organisations

Campaigning organisations such as Rights of Women, the Equal Opportunities Commission and the Joint Council for the Welfare of Immigrants offer legal advice in specific cases. Some have special telephone advice sessions and details can be obtained from the individual organisations. The depth of advice given will vary between the different groups.

In addition, women's units, either independent or attached to local authorities, may be able to provide information. Women's refuges will also be familiar with appropriate legal procedures for those in their care.

THE COURTS

There are three kinds of courts in England and Wales: Magistrates Courts, County Courts and the High Court. Each one deals with slightly different types of cases.

Magistrates Courts

Locally based, Magistrates Courts tend to be used for criminal proceedings such as speeding fines, unpaid parking tickets, assault, burglary and trespass cases. They can also be used for applying for child custody orders and local authority care proceedings.

Cases are heard by *magistrates*, sometimes known as *JPs* (*Justices of the Peace*). These are lay people who are approved by the Lord

Chancellor and undergo special training courses. In theory magistrates are supposed to reflect the background and experience of the community in general. Unfortunately this isn't always true. Most cases will be heard by three magistrates, one of whom will act as chairperson.

Some Magistrates Courts in larger towns may have full-time professional magistrates, known as *stipendiary magistrates*, who will sit alone.

Evidence must be given orally in the Magistrates Court. For some people, particularly women seeking an injunction against a violent partner (see pages 218–219), this might be quite an unpleasant experience.

Juvenile Courts
Juvenile Courts are part of the Magistrates Court system and are used to deal with criminal cases involving children.

County Courts
Once again these are locally based courts found in most towns and cities throughout the country. They deal with civil as opposed to criminal cases. These include disputes between landlords and tenants, shopkeepers and dissatisfied customers and also between neighbours, the kind of problems that arise in everyday life.

Cases in the county court are dealt with and decided by *Circuit Judges* and *District Judges* who are drawn from the ranks of senior lawyers.

Each court has a large staff. Some of them deal solely with vast amounts of paperwork. Others, particularly court clerks and the ushers, are there to ensure the smooth running of court business and to make sure those attending court hearings are in the right place at the right time. While they obviously can't advise you on the legal details of your case, the court staff can help you get the right forms and explain court procedure to you. They aim to make the court system as user-friendly as possible.

The courts are open and also sit – hear cases – during normal, or slightly shorter than normal, business hours.

Divorce County Courts

There is no special family court in this country and so divorces are dealt with by a branch of the County Court system known as Divorce County Courts. Not every County Court also has a Divorce County Court. Your local court office will advise you of your nearest one. In London, the equivalent is the Divorce Registry of the High Court.

The High Court

The High Court is based in London, but you won't necessarily have to travel to the capital if your case is referred to the High Court. Judges regularly visit major towns and cities to deal with cases that arise outside the London area.

The High Court looks at complex cases, appeals against decisions reached in other courts and defended divorce cases. If your case is heard in the High Court you will probably need to be represented by a solicitor and barrister (see page 48).

How cases are heard

Cases can be heard either in open court or in chambers.

Open court

This means that the case is heard in the courtroom itself. The hearings tend to be rather formal. The barristers and judges wear their legal robes and members of the public are admitted. The press are also permitted to attend and can report details of the case in the papers.

Cases heard in chambers

These are private hearings either in the courtroom or in the judge's room at the court. Neither the public nor the press can attend and details of the case can't be reported in the papers. On the whole the procedure is much more relaxed. The lawyers don't wear their gowns and the only people there apart from the parties concerned and their legal advisers will be necessary court staff.

HOW LAW IS MADE

There are three levels of law in the United Kingdom:

- law made by Parliament;
- delegated legislation;
- common law.

What does this mean?

Law made by Parliament
Parliament has powers to make laws through Acts of Parliament on almost anything. These are also known as statutes. An example of an Act of Parliament is the one on marriage introduced by Lord Hardwicke in 1753 (see page 82).

Delegated legislation
Sometimes in a statute Parliament gives other bodies, such as government departments, the right to make rules and regulations dealing with the details of the way the law is put into practice. On occasions, these rules and regulations have to go back to Parliament for approval. For example, many of the details of the social security law have been established in this way.

Common law
Acts of Parliament need to be interpreted. In addition there are some aspects of everyday life where there are no relevant Acts of Parliament.

In order to fill these gaps, judges have powers to interpret the statutes and decide disputes. In making their decisions they must follow the conclusions drawn by other judges in previous similar cases. This is called common law.

For historical reasons Scotland has retained a separate legal system which is not based on common law, but judges in Scotland have powers to interpret legislation and deal with gaps in the law.

There is one other level of law which is that made by the European Communities.

LEGAL TERMS

The legal terms used in this book are explained as and when they appear. However there are two phrases which occur regularly.

- A *deed* is a formal document which has to be drawn up in a certain way and has to be signed in the presence of witnesses. A solicitor will be able to advise you how to draw up a proper deed or draft one for you.
- An *affidavit* is a statement made on oath. It could be a statement you have drawn up yourself or one that has been drawn up by a solicitor. To swear an affidavit you will have to take the statement along to a solicitor. You will have to sign the document in front of the solicitor and repeat a simple oath. The solicitor will then sign the document. You don't necessarily need an appointment to do this and any solicitor will oblige.

CHAPTER 6

A Roof Over Your Head

OWNING YOUR OWN HOME

Property ownership and the law

In order to understand your legal relationship to the home you own or share with your partner, you need to grasp three legal concepts: *legal title; beneficial ownership* and *trusts*.

The laws relating to property stem from what were originally two legal systems. Common law laid down the very formal rules based on who had *legal title* to – owned – the land. However, since children and, until the mid nineteenth century, women, couldn't hold legal title to land, the rules proved to be too inflexible.

Therefore a second set of rules, known as *equity*, were developed in the Court of Chancery. These new rules distinguished the legal title from the *beneficial ownership*. This meant that while one person owned the legal title to the property, in practice they held it for the benefit of someone else.

The mechanism for establishing beneficial ownership is known as a *trust*. In other words, one person holds the property in trust for another. This was particularly important for married women who, until the *Married Women's Property Act* of 1882, couldn't hold legal title to land. The woman's property was therefore held in trust for her by someone, usually not her husband, so that her husband had no control over it. This kind of trust is *expressed*, or written, in the form of a *trust deed*.

After 1882, married women could hold legal title to property in their own right. However, a new problem arose. The law was very simple: whoever held the legal title, usually the husband, owned the property. By the middle of this century many working wives were contributing to buying and paying for the home. If the family split up, the wife was left with nothing, despite her financial contributions.

To safeguard married women a new type of trust was introduced into property law – an *implied trust*. Unlike the rest of property law this does not rely on a formal, written agreement. The whole purpose of an implied trust was to enable Divorce Court judges to award a proportion of the beneficial ownership of the family home to the wife. Today, the court has wide-ranging powers to transfer the ownership of a property from one spouse to another and apportion any profits as it sees fit, regardless of who holds the legal title.

On the other hand, the court does not have the same powers over property lived in by cohabiting couples. Ownership still rests with the person who has the legal title. However, on separation, cohabitants who do not hold the legal title or have a written trust stating their beneficial ownership can use the mechanism of an implied trust to claim an interest in the home.

To sum up

1. The person whose name appears on the Land or Charge Certificate or the title deeds of the property owns or has *legal title* to that property. Up to four people can benamed as legal owners in this way.

2. *Beneficial ownership* or *equitable title* is distinct and separate from legal ownership. The law presumes that whoever owns the legal title also has beneficial ownership unless proved otherwise.

   However, someone who is not named on the title deed can acquire beneficial ownership as well as, or instead of, the legal owner. The person who has beneficial ownership has the right to profit from the sale of the property and may also have rights of occupation.

3. The mechanism whereby a person who does not hold the legal title can obtain a beneficial ownership of a property is known as a *trust*. A trust must be in writing and for your own protection should be drawn up by a solicitor.

4. Even if you have nothing in writing, you may be able to claim beneficial ownership of the property through an *implied trust*.

Owning your home with someone else

If you hold legal title to your home it will either be as the *sole* owner or as co-owner with your partner or other people.

There are two ways of co-owning your home:

– as *joint tenants*;
– as *tenants in common*.

Although they both have the same effect on your rights to occupy the home, your rights to the proceeds of the property should it be sold will depend on the type of tenancy you have. The terms *tenant* and *tenancy* in this context have nothing to do with tenanted property. Here they mean owner and ownership of a home.

Joint tenancy

This means that the proceeds of the property will be divided equally between you. When you die, your half of the property will automatically go to your co-owner.

Tenants in common

This means that the proceeds of the property will be divided according to the terms of the co-ownership. People usually split the co-ownership according to the amount of money each put into the property in the first place and the proportion of the mortgage repayment each will contribute.

However, there are reasons why one partner might not want as great a share in the property. For example, if you're a partner in a business and might have to sell your home if you went bankrupt, it would make sense either to make your spouse or lover the sole owner of the property or to retain only a very small share.

When you die, your share of the property will be distributed according to the terms of your will or the Rules of Intestacy if you die without having made a will.

NOTE: In some circumstances you may wish to change from being joint tenants to tenants in common (see page 144).

Registered and unregistered land

When it comes to buying and selling property, the law is not concerned so much about the nature of your home, whether it's a bungalow or flat or mansion, but the land on which it's built.

Traditionally, when you bought a home you exchanged *title deeds*, great dusty wads of paper detailing every past transaction of the property. This was because originally all the land was *unregistered*.

Over the past one hundred years, increasing areas of the country have been made the subject of compulsory registration. This means that each piece of land is registered with the Land Registry. The register shows a prospective buyer whether there is a mortgage or other charge against the property (see page 146) and also any other special information about the land such as the types of building that cannot be erected on it.

In order to help streamline the conveyancing process – the method by which a property is bought and sold – all property is now on registered land.

RENTING YOUR HOME

The law relating to letting and renting property is perhaps the most horrendously complex and political area of the legal system. It would be impossible to go into anything other than the barest details here.

If you have any kind of concern, either as a landlord or a tenant, you must seek specialist advice. This could be from a local solicitor who's an expert in this area of law or from a Housing Advice or Law Centre in your neighbourhood.

Your rights as a tenant will depend on whether on your landlord is:

- a private landlord;
- a local authority;
- a housing association.

The majority of rented accommodation in this country is provided by local authorities and housing associations. If you rent from either of these sources you can usually expect to have either a *secured* or an *assured* tenancy (see below).

If you have a private landlord, then your rights will also depend on the kind of *tenancy* you have. A tenancy is the agreement under which you occupy your home. You must always find out whether you have a *protected* or an *assured tenancy* (see below). If you have either of these kind of tenancies then you will have some *security of tenure*, which means you cannot be evicted without reason.

If you are neither a protected nor an assured tenant, then your rights may be very limited.

NOTE: Even if you do not have security of tenure, a landlord *cannot* throw you out of your home without following a strict legal procedure and obtaining a special court order. If you are ever threatened with eviction or your landlord harasses you, you should seek advice *immediately* from an advice centre or solicitor.

What kind of tenant am I?

Private landlords
If you can answer *true* to all of the following questions then you probably have an *assured tenancy*, if you moved in on, or after, 15 January 1989, or a *protected tenancy*, if you moved in before that date.

1. Your landlord does not live on the premises. (For exceptions see below.)
2. You and your partner have a room or rooms of your own.
3. Your landlord does not provide services such as breakfast, room cleaning or laundry.
4. The tenancy has not been taken in the name of a company.
5. You were not given a notice before you moved in stating that the tenancy was a *shorthold tenancy* – this means you have very limited rights.

If you live in a purpose-built block of flats, the landlord will only be regarded as living on the premises if you share their flat.

However, if you live in a property that has been converted into a number of flats and your landlord lives in one of those flats then it is unlikely you will have an assured or protected tenancy.

Local authorities
If your landlord is a local council or one of a number of public authorities, you are probably a *secured tenant*.

Housing associations
If your landlord is a housing association and you moved in to your home on, or after 15 January 1989, then you are probably an *assured tenant*. If you moved in before that date, you probably have a *secured tenancy*. The law changed in 1989 and secured tenancies became assured tenancies. Both offer you more or less the same level of security of tenure but the new, assured, tenancy gives you slightly fewer rights.

Your rights as a tenant
Only the person or people whose names appear on the rent book or tenancy agreement are responsible for paying the rent. Unless you are married, only the person named on the rent book or agreement has the right to occupy the property.

As is often the case with legal issues, what happens when the relationship falls apart is mostly governed by what action you took at the start. If you already live in rented accommodation, or you're about to sign a tenancy agreement, you should look at the relevant chapters in Part Three: Getting Together.

CHAPTER 7

Life After Life

There can be few people who enjoy the thought of making a will or considering their own funeral arrangements. Nobody likes to contemplate their own mortality. The real problem with death is not so much the possible pain and anguish that goes into organising your affairs but the utter chaos that can ensue if you don't.

Once you're dead, you won't be around to see justice done. And there's a good chance that with the connivance of vengeful relatives, insensitive friends and an inflexible law, it simply won't happen. Don't leave it until tomorrow to make provision for the future, do something about it today.

There are three broad pieces of law which govern what happens to your property and your assets after you die.

- A will.
- The *Intestacy Rules*: how your assets are divided up if you don't leave a will.
- The *Inheritance Act*: how your family or dependants can challenge your will or the Intestacy Rules if they feel they haven't been adequately provided for.

In addition there are very strict rules about how a will is administered; these are known as *probate*.

WILL POWER

A will is a document that states what you want to happen after your death. It can contain a number of elements.

- In your will you divide up your *estate* – everything that you own – amongst your *beneficiaries*. These are the people who inherit your estate.

- You can leave *legacies*, particular gifts or sums of money to special friends, relatives or charities.
- If you make a legacy or legacies, you can then leave the *residue* – everything that's left over after the special gifts, expenses and taxes have been paid – to one person or divided up amongst a number of people.
- You can also state what kind of funeral you want and whether you want to be buried or cremated. However, it's probably best to make your family aware of your wishes beforehand rather than leave the information solely in your will.
- You should also appoint *executors* of your will. These are the people – usually there are two – who will administer the wishes expressed in your will. The job is more than a mere formality so you should think carefully about whom you appoint. No one can be forced to be an executor so you should always seek their permission first. It's best to get someone younger or the same age as you, since you want someone who in the normal course of events will survive you. Solicitors or banks will also act as executors but they will make a charge for the service and may not be as sensitive to your wishes as someone who knows you well. Banks in particular can be very expensive.
- If you have young children, you will also want to appoint *guardians* – people who will look after your child or children in the event of your death (see page 245).
- You can always change your will. If it's simply a minor amendment then you can add what's known as a *codicil* or supplement. The same strict rules that apply when signing and witnessing a will apply to making a codicil.

NOTE: You ought to be aware that regardless of the terms of your will, a family member or dependant can challenge them after your death under the Inheritance Act (see page 76). You cannot specifically exclude anyone from benefiting from your estate. However, if you have particular reasons for not wanting someone to inherit from your estate when you die, you should put the facts and the reasons in a signed letter and leave it with your will.

Do you need a solicitor to draw up a will?

Strictly speaking, no. There are plenty of do-it-yourself kits around. However, be wary of simply completing a standard pre-written form; they can never be appropriate for every situation. The danger is that when your nearest and dearest discover an omission, it'll be too late to do anything about it.

If you decide to draw up your own will, then you must ensure that it is properly witnessed. If it isn't, the document will be invalid. Beneficiaries cannot witness a will.

If you own property or have young children, then it's best to get professional advice.

THE INTESTACY RULES

If you die without making a will, in other words *intestate*, then your estate will be divided up according to the *Intestacy Rules*. These are strict rules governing who inherits what; they make no allowances for each individual's circumstances and therefore they may not reflect your wishes.

Under the Intestacy Rules how your estate is divided up will depend on who survives you. Provision is only made for *whole blood* relatives and half sisters and brothers. There is no provision for cohabitees, lovers or friends.

Money inherited by young people is kept in trust until they are eighteen or get married.

If your children die before you, then any money due to them becomes payable to their children or their grandchildren.

What happens if . . . ?

Your spouse and children survive you

Your spouse receives: all personal chattels; £75,000 (this figure changes periodically) or the entire estate if it is less than this amount;

half the remaining worth of the estate which is invested and the income paid to your spouse during their lifetime.

Your children receive: the other half of the remaining worth of the estate divided amongst them in equal shares; after the death of your spouse, the invested half which is divided into equal shares.

Your spouse survives you but there are no children
Your spouse receives: all personal chattels; £125,000 or the entire estate if it is less than this amount; half of the remaining worth of the estate.

If your parents survive you they receive the other half of the remainder of your estate.

If your parents are dead your brothers and sisters, or, if they predecease you, their children, receive the other half of the remainder of your estate.

Your spouse survives you but there are no children and no parents, sisters or brothers or their children alive
Your spouse inherits your whole estate.

Your spouse dies before you
Your estate is given to your surviving relations in the following order: your children; parents; brothers and sisters and if they are dead, then their children; half brothers and half sisters and if they are dead, then their children; grandparents; uncles and aunts and if they are dead, then their children; half brothers and half sisters of your parents and if they are dead, then their children; the Crown, the Duchy of Lancaster or the Duchy of Cornwall, depending where you live. Each preceding group must all be dead before the estate can go to the next.

In practice very few estates end up going to the Crown as it's usually possible to track down beneficiaries, even if it takes a great deal of time and money.

THE INHERITANCE ACT

The Inheritance (Provision for Family and Dependants) Act 1975, or the Inheritance Act as it's commonly known, lays down who can challenge the terms of a will or the effect of the Intestacy Rules, how they do it and time limits in which they must apply to the court.

Who can apply?

There are five groups of people who can make an application to the court:

- a husband or wife;
- a former husband or wife who has not remarried;
- the deceased's children;
- any person treated by the deceased as a child of the family whether in an existing or former marriage;
- anyone who was living with the deceased immediately before their death and was financially dependent upon them.

If you think you are eligible to apply, then it will be up to you to prove your claim. Bear in mind that the people who benefit from the will are likely to oppose your application.

If you are making a claim and you also have a child who is eligible to apply, then you should both make independent claims.

Time limits

Tight time limits are in force for anyone wishing to make a claim. Applications should be made within six months, although exceptions might be made in outstanding circumstances. It's best to apply as soon as the person dies.

Although the solicitor handling the administration of the deceased's estate will probably be able to answer any basic inquiries you might have, remember they are acting on behalf of the personal representatives of the dead person. You should instruct your own solicitor to act in your best interests.

For more information on the effect of the Inheritance Act and how to make a claim see pages 227–229.

DEALING WITH AN ESTATE: PROBATE

Whether or not you make a will the procedure for dealing with your estate is much the same. If you have made a will then you will have already appointed an executor (see page 73) to administer your estate. If you die without making a will then one of the people entitled to your estate under the Intestacy Rules (see above) will be appointed as an *administrator*. Executors and administrators are also called *personal representatives*.

Before your personal representatives can carry out the terms of your estate they will need to get *probate*, if there's a will, or *letters of administration*, if there's no will. These are basically authorisations from the court enabling your personal representatives to administer your will. Without this authorisation, banks, building societies and other institutions are unlikely to be willing to release money or other assets.

You can obtain probate from the Probate Registry. You will need to apply in writing and enclose a copy of the will, if there is one. If there is any inheritance tax due, it has to be paid when you apply for probate.

Until probate is obtained none of the deceased person's property can be sold or, strictly speaking, given away. If you are acting as a personal representative, you should inform the deceased's bank, the Post Office and anywhere else they had savings to ensure that all cheques and banker's orders are stopped and savings frozen. You should also notify the tax office.

Once you have probate you will have to pay off any outstanding debts as well as obtain payments of any life insurance or other policies. You'll also need to arrange the disposal of any property and personal belongings. You must keep a list of any expenses you incur so that these can be deducted from the estate.

PART THREE:
Getting Together

CHAPTER 8

A History of Getting Together

Once upon a time in Merrie Olde Englande, long-term relationships were altogether more simple. There were few legal and social niceties to observe. Late-night soul-searching about whether to cohabit or get married; tortuous family discussions about white weddings and Register Offices were things of the future.

Traditional customs
Before the mid 1500s, all that was necessary to tie the marital knot was for the couple to declare that they took each other as husband and wife, in which case the marriage became binding immediately. If not that, then they could agree to take each other as husband and wife sometime in the future, in which case the marriage was binding as soon as it was consummated.

From the mid 1500s it became customary for the marriage to be contracted at the church door in front of a priest, following the publication of banns (see page 114). It's hardly surprising that the law favoured this public form of marriage since property rights and legitimacy were important consequences of any union.

However, by the 1700s, the banns and the public nature of weddings were largely dispensed with and couples exchanged their simple vows in front of a priest or clerk in holy orders.

You can imagine the chaos that these *ad hoc* arrangements created. Wives who thought they'd been legally wed for years would suddenly discover the marriage was null and void; their husbands were already wed in a clandestine ceremony they knew nothing about. Minors married without their parents' consent and many a young heiress's fortune disappeared into the night in secret unions with unscrupulous cads. The 'Fleet' parsons thrived. These profligate clergy would roam the countryside trading in clandestine marriages.

The first Marriage Act

Into this great evil abyss strode Lord Hardwicke, who in 1753 introduced an Act of Parliament to put a stop to these abuses. Parliament decreed that no marriage would be valid in England and Wales unless it was performed according to the rites of the Church of England in the parish church of one of the parties, in the presence of a clergyman and two witnesses.

These requirements, along with others he introduced, proved so stringent, and the consequence of avoiding marriage so harsh, that many couples fled north of the border. In Scotland the marriage laws were far less rigorous. In the next seventy years Gretna Green secured its place in romantic history.

To stop this marriage traffic a new Act came into force in 1823. This made little change to the details of Lord Hardwicke's original Act, but declared that a marriage was only void if a couple knowingly and wilfully broke the terms of the law.

The first civil marriage

In the nineteenth century the Marriage Act was slightly amended a couple of times. With the growth of religious tolerance in England, Roman Catholics and Protestant dissenters increasingly voiced their repugnance at being made to undergo a Church of England marriage. Jewish and Quaker marriages had always been exempt from the Acts (see page 121).

New Acts brought into existence the Superintendent Registrars of Births, Deaths and Marriages. This enabled people of other faiths to get married without publishing banns or obtaining an ecclesiastical licence. For the first time since the Middle Ages, English law recognised a purely civil marriage.

However, by the middle of this century, the law governing marriage had become such a confusing web of legal statutes that in 1949 a 'clean-up' Act was introduced. This aimed to consolidate and rationalise existing legislation. Since that time there have been a few minor amendments, for example allowing people who are too ill to move to get married from their sickbed.

Marriage – the backbone of society

Lord Hardwicke's 1753 Act drew the first and final distinction between marriage and cohabitation. While in Scotland, *common law marriage* or *marriage by habit and repute* remained legally valid, the new Act in England confirmed that families within marriage, and not outside it, were the only acceptable way of maintaining the structure of society.

With the formalisation of the legal process, marriage became the only lawfully acceptable form of sexual relationship. An attitude which was reinforced in the eighteenth century by a particularly notorious and repressive sexual code – for women.

Whereas unmarried mothers had traditionally been able to go before the magistrates to claim maintenance from the father of their child, for a short while in the 1830s this law was repealed on the grounds that it encouraged blackmail and immorality. However, although this right was reinstated a short while later, the famous Poor Laws, now revised, continued to discriminate between unmarried mothers and their illegitimate children and widows and deserted wives.

There have always been couples who preferred cohabitation to marriage. The extent to which such a choice was tolerated probably had a great deal to do with your position in society. The sexual mores and relationships of well-to-do intellectuals, such as the Bloomsbury Group at the beginning of this century, are well documented. Their behaviour appeared acceptable – to their own small circle. On the other hand, appalling examples of the treatment of unmarried mothers abound, even today.

Before the advent of the Pill, when contraceptives were unavailable or denied to unmarried women, when there was a great deal of ignorance about pregnancy, it was women, not men, who suffered in a society which upheld a sanctified view of holy matrimony and prized chastity above humanity.

Attitudes are changing today. But the legal legacies of Lord Hardwicke and the social legacies of the Victorian era have produced a yawning gap for cohabitation law. Society is still not sure how to treat couples who choose not to marry and the law reflects this confusion.

CHAPTER 9

Cohabitation

Cohabitation is taken to mean two people who live together as 'man and wife' but remain unmarried.

POPULAR MYTHS

Let's explode these right away!

- Common law marriage. *This doesn't actually exist; it was abolished in the early 1700s.*
- Living together as man and wife gives you the same rights to the family home and to maintenance as married people. *Nonsense! Cohabitees have no automatic right to the family home and no right to maintenance.*
- The longer you live together, the more rights you acquire. *The length of time you live together makes no difference to your legal status.*
- As cohabitees you automatically inherit your partner's estate when you die. *You won't, unless you make a will.*
- Living together is much easier to walk away from than marriage. *It isn't. If anything, it's messier.*

The legal position of cohabitees is inconsistent. In some instances, for example domestic violence, you are awarded equal status and protection comparable to that of a married couple. In others, for example the right to occupy a home, you have little or no automatic legal protection.

Since the law will not automatically protect you, you must protect yourself.

Cohabitees must look to their future. However unpalatable or ridiculous the notion is to you, you have to consider your financial and legal position at the *start* of your relationship. It may be unromantic to discuss trust deeds and wills and contracts when all you want to do is talk of love. The harsh reality is that many cohabitation relationships do not last for ever. And you have no guarantee that yours will be any different. Should you come to part, you may find yourself in very different circumstances from those in which you embarked on your relationship.

A Cautionary Tale

Cindy met Mark when they were both in their twenties. Cindy worked in advertising as a PA and Mark ran a computer company. Mark's business was doing well and he owned his own house. Cindy rented a flat with some friends. They decided to start living together and Cindy moved in with Mark.

Even when Cindy became pregnant two years later, they decided that marriage was not for them and continued to cohabit. When their first child was born, Cindy stopped work. She stayed at home to look after her son, and a daughter who was born a couple of years later. Mark continued to support the family.

Six years after they met, Cindy discovered that Mark was seeing another woman. Mark told Cindy their relationship was over. He wanted her and the children to leave his house. Never imagining that their relationship could ever end, Cindy hadn't given a thought to where she would stand if the worst happened.

She had no income, no home and two children to support. The only thing she could be reasonably sure of was getting the court to order Mark to pay maintenance to their children. As for the rest, nothing was guaranteed.

But, think you, that will never happen to us. Even if it doesn't, even if you go on living together until a ripe old age, death is still no respecter of the loves and desires of cohabitees. Unless you consider the future, make your wills, insure your lives and organise your property, you too have no guarantee that you will be provided for when your lifelong companion is no longer there.

As far as relationships outside marriage are concerned, the Boy Scout motto, 'Be Prepared!' was never more appropriate.

If you are already living with your partner or about to enter a long term cohabitation relationship, then you ought to read this section in conjunction with Part Four: Breaking Up, Chapter 13 Cohabitees.

THE LEGAL POSITION

The law doesn't recognise cohabitation as a legally valid union between two people. The popular phrase common law wife or common law husband has no legal significance. The fundamental difference between marriage and cohabitation is that a husband and wife have an obligation to maintain one another during the marriage – and perhaps also afterwards. The unmarried couple have no duty to maintain their partner either while they are living together or after they have broken up.

Why cohabit?

Many couples live together as a prelude to getting married. It's a very sound method of finding out if you're really suited. Being with someone twenty-four hours a day is a sure-fire way of finding out whether you can accommodate their peculiar quirks.

Other people choose to cohabit because they oppose the principle of marriage. These relationships represent long-term commitments, in no way less meaningful than a traditional marriage. Some couples mark their commitment in a ceremony which, while it has no legal basis, certainly has equal significance to a wedding service.

And some partners live together because they have no alternative. For whatever reason, they cannot legally get married.

PROTECT YOURSELF: THE ESSENTIALS

There are three areas where cohabitees are particularly vulnerable. Although all these points apply equally to men and women, it is in fact women who are more disadvantaged because they tend to be economically weaker.

1. Your home
Unless you legally own the home you share with your partner, you have no automatic right to claim either occupation or a financial interest.

2. Your money
If you decide to dispense with individual bank and savings accounts and put all your cash into a joint account, beware. You may not get out what you put in, should you split up.

3. If your partner dies
If you or your partner die without making a will, then your estate will be divided up according to the Intestacy Rules (see page 74). These laws only recognise blood relations, they make no provision for cohabitees. (For information about making a will and what happens when one partner dies see pages 72–77).

There are also other considerations such as life insurance, maintenance after separation and so on. These are dealt with in more depth in the following pages.

YOUR HOME

Explanations of the legal terms used here are given in Part Two: Everyday Legal and Financial Basics. See pages 66–71.

Owning your home
In order to ensure that you have a roof over your head and some kind of financial security if your relationship doesn't work out, you will need to:

- legally own your home;
- or take legal steps to secure an interest in it.

Unless you're the sole owner of a property, you have two options:

1. You can hold *legal title* to the property either as *joint tenants* or *tenants in common* (see below, 'Co-owning your home').
2. You can acquire *beneficial ownership* of the property by means of a written *trust deed* (see below, 'Creating a beneficial ownership').

The first option gives you the most security and is by far the more preferable.

If you're already living with your partner, there's nothing to stop you taking either of these steps – to secure a legal interest for yourself or your partner. If your partner is reluctant to let you become a co-owner or stake a beneficial ownership, you ought to reconsider the basic foundations of your relationship.

NOTE: Even if you are in a relationship and neither hold legal title nor have beneficial ownership of your home, you may still be able to claim some financial interest in the property (see page 67). However, there are no guarantees that you will succeed and these measures should only be used as an absolutely last resort. Do not rely on them.

Co-owning your home
The most secure position you can have in relation to your home is to hold the legal title to it, either as the sole owner, or jointly with your partner. There are three key advantages to this form of ownership.

– The property cannot be sold without your consent.
– You have the right to occupy the home and cannot be evicted or asked to leave.
– You have a right to claim a share of the profits if you decide to sell the home.

If you are thinking of buying a property in which you can both live, it will be much cheaper in the long run to become co-owners at the very start than to transfer the legal title at a later date (see below).

You will need to consider:

- whether to become joint tenants or tenants in common (see below);
- what would happen in the event of your death and make provision for any children you might have (see page 247).

When you agree to share the legal title to your home, you should also ask your solicitor to draw up a trust deed stating what will happen to the property in the event of a break-up: should it be sold and if so when, what would happen if you had children?

If you are tenants in common, the deed should also state the proportion of each of your shares in the property.

Joint tenants or tenants in common?

If you're joint tenants and you die, your half of the property will go directly to your partner. On the other hand, if you're tenants in common, your share in the property will go to your estate and be divided up according to your will or the Rules of Intestacy.

A tenancy in common means that you can each claim a share in the property that reflects your personal contribution, particularly if one person is putting in more money than the other. You must specify in writing what these shares will be. Your solicitor will do it for you as part of the conveyancing process when you buy the property or you can draw up a separate deed (see above).

Transferring ownership

If one partner is the sole owner of a property, the other partner can ask for the home to be transferred to them both jointly as co-owners. The transfer might involve the new owner 'buying into' the property and you should get advice from a solicitor before you undertake a transfer.

A tenancy in common may be the best way of reflecting the fact that the original owner will probably have made a greater contribution to the buying and maintenance of the property than the new co-owner.

Before you can transfer the title, you will have to ensure that the building society or other mortgage lender agrees to the change. They may amend the existing mortgage but will probably insist that you take out a replacement. This won't necessarily involve you in all the original costs such as valuation fees and so on.

If you want to transfer the legal title, you must expect to incur some costs. If the property is mortgaged, then the transfer will most likely be regarded as a sale and therefore you will have to pay Stamp Duty if your share is £30,000 or more of the market value of the property. (For more information on transfers and mortgages, see page 93). You will also need to pay Land Registration fees and, of course, your solicitor's charge. The mortgage lender may also make a charge.

Acquiring beneficial ownership
If you and your partner agree that you should both have a claim on your home, but for whatever reason don't want to include your name on the legal title or to alter an existing legal title, you can acquire beneficial ownership of the property. The most secure means of doing this is by a trust deed professionally drawn up by a solicitor. The advantage of a trust deed is that it gives you a claim to any profits from the sale of the property.

The major disadvantage of beneficial ownership is that, unlike holding the legal title, it may be difficult to stop the legal owner selling or mortgaging the property without your consent – even if it breaks the terms of the trust.

There are two parts to acquiring beneficial ownership. The first is about the amount of money you would get from any sale; the second concerns the terms under which the property can be sold: whether there is a time limit on your option to buy out your partner or what happens to the sale if you have young children.

Safeguarding your interest

You should ensure that the trust deed specifies what happens to the sale of your home if you split up.

In addition, you should get the legal owner to write to the Land Registry and ask for a *restriction* to be entered on the Register. This means that your home cannot be sold without your knowledge and safeguards your financial interest in the home. Whether or not your trust deed specifies what happens if you split up, you must still cover yourself by entering a restriction on the Land Register.

If your home is on unregistered land, then you will have to ask your solicitor to endorse a note of your trust on the title deeds. Again, this can be done only with the consent of the legal owner.

If the relationship does break up and you haven't had a restriction entered, there are still a number of steps you can take to protect your interest (see page 146). These are very unsatisfactory and should not be relied on as substitute measures.

As a last resort you could take legal action to reclaim your share of the proceeds from the sale of the property. However, this won't be much comfort if your ex-partner has escaped to foreign lands with all the money.

Other considerations

If the house is mortgaged, the lender may well insist that your name appear as a joint mortgagee. Be aware that whatever happens, the mortgage lender always has first claim on the proceeds of a property when it's sold. You should always check with your solicitor if you are asked to sign any form from the mortgage lender.

The law regards beneficial ownership trusts like any other transfer of property. If your share of the property exceeds £30,000, then you will have to pay Stamp Duty. If duty is payable, you must ensure that the trust deed is officially stamped. If it isn't, you won't be able to use it as evidence in court, should you need to sue the legal owner for your share of the proceeds of the property. If your share of the property is worth less than £30,000 then you simply need to certify this at the bottom of the trust deed; your solicitor will advise you what to do. The only way to avoid paying Stamp

Duty is if the legal owner gives the beneficial ownership as a gift. In other words you do not 'buy into' the property nor take over any responsibility for the mortgage.

At the end of the day, by the time you've paid a solicitor to draw up a watertight trust deed and also paid Stamp Duty, you might find that acquiring beneficial ownership is actually no cheaper than transferring the legal title. And that, in the long run, is the much better option.

Mortgages
Once you become jointly responsible for paying the mortgage you take on certain obligations and rights.

Even if you and your partner have a legally binding agreement about how you divide the mortgage repayments, such an agreement won't be binding on the mortgage lender. The lender is only really interested in securing the full amount of the repayment each month, not how that payment is made up. Therefore, if one partner defaults on their share of the repayments, the lender is quite within their rights to chase the other partner for the full sum.

On the other side, as joint mortgagee you will be kept informed of any mortgage arrears or a repossession order. If you find the account is in arrears then there's nothing to stop you making up the payments yourself or negotiating with the mortgage lender. You could then pursue your defaulting partner in an attempt to recover the extra money you have paid out.

If you are transferring the legal title of your home or acquiring beneficial ownership, it is highly likely the mortgage lender will insist on making the new co-owner jointly liable for the mortgage. Since the mortgage lender is not interested in who actually makes the repayment, this does not commit the new partner to making any payments, so long as one of you can cover them.

If you're not named on the mortgage, then you are not liable to the mortgage lender for any of the repayments, even if you have agreed with your partner to contribute towards them. The lender cannot pursue you for any arrears – and neither do they have to notify you of them.

However, if you find that the lender is about to take action against your partner for non-payment of the mortgage you can ask to be made a *party to the proceedings*. This means that you can ask the court if you can remain in the house on the condition that you make the repayments. If you find yourself in this situation you should consult a solicitor.

NOTE: Watch out that you don't get caught in the *I'll pay the mortgage, you pay the bills* trap. If you split up, the court will be interested in who actually paid the mortgage in a dispute about property. You would be well advised to consider opening a joint bank account to which you both contribute, to pay your mortgage and your bills.

Renting your home
The position for cohabitees who rent their home is much the same as for married couples. You should look over the information given on pages 69–71.

However, there is one notable exception. Unlike married couples, you have *no right* to live in the property if the tenancy is in your partner's name only. Your partner can ask you to leave at any time although they must give you a reasonable amount of time to pack your bags and find somewhere else to live.

As a cohabitee it's best if you get a tenancy in your name alone or in your joint names.

COHABITATION CONTRACTS

There is a peculiar contradiction in the English legal system. On the one hand the law upholds the inalienable right of individuals to make contracts between themselves. This implies that the concept of cohabitation contracts would be highly desirable. However, on the other hand, there is family law, which argues that it is not in the interests of public policy for families to draw up private contracts about their individual rights.

With this contradiction in mind, it's impossible to determine whether an individual court would hold a cohabitation contract legally binding or enforceable. But do not be put off. The way the law is interpreted is continually changing. Some elements of cohabitation contracts can be enforced, especially those that concern property and are drawn up in the form of a trust deed (see page 66).

Whatever you do, you should ensure that your contract is made in a form which would be acceptable to a court. For this reason, it's important that contracts to do with property and money are drawn up with the advice of a solicitor.

What is a cohabitation contract?

A cohabitation contract is a private agreement made by a couple, stating the fact that they intend to live together and setting out the terms of their relationship.

While similar contracts elsewhere in the world are known for including everything from who does the washing-up, how many nights a week the couple spend apart and the terms of the couple's sexual relationship, the English courts are somewhat conservative. You would be wise to stick to the essentials of property and finance!

However, there's nothing to stop you considering the other points and putting your ideas down on another, less formal piece of paper (see 'Informal lifestyle contracts' below).

The contract should be one which the couple intends to be legally binding. That way if either person breaks the terms of the contract, the other can go to court to have the agreement enforced or be compensated for any loss. However, bear in mind what the courts will and won't enforce.

Some couples draw up a very informal agreement as a statement of their beliefs and expectations of their life together. Although this is a beautiful idea while the relationship is blossoming, it might not offer much practical and legal comfort when the bloom goes.

Why draw up a cohabitation contract?

Unlike married couples, cohabitees have no automatic rights to the courts' help if the relationship doesn't work out. Since the courts decide on facts rather than fairness when cohabitees split up, co-habitation contracts dealing with property and money are a very important insurance policy.

There's no reason why a court won't consider those terms of a cohabitation agreement which deal with property and finance. What the court is highly unlikely to enforce are 'lifestyle' clauses: for example, who does the household chores. In fact, if you insist on including statements about, for example, how often you have sex, you might find the whole document thrown out of court.

Aside from the legal safeguards there are other positive reasons for writing a contract, even an informal one.

- Drawing up a cohabitation contract is one of the most useful tools you have to help you determine the future success of your relationship. It's an opportunity for you both to sit down and discuss how you view your partnership: how you feel about each other; whether you trust your lover; the extent to which you are each prepared to share your possessions; your opinions about having children and sharing domestic responsibilities. More and more people are advocating pre-nuptial agreements in this country for the same reason.
- In some ways, drafting a cohabitation contract at the beginning of a relationship has its drawbacks. Inevitably, as partnerships mature, individual goals sometimes become less important than joint, family goals. There's more give and take, you learn where you can compromise. If it's a good relationship, it feels more comfortable, you forget about the habits that once irritated.
- If discussing the contents of a contract highlights some funda-mental differences that, in all honesty, are unlikely to be resolved with time, then perhaps the relationship was never meant to be. If your partner tells you they desperately want children and you don't, or your lover expects you to give up your hard-won career to stay at home, then maybe it's better to get out before you commit yourself further.
- If you haven't got the confidence to let your partner become a co-owner of your home or your cohabitee shows reluctance to

let you acquire beneficial ownership of their property (see page 67), it may not be the right time, or the right person with whom to start sharing your life.

The formal requirements
For any contract to be binding in court, it has to contain certain legal requirements.

- It must be clear that both parties have agreed to the terms of the contract.
- It must be clear what both parties have agreed to.
- You should make the contract a *deed*.
- If you intend drawing up a contract, especially one that involves property or other assets, you ought to consult a solicitor.

What should you put in a cohabitation contract?
There are many things which could be included in a cohabitation contract. Some of them are to do with the fundamentals of property and money. Others are about lifestyle. You would be well advised to make out two documents: one a formal deed concerning your home and other assets; the other an informal agreement covering how you will conduct your relationship. Clauses about children can never be binding.

While the whole point of a lifestyle agreement is to let you both know where you stand, don't let the terms of your agreement become a rigid rule book. There's no point feeling frustrated or rowing just because something you agreed on three years previously no longer applies. Relationships do move on and you should acknowledge when you may need to rewrite part of the document. Don't be afraid to admit that you've changed your mind or that your circumstances are no longer the same.

Informal lifestyle agreements
You might want to include statements about the following:

- The purpose of the relationship and drawing up the contract.

- The duration of the contract: is it for life or for a certain fixed period? It's probably worth setting a time limit, say one or two years and then reviewing the situation.
- General information about each partner: age, work, income, financial situation and so on.
- Money*: will you have joint or individual bank and savings accounts; how will you pay the bills; do you intend to save; what happens if you get into debt?
- Work: what are your priorities; what happens if one partner is transferred; whose career comes first; what happens if one person loses their job?
- Home*: where will you live; will you share the ownership of your home; what will you do about furnishing and equipping it?
- Domestic responsibilities: how will you share the housework; what happens if one person stops working?
- Surnames: do either of you intend to change your name; what surname will your children take?
- Children: do you want children; how many; when; how will you care for them; what happens if you can't have children of your own?
- Religion: do you have the same or different beliefs; how would you bring up any children?
- Family: do you have particular responsibilities, financial or otherwise to your respective families; what about visiting your family on high days and holy days?
- Sex: how do you view your sexual relationship; what if you had problems; what about fidelity?
- Hobbies: do you have hobbies, how much time will you devote to them? You could also consider other things like what do you do if one person smokes or snores uncontrollably.
- The future: what will you put in your wills; have you made financial provision through pensions and life insurance policies?
- Resolving disagreements and breaches of the contract: what will you do and where will you go for help?
- Dissolving the relationship*: how will you go about ending

your relationship; how will you divide up your property, finances and belongings?

*The nuts and bolts of these issues should be dealt with in formal documents. However, you might want to include some statements in your informal agreement just the same, particularly if you talk about your attitudes to and general views on these matters.

YOUR MONEY

Your money – how you save it, spend it and share it – is going to be one of the biggest considerations for cohabitees. It's certainly an area which you need to think about, from who pays the milkman to how to protect your own personal fortune, should the big break ever come.

For more ideas about money management see Part Three: Getting Together, Chapter 10, Marriage, on pages 127–133.

Savings
You can either retain your money in individual accounts or open a joint account. If you want to keep individual accounts, then think hard about how, practically, you're going to pay for household expenses. Consider whether it would be worthwhile opening up a joint account for these purposes (see below).

Joint accounts
If you open up a joint account to cover daily expenditure on the mortgage repayments, rent, food, domestic appliances and so on, the law will regard this account as a *common purse*. In other words, the money is always intended for your common benefit. This means that if you split up, the court may well divide the contents of any such joint account equally between you, regardless of what you each contributed in the first place.

If, in the event that you separate, you want to ensure that the contents are divided up in unequal shares, perhaps to recognise different contributions to the account, make sure you tell your solicitor in advance and get an appropriate deed drawn up. The same applies to any shares or other assets you might have.

The advantage of having one joint household account, while each retaining your own personal accounts, is that you can make sure that the important bills are paid and avoid arguments about who spent the milk money on the latest album or a fancy hairdo.

If you have a joint account, then there is an assumption that you trust each other. Anything bought by one person for their personal use, say an item of clothing, even if it is paid for with money from the joint account, will be regarded as belonging to that person (see page 151).

Remember, if you have a joint account you will both be liable for any overdraft.

Credit and loans

It doesn't matter whether you've just bought a three-piece suite on your credit card or you owe BT for your last telephone bill – it's all credit. Unless you plan ahead, you may be the one shelling out all the cash.

If your name appears on the account or agreement, then you're liable for the debt. So, even if you come to a private arrangement with your partner to halve all the main bills, if you signed the agreement with the gas company, then it's your responsibility to pay the bill. And if you don't, it's you they'll sue for the unpaid arrears. If you don't want this to happen, you should make sure that you both sign any agreements. That way, you'll both be liable for any unpaid bills (see page 29).

If you have a credit card, you might want to nominate your partner as an authorised user. This means that they get a card of their own and can go off on an independent spending spree. However, as far as the credit card company is concerned, you will be liable to foot the bill.

If you're about to use credit to buy your lover an expensive gift that's going to take you a long time to pay off, make sure the agreement doesn't outlast your relationship. There's a big difference between who owns an item and who's paying for it.

Ted decided to buy his live-in lover, Sarah, a colour television. In order to do so he took out a credit agreement with the local TV store. It would take him three years to pay off the loan. Unfortunately, shortly after Ted gave Sarah the TV she went off with a satellite dish salesman. Sarah argued that the TV was a present to her and she kept it. Ted, in the meantime, had to carry on with the repayments.

To avoid these sorts of problems, try and think about who would keep the item if you split up and make sure that any loan agreement is in that person's name. That doesn't stop the other partner from physically making the repayments while the relationship is still going strong. It may take the romance away from extravagant present-giving, but it sure takes the sting out of post break-up debts.

If you've been given any kind of large loan or gift from your family, perhaps as a deposit for your home, you must get it recorded in a trust deed. If you don't, then there's a chance that your family's generosity might end up, by default, in your partner's pocket should you separate.

Geraldine and her partner, Bruce, were looking for somewhere to live but without much success. They'd seen a flat which was ideal but they just couldn't afford it. Even with a hundred per cent mortgage they were still £10,000 short of the asking price. Geraldine's father agreed to lend them the money and they bought the flat as joint owners. They never recorded the fact that Geraldine's father had lent them a substantial sum of money to buy the property.

Since Geraldine had a steady job and Bruce was just starting up his own business, Geraldine paid all the household bills.

After two years, the relationship fell apart and Bruce left. He insisted the flat was sold. As the house was in their joint names and the £10,000 had not been properly acknowledged, the £18,000 profit from the sale was divided equally between Geraldine and Bruce, much to chagrin of Geraldine's father.

Your belongings

Essentially items that are given to you personally, or you buy with your own money, are yours. Things that are bought jointly belong to both of you.

If you bring things of particular monetary – or sentimental – value to your joint home, then it's worth putting down on paper your special claim to those items in case any misunderstandings arise later on. These might include equipment such as a computer that you need for your work, or pieces of furniture given to you by your friends or relations.

Pensions

Unlike a married person you will not automatically benefit from your partner's occupational pension scheme. If you contribute to an occupational pension and want to make some provision for your partner then most schemes allow you to nominate a beneficiary. You should check the terms of the scheme and make the nomination as soon as possible. If you later split up, you can cancel or change the nomination.

If you have a personal pension plan, then the same applies. If you don't already have a PPP then this is something you might want to consider doing in any case (see page 38).

Life insurance

Husbands and wives are automatically deemed to have an insurable interest in each other (see page 41); cohabitees are not. In order to take out life insurance on your partner's life you will have to demonstrate an insurable interest. As far as specific liabilities such as a joint mortgage is concerned this should be straightforward.

Proving an insurable interest in other circumstances might be impossible. Therefore, if you want to provide for your partner after your death by way of an insurance policy you will have to take out a policy on your own life and do one of the following:

- name your partner as the one entitled to the benefit paid out when you die;

- provide that the benefit is held in trust for your partner;
- assign the benefit of the policy to your partner.

However, if you do any of these things, then you will not be able to change your mind at a later date without your partner's consent. Even if you stop paying the premiums the policy will still belong to your partner.

Alternatively, you can take out a policy on your own life so that the benefit forms part of your estate on your death. By making a will, you can then ensure that your partner receives the benefit from the pension plan or life insurance.

NOTE: Whatever you decide to do you should take good, independent advice to ensure that your partner is provided for and your interests are safeguarded in case you separate.

COHABITING WITH SOMEONE WHO'S DIVORCED

If you or your partner are divorced you may find your relationship affected by the divorce, at least in financial terms.

When the court makes a financial settlement in a divorce they will want to know if either spouse is already, or is intending to cohabit or marry a new partner. They will want to know the financial position of that new partner and whether they will be maintaining the spouse and to what extent.

In the same way, if you or your partner receive maintenance payments from a former spouse, then they can apply to the court to have the payment varied if they believe their ex-husband or wife's circumstances have changed.

Other rights, for example to remain in the marital home, may also be challenged if a former spouse starts living with another partner on what appears to be a formal basis.

LESBIAN AND HOMOSEXUAL COUPLES

Since the law does not recognise lesbian or homosexual 'marriages', your legal position as a couple is more or less the same as any other two people who cohabit. There is no obligation upon you to maintain each other and by the same token you have no automatic rights to property or to be provided for when your partner dies.

However, lesbians and homosexuals are in many respects in a far more vulnerable position. This is due not so much to the law but to its interpretation and prevailing attitudes towards sexuality. There are two areas where lesbians and homosexuals may face particular difficulty:

- When a partner dies without having made a will and declaring how they wished their funeral arrangements to be handled. Their surviving companion may face huge difficulties in dealing with and being accepted by the deceased's family. This is particularly true if the family did not know, or refused to accept, that the deceased was gay. The same may apply where one partner is severely ill and the family intervenes in their care.
- In custody cases where, usually, the lesbian mother leaves her husband who then uses her lesbianism against her when she seeks to continue to care for her children.

For lesbians and homosexuals in these situations, it's not a question of what the law says, but the specific techniques you need to use in order to make your case successfully. To do this, you should contact the specialist agencies and publications who can give you detailed, practical advice and support. Suggestions of organisations that may be able to help are given in the resource section of this book.

TAX NOTES

See pages 42–47 for basic explanations of the technical terms.

1. Each cohabitee is liable to pay income tax and capital gains tax

on their own income and capital gains.

2. If you have any joint savings accounts or other investments, you will each be liable for fifty per cent of the tax payable on that account, regardless of how you split the interest or dividends.

   It's sometimes possible to split the tax liability on joint accounts according to the way you will share the profits. If you want to do this, you should write to your tax office.

3. If one of you is earning and the other isn't, you might consider putting all your savings into the account of the non-earner. As a non-tax-payer, they will be able to reclaim any tax already deducted from the interest on the savings.

   However, in order for this to work for tax purposes, the earning partner must have no legal or beneficial interest in the savings. In other words, the account must be in the sole name of the non-earner and you mustn't draw up a trust deed saying that you both have a right to a share in the savings. If you were to split up, the earner couldn't demand the contents of the account even though they made the major contribution to it.

CHAPTER 10
Marriage

Despite the impression given in glossy magazines, marriage is not simply about candlelit proposals, fairytale wedding dresses and sun-kissed honeymoons. The law lays down some fairly tough rules about who can marry and how they can do it.

ENGAGEMENT

Engagement has no legal effect and therefore the law attaches little significance to it. Unlike marriage, there are no legal formalities or requirements. You can become engaged before you're sixteen and don't need anyone's consent.

The engagement's off!
Up to 1970, a contract to marry, in other words, an engagement, was regarded much like any other contract. If it was broken, the rejected suitor could sue for breach of contract. That right has now been abolished, and an engagement is no longer a legally binding contract. What's more, the jilted party cannot sue for any expenses or losses they've incurred planning the cancelled wedding.

Carina Roberts and Jeremy Silver fell madly in love and decided to tie the knot just as soon as they could.

Carina's excited parents went ahead and booked the church, a hotel for the reception and ordered the printing of the invitations. Jeremy put down a deposit for two romantic, sun-drenched weeks in the Caribbean.

Unfortunately, no sooner had he done this than Jeremy began to get cold feet. Was Carina, after all, the woman for him? Perhaps not. So he called the whole thing off.

Carina's father was furious. He'd just spent a fortune making the

*wedding arrangements. Although he got some of his money back, he was
still well out of pocket. Unfortunately for Mr Roberts, there was nothing
he could do. Justifiably angry as he was, he couldn't sue young Jeremy
for pulling out of the deal. For as far as the law was concerned, there
was no deal.*

What about returning gifts?

The law makes the assumption that engagement (and wedding) gifts
are given on the understanding that the couple are to be married.
Once the marriage is called off, the couple are no longer entitled to
the presents. So, if you receive presents and then decide to cancel
the wedding, you should return the gifts to the people who gave
them. However, if they say they don't want them back, you may
each keep those gifts given to you by your own relatives.

The same rule applies to gifts given by the couple to each other.
If the wedding's off, those presents should be returned, regardless
of who's 'at fault'. Gifts such as birthday and Christmas presents
will not normally have to be returned since these are usually given
for reasons other than the impending wedding.

However, there is one notable exception to the gift rule . . .

The engagement ring

The giving of an engagement ring is presumed to be an absolute
gift and as such is non-returnable – even if the prospective bride
jilts her fiancé. However, the ring should be returned if it was given
on the understanding that it must be handed back to the man in
the event of the marriage not taking place.

If you have a family heirloom, of sentimental or monetary worth,
you may want to think about this before you put it on the finger of
your betrothed.

Prenuptial property

When you break off the engagement, you may already have set
about buying a home and furnishing it. If you can't decide what to
do about selling or dividing up your property then you can ask the
court to do it for you. The court will treat you as if you had been

married (see page 173). However, it will be greatly to your advantage if you can sort things out between you rather than resorting to the court. It will save you a good deal of expense.

GETTING MARRIED

Gone are the days, but not so distant, when marriages in this country were decided by parents and sums of money. Today, on the whole, people marry for love.

Valid marriages

To be legally valid, a marriage must be:

- voluntary;
- between two single people;
- who are at least sixteen;
- mentally and physically capable;
- of the opposite sex;
- not closely related.

What do these six phrases mean?

Voluntary

Both the man and the woman must agree voluntarily to marry and be capable of understanding the meaning of their consent. A marriage will not be valid if one or other party has been forced by fear or undue duress to consent. In the same way, if the man or woman does not know what they are doing perhaps because they are drunk or their understanding is impaired by old age, then, again, the marriage will be invalid.

Although there are some exceptions, social pressure and desire to please your parents are not enough to invalidate the marriage. This can be a particular issue for those who submit to arranged marriages.

For example, in one case where a Sikh girl went through an arranged marriage out of obedience to her parents and a proper sense of duty, the court decided that there had been valid consent.

In another similar case, the court annulled a marriage where a young Hindu girl was forced into marriage with the threat that if she did not agree her parents would throw her out of the house, leaving her homeless and penniless.

Similarly, if one partner is mistaken about the identity of the other partner, then the marriage is invalid.

Samantha was due to marry Peter who was one of identical twins. Samantha went through with the wedding ceremony, only to discover on closer inspection afterwards, that in fact she'd married Andrew, Peter's twin brother. Samantha's marriage was invalid.

However, you can't claim mistaken identity just because you find out later that your partner wasn't all you thought they were.

Christopher was looking forward to marrying his fiancée, Julia. She was always immaculately groomed, drove a flashy car and was something important 'in the City'. Christopher assumed Julia was a woman of some means and, from her rather upper-crust accent, he also thought, of some social standing.

Once they were married, Christopher was sorely disappointed. Julia was very much a self-made woman. A high flyer, unfortunately Julia lost her job during a recession and with it her flashy company car and her fast-lane lifestyle. Christopher claimed he was mistaken about Julia's wealth and social status and wouldn't have married her had he known the true situation. His marriage to Julia remained valid.

Between two single people

Both parties must be single, widowed or divorced. If either the man or woman is already married at the time of the wedding ceremony, then the marriage will be void. What's more, one or both of the parties will have committed *bigamy*. These days prosecutions for bigamy are rare. The police only tend to pursue the case if the bigamist is acting maliciously or fraudulently.

Problems sometimes arise when someone who's married, but has been separated from their spouse for many years, wishes to remarry. To avoid risk of a bigamy prosecution, you should ask the court to grant a divorce based on five years' separation (see page 160). Without such an order, there is a risk that the second marriage may be decreed void. Spouses who have not heard from their partners for more than seven years, and who have no reason to suppose that they are still alive, have a special defence in bigamy cases, but this still may not save the new marriage.

The legal position of *polygamous* marriages is complicated. Although a marriage where one partner is already married is not valid, the courts will recognise all marriages if:

- The marriage complied with the laws of the country in which it took place.
- The spouses were capable of marrying according to the laws of their respective country of *domicile* (the country you regard as your home).

If you are in any doubt about your legal position or the validity of your marriage, seek the advice of a solicitor.

Who are at least sixteen
Since 1929, the legal minimum age for marriage has been sixteen. If either the boy or girl, or both, are under sixteen, the marriage will be void. In addition, the child will have committed a criminal offence.

Before the age of eighteen, young people need consent in order to marry. If the consent is forged, or the young person lies about their age in order to do away with the need for consent, they will have committed a criminal offence. However, in this case the marriage will remain valid.

Young people under eighteen need the signed consent of each parent still alive who has parental responsibility, unless there are special circumstances.

- No parent alive with parental responsibility but child is not adopted: consent from guardian.
- Parents are divorced or separated: consent from parent (or both parents); whoever has a residence order.
- Child is adopted: consent from adoptive parents.
- Child is a ward of court: consent from the court.
- Child is in local authority care: consent from local authority as well as from parents or guardian.

If, for some reason, your parents cannot give consent, perhaps because they cannot be traced, then the Registrar of Marriages will give you information on how to apply for *special consent*.

If your parents refuse to give their consent, you can ask the court to give its consent instead. This is best done through your local Magistrates Court (although the County Court and High Court will also accept applications). Your local court office will tell you what you need to do.

Mentally and physically capable
In order for the marriage to be deemed valid, both parties need to understand what they are doing at the time of the marriage. The law isn't particularly interested in the state of someone's mind, before or after the ceremony, merely that they are lucid during it.

The law also accepts that it is not very difficult to understand the concept of consenting to marriage and therefore you don't need to be super brilliant to enter into matrimony.

'Physically incapable' means the inability to consummate the marriage. However, if you marry someone in the full knowledge that they cannot consummate the marriage, then you cannot later have the marriage annulled (see page 157).

Of the opposite sex
Homosexual and lesbian marriages are not legally valid. Marriages where one partner has undergone a sex change are also not legally valid.

Some years ago a man who had undergone a sex change got married. His 'husband' knew about the operation. However, three months later, the 'husband' asked that the marriage be declared null and void on the grounds that it was a marriage between two men. The court agreed to an annulment saying that a sex change did not alter a person's biological or 'legal' sex.

Not closely related

The law prohibits marriages between certain family members. These are known as the *Prohibited Degrees*.

A man cannot marry his:

mother	grandmother
stepmother	wife's grandmother
mother-in-law	grandfather's wife
daughter	grandsons's wife
daughter-in-law	sister
stepdaughter	aunt
granddaughter	niece
wife's granddaughter	

A woman cannot marry her:

father	grandfather
stepfather	husband's grandfather
father-in-law	grandmother's husband
son	granddaughter's husband
son-in-law	brother
stepson	uncle
grandson	nephew
husband's grandson	

Any of these marriages would be void.

NOTE: In addition to fulfilling these qualifying terms, you will have to observe the proper formalities of the marriage procedures (see below).

The formalities
In England and Wales, there are only two ways to wed legally.

1. In a civil ceremony performed in accordance with the statutory requirements.
2. In a religious ceremony performed in accordance with the rites of the Church of England or other recognised denomination.

Essentially, the Church of England lays down how Anglican weddings are formalised; and the state sets out regulations on how and where all other marriages are carried out. This includes civil, nonreligious ceremonies, as well as weddings performed by Roman Catholics, nonconformist Churches and other faiths. However, the rules vary according to each religion.

All these regulations governing the form of marriage ceremonies are subject to the basic laws about who can and cannot wed and what constitutes a valid marriage (see above).

Regardless of where you get married, you will need two witnesses to attend the marriage and sign the marriage register.

Where?
Since Lord Hardwicke's Act in the early 1700s (see page 82), marriages must take place in public places with unbarred doors. Therefore you cannot marry in a private home and church doors should remain unlocked. The only places currently recognised for the solemnisation of marriages are churches, Register Offices and some other venues used for religious worship, such as synagogues, which are licensed for the purpose. Although the law is being reviewed, there are unlikely to be any drastic changes.

When?
As a rule marriages should take place between 8 a.m. and 6 p.m. However, Jewish and Quaker weddings do not need to abide by

this and exceptions can be made in special circumstances.

CHURCH OF ENGLAND WEDDINGS

Before you walk down the aisle, you'll need to comply with some basic legal formalities or *ecclesiastical preliminaries*, as they're referred to by the Register Office. If you intend to have a church wedding, your local vicar will guide you through the regulations.

Legal necessities
In order to go ahead with the marriage ceremony, you will need to have obtained one of the following.

Calling of the banns
Banns are the official notice of the impending marriage. The banns are written in a standard form according to the Book of Common Prayer and are 'published' by being read aloud in church for three successive Sundays preceding the marriage. The ceremony must take place within three months of the publication of the banns.

If you live in a different parish from the church in which you intend to get married, then the banns will also be read there. You will be expected to attend the church to hear the banns being read out on at least one of the Sundays.

Common licence
A common licence, or an ecclesiastical licence, dispenses with the need to call the banns and will enable you to get married with only one day's clear notice. However, you will need to have lived in the parish for at least fifteen days prior to the application.

In addition, you will have to swear an affidavit – a sworn statement – declaring that there is no legal reason why the marriage shouldn't take place and that the other party consents to the wedding.

For more details about applying for a common licence contact your local Diocesan Office.

Special licence

Issued by the Archbishop of Canterbury, this allows a marriage to take place anywhere, at any time. Very few are granted each year and tend to be for special and urgent reasons; for example, if someone is too ill to leave their hospital bed or is dying. To obtain a special licence you should apply to the Registrar of the Court of Faculties.

Superintendent Registrar's certificate

Rarely used for Anglican church weddings since publishing of the banns would be the usual practice. You will have to give the same assurances as for a common licence, except that a solemn declaration rather than an affidavit will suffice. The notice will be displayed for three weeks at the Registrar's Office and if there is no objection, you will receive your certificate enabling the marriage to take place.

The Church's requirements

Vicars are required by law to marry every couple who asks them to do so, providing both prospective bride and groom are legally free to marry, live within the parish and neither has been divorced. This doesn't mean that if you don't live within the parish or this is your second marriage you can't get wedded in church, only that the vicar doesn't have to comply with your request for him to marry you.

If you satisfy all the other basic requirements, then the only grounds on which a clergyman could refuse to marry you is if neither bride nor groom has been baptised. This get-out is known as the conscience clause.

You don't need to believe in Christianity to get married in church: it's a matter for your own conscience. However, the vicar will probably probe the depth of your Christian commitment when you meet to discuss the service.

The Church lays down standard forms of the marriage service and exchange of vows. If you want to alter any part of the service, for example to omit the words 'obey' from the traditional female response to the vows, then you should discuss this with your vicar.

Up the aisle

For anyone contemplating a church wedding, it's usual to make an appointment to meet the local vicar. If you're unfamiliar with churches in your area, take the time to go to a couple of services to get the feel of the place and the style of the clergyman.

At your first meeting the vicar will ask you routine questions about your name, address and so on. If there are any difficulties about getting married in church they will tell you. You may also be asked whether or not you've been confirmed and if you have a confirmation certificate.

At this first appointment, the vicar will give you details about the fees and special arrangements for counselling and the rehearsal. This is also your opportunity to discuss other important issues such as the music, hymns and flowers. You ought to check early on whether there are any restrictions on videos, photography or confetti.

Pre-marriage counselling

Most vicars will offer some kind of pre-marriage counselling. This might be anything from a ten-minute cursory discussion on Christian beliefs to a series of workshops with other engaged couples over a period of a few weeks.

The rehearsal

If you marry in church you will probably be asked to attend a rehearsal of the wedding ceremony. For some this will be the full number with bridesmaids, page boys and honoured guests turning back and forth; for others, an informal chat between bride, groom and vicar.

The rehearsal is a valuable opportunity, not only to find out who stands where, but also to get a feel of the church and find out about any awkward steps or uneven flagstones before you get bound up in white tulle or paralysed by prenuptial nerves. It's also a good chance to iron out any last-minute difficulties. Don't be afraid to ask questions and clear up anything you're unsure of or unhappy about.

CIVIL WEDDING FORMALITIES

These *civil preliminaries* apply equally to all non-Anglican denominational ceremonies as well as to non-religious Register Office marriages.

Before you can get married in a civil service or a synagogue, mosque or other place of worship, you must enter what is known as a *Notice of Marriage* at your local Register Office. There are then three ways in which you can obtain a certificate or licence to enable you to go ahead with the marriage ceremony.

1. Superintendent Registrar's certificate without licence
Both the bride and groom must have lived in the registration district for at least seven days before they give notice. If you live in separate registration districts, then you will each need to go to your respective Registrars and give notice. The seven-day rule still applies.

The Registrar will want to know exactly where the ceremony will be performed and it must be within the registration district in which at least one of you lives. There are certain exceptions to this, if the marriage is to be held somewhere other than a Register Office. Twenty-one clear days after the Superintendent Registrar has entered the notice in the notice book, they will issue a certificate. The marriage can then take place at any time within the following three months.

2. Superintendent Registrar's certificate and licence
This is much the same as the plain certificate except it can be granted within forty-eight hours. However, the residence qualifications are different. So long as both the bride and groom normally live in England and Wales, only one of them has to have lived in the registration district for at least fifteen days prior to giving notice.

One clear day, excluding Sundays, Christmas Day or Good Friday, must elapse between giving notice and the Superintendent Registrar issuing the licence for the marriage. The licence is again valid for three months.

3. Registrar General's licence

Like the ecclesiastical Special Licence, the Registrar General's licence is only issued in very special circumstances, for example where someone is too ill to be moved to a Register Office or other registered building.

To obtain a licence either the bride or groom will have to go personally to the Superintendent Registrar of the district in which the marriage is to be solemnised. If there is sufficient reason to grant a licence it will be done immediately. There is no residence qualification.

REGISTER OFFICE WEDDINGS

For some people a Register Office wedding is a matter of choice, for others a necessity, either because they are unable to participate in a religious ceremony, or as a legal prelude to religious celebrations.

Register Office marriages are short and simple. Traditionally, they've had a bad reputation, criticised as wedding conveyor belts, for shabby rooms, windows overlooking garbage depots with little thought for the sensitivities of the bridal couple on their special day. However, times are changing. Registrars are looking to make the Register Office more inviting and give meaning to the short ceremony. Register Office weddings may be brief but they can also be beautiful.

When you've completed the civil preliminaries (see above) and are granted your certificate, the Superintendent Registrar will fix a date for the actual wedding. In some popular districts there may well be a waiting list, particularly for Saturday marriages. You will also be told what time you and your guests need to be at the Register Office, the number of guests you can invite and whether there will be any restrictions on photography or videos. You'll also be reminded to bring along two witnesses.

The marriage service

When you arrive the Registrar will check to make sure that all your details to be entered in the marriage register are correct. You'll also need to pay any outstanding fees. Your guests will probably be assembled in a waiting room and will then be asked to join you in the marriage room. Your witnesses will be placed either side of you and your wedding rings, if you have them, on a velvet cushion.

There are in fact only a dozen lines in the marriage ceremony that are required to be said by law. The rest of the ceremony is at the discretion of the local Superintendent Registrar, providing that nothing of a religious nature is included.

Below is a model Register Office marriage ceremony suggested by the General Register Office. The statutory words are in bold.

The Superintendent Registar (SR) stands and says to the bridal couple and the guests, who remain seated: *This place in which you are now met has been duly sanctioned according to the law for the celebration of marriage. You are here to witness the joining in matrimony of Romeo Montague and Juliet Capulet. If any person present knows of any lawful impediment to this marriage, he should declare it now.*

SR askes the bride and bridegroom to stand. To the man: *Is your full name Romeo Montague?*

To the woman: *Is your full name Juliet Capulet?*

To both: *Before you are joined in matrimony I have to remind you of the solemn and binding character of the ceremony of marriage. Marriage according to the law of this country is the union of one man with one woman, voluntarily entered into for life, to the exclusion of all others.*

Now I am going to ask you in turn to declare that you do not know of any lawful reason why you should not be married to each other.

To the man: **Will the bridegroom please repeat after me: 'I do solemnly declare that I know not of any lawful impediment why I, Romeo Montague, may not be joined in matrimony to Juliet Capulet'.**

To the woman: **And now the bride. 'I do solemnly declare that I know not of any lawful impediment why I, Juliet Capulet, may not be joined in matrimony to Romeo Montague.'**

SR to all witnesses: *Now the solemn moment has come for these two persons to contract the marriage before you, their witnesses. Will you please stand.*

Where a ring is to be given, the SR instructs the man to put it on the woman's left hand and hold it there while repeating: or if no ring is to be given the SR instructs the man to take the woman by the hand and repeat: *I call upon these persons here present to witness that I, Romeo Montague, do take thee, Juliet Capulet, to be my lawful wedded wife.'*

Then the SR instructs the woman to take the man by the hand while repeating: *'I call upon these persons here present to witness that I, Juliet Capulet, do take thee, Romeo Montague, to be my lawful wedded husband.'*

Romeo Montague and Juliet Capulet, you have both made the declarations prescribed by law, and have made a solemn and binding contract with each other, in the presence of the witnesses assembled here. You are now man and wife together.

Will you all now please be seated while the register is signed.

OTHER FORMS OF RELIGIOUS WEDDINGS

Once you get beyond Anglican church weddings or civil Register Office ceremonies, the legal requirements are somewhat more complex.

You will need to satisfy three provisions before you can carry out the ceremony:

- Regardless of where you actually get married, you will need a Superintendent's certificate or licence first (see page 117).
- The place in which you get married must be registered for religious worship and be registered for the solemnisation of marriages. In practice this applies to almost all churches, Catholic and non-conformist.
- The ceremony must contain the statutory words which have to be repeated in front of the district Registrar or other authorised person, which includes most priests.

If you cannot fulfil the last two qualifications, you will have to have a civil service in a Register Office to satisfy the legal requirements before you have your religious ceremony.

Exceptions to the rule: Jews and Quakers

For historic reasons, Jewish and Quaker weddings are treated somewhat differently. Jewish marriages can take place anywhere, at any time, even in a private home, providing they are carried out under the auspices of an authorised person. In practice this is usually the marriage secretary of the synagogue of which the bridegroom is a member. In addition, there is no requirement to include the statutory words. The ceremony comprises the traditional Jewish marriage service.

In the same way Quaker weddings do not have to adhere to the regulations governing other weddings and can be held in any Friends Meeting House or other place where religious worship is regularly held. Again, the ceremony doesn't have to include the statutory lines.

In both cases the couple will have to obtain the Superintendent Registrar's Certificate or Licence first. The proviso to these exceptions is that bride and groom must prove they are members of the faith, or in the case of Quakers must receive a special dispensation from the Society of Friends.

YOUR MARITAL RIGHTS AND OBLIGATIONS

You might think that once you've got your licence, paid your fees, bought your rings and invested mountains of money, time and energy into choosing what to wear, what to eat and what to dance to, that you've just about paid your dues. However, that's only the beginning.

If you believe in your vows to love, cherish and support each other, then your legal rights and obligations as a married couple won't be too onerous. For the record, here they are:

- Your consent to marry each other implies an agreement to live

121

together. This is known as the *duty to cohabit*.
- You have a duty to maintain each other.
- You have a duty to have sex together.

However, the court would never force you to do any of these things other than maintain each other. It's likely that if you had any major disagreements about these obligations that cannot be resolved, the marriage would no longer be workable and you would be seeking a separation.

Marriage also has other effects on the way you live your life: whether a woman changes her name; how you organise your home and your money; your tax position, pension rights and your will. These points are covered in the rest of this section.

A CHANGE OF NAME?

Tradition has decreed that a woman take her husband's surname on marriage. Contrary to popular belief, there is no legal requirement for her to do so.

Taking your husband's name
Although increasing numbers of wives retain their maiden name, the majority continue to adopt their husband's name when they marry. You are entitled to keep your husband's name – and any title – even after his death or in the event of you both getting divorced.

If you are planning a honeymoon abroad and intend to take your husband's name when you marry, the Passport Office will issue you with a new passport in your married name before the actual wedding.

Changing your name(s)
In English law, you can call yourself any name you choose and you can change your name as and when you wish. The only restriction is that the name change should not be with intent to mislead; for example, so you can sign someone else's cheques. The only name

you can't change officially is one you were given at baptism.

For a variety of reasons some couples consider changing both their surnames to a new one. Double-barrelling some surnames becomes absurd. Try sewing a Montmorency-Chillingworth name label into a school sock! Others recognise that while they retain their own names for work and personal reasons, when they have a child they will have to decide which surname it will take.

How to change your name
Although in theory you can simply wake up one morning and decide to call yourself 'Rupert Bear', in practice you need to produce an official piece of paper to this effect. There are three ways of doing this:

1. A statement signed by a respected member of the community
'Respected' members of the community include: solicitors, JPs, doctors, clergymen. The statement should confirm that the new name is the name by which you are commonly known. However, this sort of informal statement is unlikely to be accepted by banks and similar institutions.

2. Deed poll
The most formal means of regularising a change of name. For a charge a solicitor will prepare an official document or deed, which will then need to be registered at the High Court. Some professions, for example, the legal profession, insist that their members formalise their name change in this way.

3. By statutory declaration
This is an official way of formalising your name change and is basically a sworn statement. A solicitor will prepare one for you for a fee, or you can draft one yourself and take it to a solicitor to have it sworn. A standard example of a statutory declaration follows.

STATUTORY DECLARATION
OF
REGINALD BLOGGS – RUPERT BEAR

I, *REGINALD BLOGGS of Rose Cottage, Little Snoring, Hertfordshire, a bagpipe player*, do solemnly and sincerely declare that:

1. I absolutely and entirely renounce, relinquish and abandon the use of my former name of *Reginald Bloggs*, and assume, adopt and determine to take and use from today the name of *Rupert Bear* in substitution of my former name of *Reginald Bloggs*.

2. I shall at all times after today in all records, deeds and documents and other writings and in all actions and proceedings as well as in all dealings and transactions and on all occasions use and sign the name of *Rupert Bear* as my name in substitution for the former name of *Reginald Bloggs* so relinquished as set out above to the intent that I may from today be called, known or distinguished not by my former name *Reginald Bloggs* but by the name of *Rupert Bear* only.

3. I authorise and require all persons at all times to designate, describe and address me by the name of *Rupert Bear*.

I make this solemn declaration conscientiously believing the same to be true and by virtue of the Statutory Declarations Act 1835.

Declared by the above named

Signed *Rupert Bear*

at *49 The High Street, Great Snoring*
this *seventeenth*
day of *October*
1992

before me *Louby Loo*
a solicitor empowered to administer oaths

NOTE: You should replace the fictional details given in italics with your own name and personal information. Your solicitor should then sign the document.

MARRIAGE CONTRACTS

If you've watched one too many American legal soap operas on TV, you might be wondering why you haven't drawn up a prenuptial agreement or a marriage contract.

Well, how many times have you heard the words prenuptial agreement mentioned in a British drama series? None? Precisely. Marriage contracts, like cohabitation contracts, although recognised in other parts of the world, have no legal standing here. They cannot be legally binding. While a court may take into account the terms of your contract, it will overrule them if it sees fit.

However, that's not to say that it's not worth your while sitting down with your spouse-to-be and drawing one up. The reasons for making such a contract when you get married, or even if you are already married, remain as valid as if you were cohabiting. A contract gives you a chance to set out the parameters of your relationship, to discuss how you perceive your marriage developing. It also provides a framework to discuss the nuts and bolts of your relationship, like money, careers, domestic responsibilities and children. These might be issues about which you find it difficult to communicate. Don't view a contract as written in stone. Use it as a guide. Review it as the relationship matures.

If you want to consider making a marriage contract, look back over the information and advice to cohabitees on pages 94–99.

YOUR HOME

For people who choose to cohabit without getting married, who owns their home and how they own it are of paramount importance. For spouses, the situation is less critical. Ultimately, the court can decide what happens to your marital home and who, if anyone, lives in it should you split up.

How the court arrives at its decision will depend on your individual circumstances, whether or not you have children, the value of your marital home, your savings and your earning power. These are described in more detail on page 173 in Part Four: Breaking Up.

Owning your home

Even though the court will ultimately determine what happens to your home if the relationship doesn't work out, it may not always reach what you might consider a fair judgement. If you split up within five years or so, while you're still young and able to earn and you don't have any children, the courts are likely to take the attitude that you should only get out of the relationship what you put in.

To find out more about the legal technicalities of owning and buying a property look back over the reference section in Part Two, starting on page 66 and also at the advice given to cohabitees, beginning on page 88.

If you are buying a property together your best option is to put it into joint names, even if only one of you actually pays the mortgage. If one spouse already owns a property which you then use as your marital home, consider transferring the legal title and beneficial ownership into both your names.

If the property is in the name of only one spouse who then defaults on the mortgage payments, the building society or other lender must accept repayments from the other spouse. If this problem arises, you should see the mortgage lender immediately.

Renting your home

You can take out a tenancy either in one spouse's name or in both your names. If the tenancy is taken out in one name only, then only the person named in the rent book or the agreement is responsible for paying the rent. If the tenancy is in joint names, then both of you are responsible for paying. If one doesn't pay up, then the other must, including any arrears.

126

Whether the tenancy is in one name or joint names, both husband and wife have a right to live in the home. Neither can make the other leave, except in very exceptional circumstances such as domestic violence (see page 217).

If your spouse is already the tenant of a property, you should transfer the tenancy into your joint names immediately. However, you may need the landlord's consent before you do.

YOUR MONEY

Money is one of the biggest causes of marital arguments. The other is who does the washing-up. The odd thing is, the two often go together.

Money talks

Money is power. The person who earns dictates how it should be spent. The person who doesn't earn, or earns less, usually cleans the toilet bowl. Cynical perhaps, but unfortunately there's at least a grain of truth in it.

People play manipulative games with money, like they play games with sex. They pretend they're richer or poorer than they really are, they throw it around, they hide the fact they've spent it.

Your partner and money

Part of your partner's attraction is to do with their attitude to money, whether or not you consciously recognise it. It may be that you feel secure because you know they're cautious or you may love them for their extravagant habits; they may reflect your own attitudes or you may be attracted because they're your opposite. If you want to avoid money mayhem, then you need to address these issues. Sort out how you save and how you spend. Don't push bills and tax demands to one side. Be professional about the way you manage your finances.

As with property matters, married couples do not have to think ahead to quite the same degree as cohabitees. Ultimately, the courts have the power to provide a just settlement if you break up.

However, the same words of caution apply: if the marriage finishes while you're still young and childless, you are likely to get out of the relationship only what you put in.

Part Two of this book deals with essential legalities and financial facts so have a look back over pages 25–47. The following pages look at ways to manage your money.

Money management

You cannot manage your finances properly unless you make a thorough budget. It's not something you can do while strap-hanging on your way in to work; neither should you wait until you're drowning in debts (see page 31).

Setting out a budget stops you: finding you're completely broke at the end of the month; arguing about one person buying an Italian designer suit when there's not enough money left for the rent; living off dry bread and water when you've got enough money to go out and buy a steak. Unfortunately the last-mentioned rarely happens!

Calculating your budget

MONTHLY INCOME	*MONTHLY EXPENDITURE*
His earnings	Mortgage
Her earnings	Rent/ground rent
Any additional earnings	Tax/NIC (if self-employed)
(give an average)	Average monthly bills
Income from investments	– water
State benefits	– gas
Other	– electricity
	– telephone
	Loan, HP, credit card repayments
	Insurance
	– house
	– contents
	– car
	– life
	Pensions
	Savings plans
	Household goods/food
	Car
	– tax
	– petrol
	– service
	Transport
	– to work
	– other
	Personal spending
	– clothes
	– cosmetics
	– hobbies
	– subscriptions
	– entertainment
	Planned savings
	– holiday
	– other
	Other
	10% cushion*
TOTAL AVERAGE MONTHLY INCOME	*TOTAL AVERAGE MONTHLY EXPENDITURE*

RESULT (SURPLUS OR DEBIT)

*If you can add a ten or five per cent cushion to tide you over on a rainy day – in case the interest rates go up, your insurance increases and so on – then so much the better.

129

Your account or mine?

How you organise your money will depend on your personal financial situation, both as a couple and as two individuals, and the extent to which you trust your partner. There are three ways to do it: each has its pros and cons.

1. Two singles

Particularly at the start of your relationship, you might want to keep your finances separate. This isn't just about trust; independence plays an important part too.

- If you each have your own personal account you won't have to worry that your partner's keeping tracks on your spending habits.
- If you each tend to spend money in a different way or one of you has a hobby the other doesn't entirely approve of, then separate accounts let you control your own financial destiny.
- However, the big drawback is what do you do about the household bills. With large bills that you can predict in advance, like the mortgage, you could arrange a standing order from one of your accounts.
- The problem is you have to be incredibly well organised to run your joint finances in this way. If you're at all slapdash, absent-minded, or constantly broke, this arrangement is probably not a wise idea.
- You also need to consider what happens if one person stops earning. This arrangement is unlikely to continue to be viable.

2. One joint

If you have a single common pool of money then it becomes much easier to ensure you meet all your household bills. You can plan in advance and you won't be splitting your income in a number of different accounts. The result is that you are less likely to find yourself suddenly without sufficient cash to cover the essentials.

- The drawback is that you have no privacy at all. Each knows

how much the other is spending. You may feel more reticent about purchasing something extravagant for yourself out of a joint account.
- Problems can arise where one person isn't working and, not having contributed to the joint fund, may feel awkward about taking money out of it for their personal use.

3. Two singles and a joint

This is probably the happy medium. You have a joint household account to which you both contribute while each keeping a personal account for yourself.

- To do this successfully you must ensure that you have a standing order from your personal account to the joint account. You need to get the timing right to ensure that large payments like the mortgage get paid only once there's money in the account.
- The danger is that you can sometimes find yourself with money in the account, but not at the right time; consequently you incur bank charges for being overdrawn. Discuss the matter with your bank manager first to make sure you get a smooth flow of money in and out of the account.
- For this reason you shouldn't try to transfer money from numerous accounts in some fancy configuration each month. Unless you're extremely smart, the bank charges will inevitably catch you out.

And now for a novel idea!

Separate but equal

This is a similar scheme whereby you have a joint household account while each retaining individual accounts. But there's one big difference. You each contribute the same amount to the joint fund and you each have the same amount left in your personal account regardless of the earning powers of each spouse. The merit of the scheme is largely psychological rather than financial.

– However, for the scheme to work well the amount of money you have coming in each month needs at least to cover your outgoings; you also need fairly predictable incomes. In addition you'll have to prime the joint account so that you have something to cushion you from month to month.

– What's more, the scheme won't work if you have problems in handling the fact that one of you earns more than the other; especially if deep down you're not willing to share what you have equally without embarking on some kind of power/guilt game.

– The advantage of the scheme is that you can both feel you are contributing the same amount to the common pot, while retaining your independence. This may be particularly important if you have little or no income of your own, when, for example, you're staying at home to look after a young family. It means you don't have to ask or account to your earning spouse for every penny.

What's the magic formula?

1. Work out your individual monthly incomes after tax etc.

Janet works part time while her son is at nursery school. She earns £7,200 a year after deductions. Her monthly wage is therefore £600.

John works full time and brings home £15,000 after tax, that's £1,250 each month.

2. Add up your total monthly incomes and divide by two.

Janet' and John's monthly incomes: £600 + £1,250 = £1,850
$$£1,850 \div 2 = £925$$

The £925 represents their individual 'earnings' when they divide their income equally.

3. Add up your total yearly outgoings and divide by twelve to get your monthly outgoings. Then divide by two so that you each end up with your half share of the outgoings.

Once you have worked out your contribution, you should each make a standing order from your individual accounts to have the money paid into the joint account every month.

Janet and John worked out that their total yearly outgoings are £13,200 – £1,100 a month. That means that they each have to contribute £550 to their joint household account.

However, that would have left Janet with only £50 in her own account each month while John would have been rolling around with £700 to spare. Hardly the point of the scheme, so . . .

4. You need to do a smart calculation. Take the highest earner's monthly wage and subtract from it the 'equal earnings' you worked out in step two. The higher earner should then make out an additional standing order to have this sum transferred each month to the lower earner's individual account.

John's monthly income is £1,250; the 'equal earnings' £925. £1,250 – £925 = £325. John had to make a standing order in favour of Janet for £325. That meant that at the end of the day they each had £375 in their personal accounts each month.

In other words the monthly calculations looked like this:
John: £1,250 – £550 – £325 = £375
Janet: £600 – £550 + £325 = £375

FINANCIAL PROVISION FOR THE FUTURE

If you're married and particularly if you have children, you ought to consider planning for the future. Pension plans, life insurance and long-term investments are worth thinking about sooner, rather than later. It's the usual Catch 22; although policies are much cheaper the younger you are when you take them out, youth (or relative youth) is precisely the time when you can least afford to think about the future.

To find out more about planning for the future look back over Part Two, pages 34–41.

MAKING A WILL

You must make a will either just before you get married or immediately after. If you made a will while you were still single, it will become invalid as soon as the marriage vows are exchanged. This obviously doesn't apply to a prenuptial will made in anticipation of your forthcoming wedding.

Don't be misled into thinking that you don't need to make a will if there are only the two of you. Not all of your property will automatically go to your spouse if you die intestate – without having made a will.

For more information on making a will and the Intestacy Rules see pages 72–77.

TAX NOTES

Basic explanations of the technical terms used are found on pages 42–47.

Until the beginning of this decade, married women were largely ignored as far as income tax and capital gains tax were concerned. Husbands were responsible for completing tax returns and paying tax for both themselves and their wives.

In 1990, independent taxation of married women was introduced. Now everyone is taxed individually and is responsible for completing their own tax returns. However, even the new tax rules distinguish between married and unmarried couples.

1. Husbands living with their wives are entitled to claim the *married couples allowance* which is an additional deduction against taxable income. If the husband does not have enough income to make full use of the allowance, then he can transfer the surplus to his wife.

2. If you marry part way through the tax year, the husband is entitled only to a proportion of the married couples allowance.

Angela and Philip got married in October. Philip was therefore entitled to claim half of the total married couples allowance for that year. (The tax year runs from April.)

3. Married couples are entitled to claim tax relief (MIRAS) on only one home.
4. You can also claim relief from CGT on only one home.
5. Gifts between husband and wife are not subject to capital gains tax or inheritance tax.

For information about tax and children see page 267.

CHAPTER 11
Remarriage

You can get remarried only if:

- your former partner is dead;
- your marriage is annulled;
- you have been granted a Divorce Decree Absolute.

When you remarry, you will once again take on the responsibilities
of a married person and, of course, be protected by the law if the
marriage doesn't work out. However, there are a number of points
that second (or more) time around brides and grooms should take
on board.

DIVORCE SETTLEMENTS AND REMARRIAGE

The key points about maintenance payments are covered below.
However, if you are about to remarry and you haven't yet applied
for, or finalised the financial element of your divorce, you should
be aware of the following facts.

- Once you remarry you are no longer entitled to start a claim for
  property adjustment orders or for a *lump sum* (see pages 172–173).
- If you have already begun your claim, then you can continue
  it after your remarriage.
- You should always check that any claims you intend to make
  are made before you remarry.
- If you have already remarried, or you have clear intentions to
  remarry, before the court decides on the terms of the financial
  settlement, then it will take your new circumstances into consideration.

MAINTENANCE PAYMENTS FROM A PREVIOUS MARRIAGE

If you receive *periodical maintenance payments* (see page 173) from a former spouse, then these will cease automatically when you remarry.

- Lump sum payments and property adjustment orders will be unaffected.
- However, if your right to remain in the marital home lasted only for as long as you remained unmarried, then that agreement will obviously be brought to an end.
- If your former spouse remarries and you continue to make maintenance payments to them after the wedding, you can go to court to reclaim whatever you have paid out unnecessarily.
- If you are making payments to a former spouse, then those payments will not be affected by your own marriage. However, if you feel that you have taken on new financial responsibilities as a result of your remarriage, you can go to the court to ask it to reduce the maintenance payments (see page 207).

RELIGIOUS WEDDINGS

Couples marrying for the second or more time after a divorce may find it difficult to have a religious wedding ceremony.

- The Church of England will not compel any of its ministers to perform a second marriage where the couple have previously been divorced. However, the prevailing trend seems something of a muddle. Some ministers will, some won't. If you find your local vicar refuses your request, then you might try another somewhere else.
- The Roman Catholic Church does not recognise divorce, full stop. However, it will marry those whose previous marriage has been annulled.
- Other Churches tend to be less strict and you should inquire directly from them.

– A Jewish woman wanting to remarry will have to obtain a *get* or religious divorce from her husband in addition to her Divorce Absolute. The *get* is a source of great controversy. The progressive synagogues will grant a *get* where the husband refuses to give one, in order to enable the woman to remarry in the synagogue.

YOUR WILL

If you're coming from one broken relationship, then you've probably already redrafted your will. As soon as you remarry, any previous will will be revoked and you should make a new one.

OTHER CONSIDERATIONS

Like any other couple, you will need to think about securing your rights to your home, protecting your money and providing for the future. Look back over the previous chapter, Marriage, which starts on page 106.

– If you have children, your position will be largely unaffected by your remarriage.
– Remember that you cannot simply change your child's name to that of your new spouse.
– You may, however, want to consider making your new spouse a legal parent of the child of your former marriage. This is explained in Part Five: Parents and Children on page 250.

PART FOUR:
Breaking Up

CHAPTER 12

Breaking Up is Hard to Do

Breaking up is hard to do. It's a time of emotional turmoil and hard decision-making. Whether instigator or victim of separation, married or not, everyone faces mental and physical stress. Even for those couples where the separation is mutual, the process is not without pain. But for each person facing a relationship break-up, the experience is unique. How well you deal with separation and how long it takes you to get on your feet again is highly individual. It may be a matter of months or it may take many years.

Understanding the legal processes, finding out how to safeguard your financial interests and knowing where to turn for help and advice may lessen the burden and enable you to begin to see light at the end of what may seem a very long and dark tunnel.

Separation feels like . . .

Exhilaration, desolation, freedom, guilt, loneliness, vengeance, running away, anger, mourning, fear, jealousy, shock, rejection, disbelief and through it all . . . doubts. The range of emotions people feel when confronting the end of a relationship is huge. For some it's a tremendous sense of exhilaration, of fresh beginnings, new loves. It's an opportunity to start again, try new things, begin living.

For others and those who have separation thrust upon them, there's a sense of regret, rejection, bitterness for wasted years, disbelief and perhaps abject terror about the future. Many tread a middle path. Knowing the relationship has run its course, mourning its loss yet looking to the future with a mix of excitement and fear.

There are no 'right' or 'wrong' feelings. It's better to let them all wash right over you, to feel and recognise them, than to shut them out or deny them.

Separation is about change

Separation, like any other aspect of a relationship, is about change. Imagine the gradual break-up like living in a straw house built on rocks. The straw slowly blows away and the foundations start to crumble. Perhaps you sense the cracks, perhaps you don't. Maybe you try to patch it up. Then all of a sudden you realise – or someone points out to you – that the foundations have all but disappeared: neither of you is left standing on very much. It is time to pick up the pieces, go through the necessary processes and reconstruct your own rock.

Change, particularly sudden or traumatic change, will provoke a stream of reactions and emotions. Usually there is a sense of disbelief, followed by denial of the situation. Then comes anger and, eventually, acceptance. There is no fixed timescale. Your emotions may keep recycling. You may take many years to accept the changes fully. Irrespective of whether you feel a great sense of trauma, give yourself time to mourn the passing of the old relationship.

Separation is more than two people

Separation is not just about two people splitting up; relationships with children, family and friends are equally affected. You may move home, job and neighbourhood. As the nature of your relationship and your status change, you too will need to evolve: from spouse or cohabitee to someone who is working through the process of separation and then on, into a different future.

GETTING HELP

If you're worried about the state of your relationship, it may be worth seeking the advice of a professional counsellor to see if you can save or strengthen the partnership. This is true even if one partner has already suggested that the relationship is over. Unfortunately there is no nationwide provision for reconciliation and counselling services. You may find yourself having to wait a considerable time to see someone, or pay privately for advice. A good place to start looking for help is your local Relate, formerly The Marriage

Guidance Council. You don't have to be married to seek their advice. Alternatively, your doctor, clergyman or solicitor may be able to recommend someone or your library or advice centre may have a list of local practitioners. Most of the major religious denominations also offer professional counselling services (see Part Six: Resources).

Even if you accept that the relationship is over for good, there's no getting away from it, divorce and separation can be traumatic experiences. If you find it hard – or impossible – to discuss the separation process with your partner, or if you're worried about dragging your children into your conflicts then it's also possible to get professional help. This is known as conciliation or mediation.

Unlike reconciliation – the service offered by organisations such as Relate, which aim to help you to try to get back together – conciliation is a counselling service which aims to help you manage the separation process with less conflict and bitterness, and without escalating legal fees. There are independent conciliation services throughout the country and the National Family Conciliation Council will be able to tell you what's available in your area.

Services can vary considerably in terms of the way they structure counselling sessions, whether or not they involve children in discussions and if they charge fees. As a general rule they will provide a neutral place for you and your former partner to meet with an impartial counsellor to work out solutions to some of the problems you might have. The service is confidential. You may also find that if you end up disputing before the court then it will refer you to a conciliation service. However, this is a relatively new practice and not standard throughout the country.

CHAPTER 13

Cohabitees: Separation

To restate the message loud and clear: the law offers no automatic protection to cohabitees. You must think ahead and protect yourselves. However, that's not much consolation if your relationship is falling apart and you've only just picked up this book.

Whatever your situation, your key considerations are likely to be: your home; your money and your children (see pages 88, 99 and 257). Where do you stand? Before you embark on the process of disentangling your relationship, there are two points you ought to consider immediately:

- If you own your home as a joint tenant you should think about changing it without delay to a tenancy in common (see page 68). The effect of this will be to ensure that should you die before you conclude the separation arrangements, your share in the property will go to your estate and not automatically to your ex-partner.
- If you've made a will under which your partner benefits, you should destroy it, amend it by a codicil (see page 72) or make another one.

YOUR HOME

Many of the points made here relate back to the basic technical explanations given in Part Two (see pages 66–71) and the specific information for cohabitees on pages 88–94.

Home owners

What happens to your home when you split up, your rights of occupation and how much money, if any, you will get from the sale of it, will depend on your legal status as an owner. If there is nothing down on paper, then who gets what is entirely open to argument. It can be incredibly difficult to prove any kind of 'right' to the proceeds of a home without written proof. Over time, verbal agreements about which partner is entitled to what percentage become distorted memories. This highlights yet again the importance of cohabitation contracts and written trust deeds (see pages 94–99).

NOTE: A general warning. If, for any reason, you and your partner cannot agree about the sale of your home or how to divide the proceeds, you will have to let the court decide for you. Going to court can be a time-consuming, protracted business, and it'll probably be very expensive, although you may qualify for legal aid. In addition you may not regard the court's decision as fair. Be pragmatic, be sensible and try and sort things out between you (see page 17–22).

Legal co-owners
If you are joint tenants, take heed of the comment made above about changing to a tenancy in common.

However you co-own your home, you have two options.

- Sell the property and divide up the net proceeds. Don't forget that you will need to deduct estate agent's fees, conveyance and any other essential costs from the gross, total, profits.
- One partner can buy the other one out. You ought to agree a time limit within which time this has to be achieved, particularly if the buyer has trouble securing the necessary finance.

If one partner refuses to sell the property, the court can force them to put the home on the market – and the court is likely to do so.

If you are tenants in common then the proceeds of the sale of the property will be divided up according to the percentages agreed in the title deeds. Where no division is specified and you can't agree between you, the court will decide for you. If you are joint tenants then the proceeds will be split fifty-fifty.

One partner has legal title to the home but the other is also a beneficial owner

If your partner has legal title to your home you may have also acquired beneficial ownership of it through a trust deed (see page 66). This deed will show how the proceeds are to be divided and may also state how the home is to be sold.

However, even though you have a right to a share of the proceeds of the home, your partner can sell the property without your consent or even your knowledge. That is, unless you have taken certain steps to protect your interest. These measures are explained on page 92.

If you haven't already considered with your partner how and when you would sell your home should you split up, then you'll need to take immediate action to trumpet loud and clear that you have an interest in the property. This is particularly important if you think there's a danger of your partner selling up and making off with the proceeds, or if you want to delay or prevent the sale of your home.

So what can you do?

Protecting your interest

Unless your partner has already registered a *restriction* on the Land Register (see page 92) you, yourself, can ask for a *caution* to be entered on the Register. This applies if your home is on *registered land*. The effect is to ensure that no one else can attempt to register the property in their name without you being notified first. Buyers are likely to be cautious about the purchase if they see that someone, other than the seller, has an interest in the property.

Even if you haven't registered a restriction or caution you may still be protected. You'll be covered providing you have been living in the property at, or since, the time when you acquired beneficial ownership; and certainly before any inquiries from a prospective buyer or their mortgage lender.

If any potential buyer or lender inquires whether you have

beneficial ownership of the property you must answer positively otherwise you will lose your protection. It doesn't matter whether their inquiries are verbal, for example when they come to look at your home, or in writing through their solicitors.

If your home is on *unregistered land*, it will be very difficult to register your interest in the same way. You will have to make it plain to any prospective buyer that you have beneficial ownership of the property. Don't assume that just because they see you living in the house, they will presume you have beneficial ownership. You must spell it out to them.

The property is in one person's name

If your partner is the sole legal and beneficial owner of the property, then they can simply ask you to leave. The law regards you as living in your partner's home under *licence* – at their invitation. If you refuse to leave, then the owner can ask for – and will get – a court order to evict you.

However, even if you have nothing in writing to suggest you have an interest in the property, you may still be entitled to claim some financial share in the home. This is a very slippery and uncertain slope to climb. It should only be used in desperation. Do not use it as a fallback position if you can at all help it.

Claiming an interest

To have any hope of staking a successful claim you have to show two things:

- You added substantially to the value of the property or greatly reduced the mortgage.
- When you made your contribution or payment it was with your *joint* intention that you should acquire an interest in the property.

What you are seeking to prove is an *implied trust* – as opposed to a written trust.

If you lent your partner money for a deposit on the property, then this won't be taken as creating a beneficial interest. In the same way, contributions towards the mortgage instead of rent have no effect.

It's also possible to claim beneficial ownership for non-financial contributions. If you're female then the fact that you carried out a traditional 'housewife' role may help your claim.

The court may well look very favourably upon a claim where you and your partner have a child, thereby reinforcing your relationship as 'man and wife'.

In a very famous case, the Court of Appeal found an implied trust even though the woman had made no financial contributions. In this case the couple, Mr and 'Mrs' Eves, intended to marry and she took his name. The house was bought by Mr Eves, in his name alone; he told his partner, untruthfully, that she was too young to own property. However, Ms Eves did a lot of work in the house, breaking up concrete, demolishing a shed, plus extensive decorations. They had one child, but after four years the relationship broke up and Mr Eves turned her out of the house. The court held that Ms Eves had acquired an interest in the property and that she was entitled to a quarter of the proceeds of the sale of the house.

If you think you may have a financial or occupational interest in your home, you should seek the advice of a solicitor immediately.

Rented homes
You need to consider three things:

- your rights of occupation;
- who pays the rent;
- whether you can transfer the tenancy.

Your rights of occupation
If you split up, and your name is not in the tenancy agreement either as sole tenant or joint tenant, you have no right to remain in the property. Your partner can simply ask you to leave, providing

they give you reasonable notice, which may be only a week or so.

If your partner is the sole tenant of the property and they leave you, you should get legal advice immediately. The legal position can be very complex in this situation and you will want to establish very quickly whether you have any security of tenure.

Whatever your situation, if you continue to live in the property, remember that the landlord cannot evict you without first getting a court order. If you receive a *Notice to Quit* see a legal adviser without delay.

Paying the rent
Only the people whose names appear in the rent book or on the tenancy agreement are liable to pay the rent.

- If you and your partner are joint tenants and one of you leaves the property, you both still remain responsible for paying the rent.
- If your partner is the sole tenant and they leave, then you do not have to continue paying the rent

However, if your partner stops making payments, the landlord may apply for a court order to force you to leave. To stop this happening, you can pay the rent yourself. The only snag is, the landlord is not obliged to accept rent from anyone other than the named tenants. So they may refuse your payments and go ahead with the court order in any case.

If you have children and the landlord does apply to the court to evict you, you can ask the court to postpone the hearing until you have sorted out your affairs (see below).

Transferring the tenancy
The courts have no general power to order the transfer of a tenancy between cohabitees.

- If your partner leaves home and the tenancy is in their sole or joint name, you cannot force them – or the landlord – to

transfer the tenancy into your sole name.
- Your partner can voluntarily *assign*, or give, their share in the tenancy to you. However, such an assignment will normally be subject to your landlord's consent, which they may not give.
- If you have children, the court has the power to transfer the tenancy to the parent with whom the children will live. This can be done through the County Court.

YOUR MONEY

The principles of savings accounts, credit, pensions and life insurances are explained in the reference section on pages 34–41. Specific information for cohabitees is contained in Getting Together, pages 99–103. Since these already cover the effect on your financial arrangement if the relationship ends, please look back over those chapters to find out your position when you separate.

If you are worried that your partner might drain the contents of any joint savings accounts, read the advice given to spouses on page 181. You can take the same action. In the same way, if you are anxious that a revengeful partner might take advantage of a joint credit card account, you should also take immediate steps to protect yourself and these are explained on pages 181–182.

As far as pensions are concerned, if you have nominated your former partner as a beneficiary should you die, then you might want to cancel this. If you have assigned the benefit of a life assurance policy to your partner, however, you might not be able to do anything about it without their consent – except stop paying the premiums.

YOUR BELONGINGS

If you have already drawn up a cohabitation contract of the kind described on pages 94–99, then that document should be your first point of call when you realise the relationship is over.

If you have such a contract, you will probably have spelt out how you organised your money and property while you lived together, and what you would do if you broke up. However, even if you have an agreement which was intended to be legally binding, there is no guarantee that the court would uphold the terms of the contract, if in fact one of you chose not to honour it.

What happens then to your money and your personal belongings if you have no cohabitation contract, or if you are not prepared to abide by what you had previously agreed?

The big split

Unlike the break-up of a marriage, the court has no power to intervene and adjust which partner has what property when a cohabitation relationship ends. Unless you have evidence that you reached agreement about who owned property bought jointly during the relationship, you – and the court – will be interested in establishing only one thing: which of you was responsible for acquiring which items of property.

The four basic rules on splitting up property are these:

- Anything you owned before you started living together remains yours.
- Anything you bought with your own money remains yours.
- Anything given to you personally as a gift remains yours.
- Anything which you bought together belongs to both of you.

There is the crunch: what do you do about things you bought together? The rules that apply to home ownership apply here. Whoever pays owns. That's really the bottom line.

You need to be sensible. There's absolutely no point in going to court over household items – furniture, domestic appliances and so on, all of which depreciate in value. Perhaps a good rule is to divide up your joint belongings on a needs basis.

MAINTENANCE

To put it brutally, cohabiting couples cannot claim maintenance. There is no obligation for cohabitees to maintain each other either during their relationship or when it ends. Even if you have a cohabitation agreement in which one partner agrees to continue to maintain the other partner should the relationship finish, there is no guarantee the court would enforce it.

The only possibility of obtaining any maintenance payments is if you have a child between you. If you're in this situation, you should read the advice given in Part Five: Parents and Children on pages 257–266.

TAX NOTES

Since cohabitees are taxed individually, separation will make no difference to your general tax position. You will only be affected if you have children (see page 267).

For a word of caution on splitting up your home and capital gains tax see page 210.

CHAPTER 14

Married Couples: The Legal Break-up

The laws on marital separation offer more than simply the means to secure a legal final exit from a marriage commitment. While some couples seek the finality of divorce, perhaps freeing them to marry new partners, others search for a temporary way of separating while ensuring financial protection.

The legal system offers you a number of options. Which one you choose will depend on the state of your relationship and the state of your finances.

The divorce who's who
Petition: the application to the court requesting a separation or divorce.
Petitioner: the person seeking the divorce who files the petition.
Respondent: the other spouse, the person being sued for divorce.
Parties: refers to both the petitioner and the respondent.
Co-respondent: in cases of adultery this is the person with whom the respondent has had a sexual relationship.
Decree: a court order.

SEPARATION: THE OPTIONS

There are four ways you can end your relationship either on a temporary basis or for good:

- separation agreements (also known as voluntary agreements and maintenance agreements);
- judicial separation;

- divorce;
- annulment.

Each has its own advantages and disadvantages.

Separation agreements
These are agreements about financial matters. They can be drawn up on a relatively informal basis by husband and wife without the intervention of a lawyer. However, if you want it to carry weight, it's worth having such an agreement drawn up by a solicitor.

Advantages
- Great if you and your spouse are on amicable terms and can agree what to do about your finances, your children and so on.
- Avoids the need to go to court (but see below).
- Good as an interim measure, to give some financial protection during a trial separation or while waiting to petition for divorce.
- A civilised way to get your financial affairs in order.
- If you do get back together again, the agreement can simply be cast aside.

Disadvantages
- Although many agreements, properly drawn up, may stand up in court, they can sometimes be overruled if one partner feels they have been disadvantaged or the court believes the arrangements for the children are not in their best interests.
- If negotiations break down, you may find you need the protection and jurisdiction of the court.
- Such agreements won't give you the final 'clean break'.

Judicial separation
Rarely used these days, it gives legal recognition of separation for people unable or unwilling to get divorced. Judicial separation also affords legal and financial protection to separated spouses.

Advantages
- Offers a formal means of separation if you cannot get divorced for religious or other reasons.
- Gives financial and legal protection, particularly as an interim measure, if you're unsure about the finality of divorce or are waiting to petition for divorce.
- The court sorts out issues which might cause conflict such as who keeps the marital home.
- You can apply for residence orders, maintenance agreements, injunctions and so on.

Disadvantages
- Judicial separation is a legal procedure so you will need to fulfil certain criteria and abide by court procedures.
- If you and your spouse argue about your interests before the court, it could get expensive.
- It will not end the marriage as far as the law is concerned, so you won't be able to remarry.

Divorce
This is a strictly regulated procedure to end the marriage legally, leaving you free to remarry if you wish.

Advantages
- The ultimate 'clean break'. You can sort out all your affairs and use the power of the courts to bargain in your own best interests.

Disadvantages
- You will have to fulfil certain criteria in order to petition for divorce and adhere to a strict legal procedure.
- Divorce is final. There is no going back. If you do reconcile with your 'ex' you will need to remarry if you want to continue as 'man and wife'.
- The process can be costly if you and your spouse dispute before the courts.

Annulment
You can only have your marriage annulled if you can prove it was illegal in the first place (see below).

SEPARATION: THE PROCESS

The following pages look at judicial separations and annulments. The divorce procedure is dealt with in the next section. If you want to find out more about drawing up a separation agreement turn to Chapter 15, The Financial Break-Up, on page 172.

Judicial separation
A judicial separation means that the petitioner is no longer under any legal obligation to live with the respondent. It is a formal recognition of separation but it does not end your marriage. As far as the law is concerned, you and your partner remain married. Neither can marry anyone else and the wife may be entitled to receive any widow's pension if the husband dies. However, if either partner dies without having made a will, under the Intestacy Rules (see page 74) the other partner will not be treated as a spouse.

Gina and Henry Peterson obtained a judicial separation. Some years later Henry died. During his working life Henry had contributed to a pension scheme, which provided for his wife in the event of his death; however, he hadn't made a will.

When he died, Gina received a lump sum from the pension company but nothing from Henry's estate which was divided amongst his children.

The procedure for obtaining a judicial separation is the same as petitioning for a divorce (see below). You do not have to show that the marriage has broken down irretrievably but you do have to prove one of the same five facts (see pages 158–160).

The other difference is that there is no interim stage or *Decree Nisi*. There is only one decree which is final.

Annulment

A decree of *nullity* is granted if a marriage is proved to be *void* – in other words, has never legally existed – or *voidable* where one partner applies for the marriage to be declared void. The reasons for this include where one partner, or both, is under age, mentally incapable, already legally married or that the marriage has never been consummated.

The effect of a decree of nullity is to treat the marriage as never having taken place in law. However, children of a marriage which is declared void remain legitimate.

Proceedings for annulling a voidable marriage must be started within three years of marriage except where the grounds are non-consummation. If you want to have your marriage annulled, you should seek the advice of a solicitor.

GETTING DIVORCED

Who can divorce?

In order to obtain a divorce (or judicial separation), you must prove four facts:

- That a valid marriage existed. In most cases an official copy of the marriage certificate is sufficient. If the marriage took place outside England or Wales, it may be necessary to produce other evidence and a certified or sworn translation of the foreign marriage document.
- That you have been married for at least a year. You cannot get divorced if you have been married for less than a year.
- That you or your spouse have been either legally domiciled, or resident in England or Wales for at least a year before divorce proceedings begin. Domicile is a legal concept which means the country which you regard as your permanent home. If there is any question about whether you are domiciled in this country or if neither you nor your spouse live here, you should consult a solicitor right away.
- That the marriage has broken down irretrievably (see below).

In addition if you have children you must also prove that satisfactory arrangements have been made for them (see pages 257–266).

Grounds for divorce

There is only one ground for divorce in this country: that the marriage has broken down irretrievably. There are five ways of proving this:

1. Adultery

There are two parts to this. First, that the respondent has committed adultery and, second, that the petitioner finds it intolerable to go on living with the respondent.

- Providing the respondent doesn't contest the petition this is often the quickest and easiest way of getting a divorce.
- However, if you continue to live with your partner for more than six months after you become aware of their adultery, you may be taken to have accepted their behaviour and will not be able to start divorce proceedings on this ground.

In the spring of 1986, Jenny McGill discovered her husband, Tony, was having an affair with a business colleague. Jenny confronted Tony and he said he would finish with the other woman.

Jenny decided to ignore her husband's past infidelity and continued to live with him for the next year. Had she then, in the spring of 1987, started divorce proceedings, she would not have been able to do so on the grounds of adultery.

However, in 1988, Jenny found out that Tony had resumed the affair and she was entitled to petition for divorce on the basis of her husband's adultery.

- A petition cannot be based on the petitioner's own adultery.
- A relationship that does not actually involve sexual intercourse is not adultery, although it may constitute unreasonable behaviour.
- For a woman to be accused of adultery, it is essential that the

sexual intercourse was voluntary. For this reason a woman who is raped does not commit adultery.

2. Unreasonable behaviour
The respondent has behaved in such a way that the petitioner cannot be expected to live with the respondent.

- Unreasonable behaviour is difficult to categorise but includes violence, alcoholism, insanity, public humiliation, excessive demands for, or refusal of, sex and meanness with money.

In one famous case a wife sued her husband for divorce on the grounds of unreasonable behaviour. The man was a DIY fanatic. He took off all the doors inside the house to alter them, including the toilet and bathroom doors, and failed to put them back.

- Again, you must show that you have not lived with respondent for more than six months after the last act of unreasonable behaviour alleged in the petition.
- Unreasonable behaviour can be hard to prove. Unless you are claiming physical abuse, for which you have ample evidence, you would be wise to seek advice from a solicitor.

3. Desertion
The respondent has left the petitioner, against the petitioner's will, for at least two years.

- You can also claim to have been deserted if your spouse continues to live in the same home as you but withdraws into one or two rooms and has nothing to do with you; this means you don't prepare or eat meals together, share a living room and so on.
- If the respondent can prove they have made a genuine and realistic offer to return, then the 'desertion' comes to an end and the petition would be dismissed.

4. Two years' separation with consent

The parties have lived apart for a minimum of two years and the respondent agrees to a divorce.

5. Five years' separation without consent

The parties have lived apart for a continuous period of five years. No consent is necessary.

Attempts at reconciliation

If you and your partner are reconciled after an initial period of separation, you may find you have to postpone your divorce. If you return to live together for a short while you can still proceed with the divorce, providing that the total amount of time you have lived together is not more than six months. If the reconciliation is less than six months then you will need to add that time on to the separation period.

Jean and Bob Marks decided to separate. Seven months later they got back together again but it lasted only three months. A year later they had a second attempt but this time they stayed together for four weeks. They finally went ahead with the divorce two years and four months after they first separated.

If you have lived together for more than six months in total, you will have to find another fact to prove the marriage has broken down or begin the two- or five-year period over again.

Which ground?

The two-year separation with consent is often referred to as the 'no fault ground'. Since it doesn't cast blame on one or other party it is probably the most amicable way to start divorce proceedings.

Unreasonable behaviour petitions and to some extent adultery can make the process more difficult and acrimonious. However, there may be good reasons as to why you can't wait for two years.

The five-year separation tends to be a last resort where the other grounds aren't possible or don't apply.

THE DIVORCE PROCEDURE

The divorce procedure is really divided into two parts. The first is about the legal process of dissolving the contract you entered into when you got married. The second concerns your home, your finances and your other assets. The following pages deal with the first part, dissolving your marriage. To find out what happens to your property and your money you should turn to page 172, Chapter 15, The Financial Break-Up. If you have children, you'll also need to look at the special notes on pages 257–267 in Part Five: Parents and Children.

Almost all divorces are undefended: in other words, the respondent doesn't contest the divorce. Even if you disagree about arrangements for maintenance or the custody of children you can still go ahead with undefended divorce. The hearings for maintenance, residence and access orders will be held separately. This is part of an effort by the courts to try and ensure that marriages which have broken down completely are ended as painlessly and as quickly as possible.

The majority of straightforward divorces are dealt with by *Special Procedure*. This means that all the documents are read and the case decided by a District Judge without the need ever to go to court. This doesn't apply if you have children because there will always be a hearing to decide their future care.

You will not get legal aid in order to be represented in a non-defended divorce, although you may qualify for help under the Green Form Scheme to enable you to complete the necessary forms (see page 52). However, that doesn't stop you from being represented through legal aid at custody or maintenance hearings.

All divorces – defended or not – begin the same way. For additional information on defended divorce see page 167.

Undefended divorce

1. The application form
The application form or *petition* is obtainable from Divorce County Courts (look for their addresses in the telephone directory), legal

stationers and CABs. You will need three or four copies of the petition: one for you, one for the respondent, one for the court and one for the co-respondent in cases of adultery.

If you have children you will also need three copies of a form called the *Statement as to Arrangements for Children* in which you need to explain your proposals for your children (see page 263).

Some general points in completing the form:

- Ensure your typing or handwriting is legible.
- Don't make any allegations which you can't prove or which you intend to drop immediately the respondent denies them.
- Keep the petition as short as possible.
- Always make sure you get a copy of every document you send to the court office for your own future reference.

2. Completing the petition

The petition is reasonably straightforward to complete. Take a copy of the blank form and write a rough draft so that you can think through carefully what you want to say and make any changes without the final application becoming a complete mass of scribbles.

You will need to give details of your marriage, the addresses and occupations of you and the respondent and the names and dates of birth of any children. You will also need to give details of any previous court proceedings relating to the marriage.

You will need to state the grounds on which you are petitioning for divorce. Be brief but also be thorough and logical. The court supplies guidance notes which you should read carefully.

Adultery: you will need to give the co-respondent's name and address (if you know them). Many people are unduly worried about disclosing the name of the co-respondent. Gone are the days when divorce cases attracted hordes of hungry scandalmongers. Unless the divorce is contested, you may never need to go to court, the names will only be stated briefly in public and no details will be given.

It is useful but not necessary to say where and when the adultery took place. You must also state that you find it intolerable to live with the respondent.

Unreasonable behaviour: you must give a precise account of the unreasonable behaviour, but you don't need to list every shred of evidence. Try to give in date order the most important incidents, particularly details of the first, worst and most recent.

Desertion: you have to show that your spouse intended to desert you and that there is no good reason why you should live apart. The fact that your partner is in prison or hospital is not sufficient reason. You must also be able to state that you always wanted your spouse to return and that you never did anything to make them leave.

Separation: you must give proof that you have been living apart for the required length of time. If you have attempted to rescue the marriage and lived together at all during the months of separation, check that you haven't ruled out divorce on this basis (see page 160).

On the last page of the petition you will find the *prayer* or petitioner's formal request that the marriage be dissolved. This is also the place to ask for care of the children, the costs of the case to be paid by the other side and orders for maintenance, lump sum payments and property adjustments (see page 172). If you are in any doubt, do not cross any of these off at this stage. If you do and then change your mind later, it may be very complicated and perhaps impossible to reinstate them.

Along with the petition you will also have to send a copy of your marriage certificate. You're probably best getting a duplicate copy from the General Register Office; for details of current charges call them directly or contact your local CAB. A photocopy is not acceptable.

Finally, unless you are exempted, you will also have to enclose the court fee. The current charge will be specified in the court literature.

Send the completed forms together with the fee and your marriage certificate to your local Divorce County Court or the Divorce Registry, if you live in London.

Once you hand in your completed petition to the court you will be given a file number. You must always quote that number on all your subsequent correspondence or visits to the court.

3. *The petition is circulated*

Before the court can go ahead and consider your request for divorce, it must be satisfied that a copy of the petition has been *served* – sent or delivered – to the respondent and, where appropriate, the co-respondent. So, once the court receives your petition it will circulate copies to the people named in it.

With the *Notice of Proceedings* – a letter informing the respondent that divorce proceedings have begun and explaining what they need to do – the court also sends out an *Acknowledgement of Service*. The respondent (and the co-respondent) must complete this acknowledgement form and return it to the court within eight days.

This form is not just an acknowledgement that the petition has been received, it also asks questions about whether the respondent wishes to defend the divorce or objects to a request to pay costs. It also gives the respondent an opportunity to ask for residence or contact orders for your children.

Where the petition is on the basis of adultery, the respondent and co-respondent are asked whether they admit to the adultery; they should sign the acknowledgement personally.

4. *Problems serving the petition*

Problems do arise and the court will inform you if they have not received the Acknowledgement of Service within fourteen days. The respondent may have moved away from the address given by the petitioner or they may refuse to sign and return the acknowledgement. Since you cannot proceed until this is done, or the court is satisfied that the petition is impossible to serve, you may have to try other means to ensure the respondent acknowledges the petition.

One way is to ask the court bailiff to serve the petition in person. You may be asked for a photograph or written description to help the bailiff identify the respondent. Unless you are exempt from paying fees there will be a small charge for the bailiff's service. The court office will let you know the outcome of their efforts.

Where this fails or you don't have an address for the respondent or co-respondent, you will need to ask the court to bypass the requirement to serve the petition. The form you need is an *Affidavit to Dispense with Service*. You will need to complete this and have it sworn in front of a solicitor before returning it to the court.

5. Request for directions to trial

If neither the respondent nor co-respondent indicates their intention to defend the case, you will be sent a copy of their acknowledgement together with two new forms to complete.

The first is a *Request for Directions to Trial* which is a simple form asking for the case to be decided by a District Judge. The form is in several parts. You will need to fill in, sign and date the first part. The rest of the form is for use by the courts.

The second is an *Affidavit of Evidence* which relates to the questions in the petition and asks you for confirmation of the statements you made as well as any amendments or additions. You can also help satisfy the court that the signature on the acknowledgement of service is the respondent's.

Once completed, both the Directions to Trial and the Affidavits of Evidence can be sent back to the court by post. However, before you do so, you will first have to go to a solicitor to have the affidavit – a formal statement witnessed by a solicitor – sworn (see page 65). Alternatively you can take the documents directly to the court where you won't need to pay a swear fee.

6. Affidavits of evidence

Where your petition is based on more than one ground you should complete separate forms for each of the grounds. The affidavit is in a question and answer form to make it easier to complete. You must answer all the questions. When you fill in the affidavit you may find yourself repeating information you put down in the petition. However, you will probably also be asked for more details.

Adultery: if the respondent has admitted the adultery on the Acknowledgement of Service or in some other written statement, then you should identify their signature and attach the document to your affidavit. If this kind of statement is not available then you might want to obtain affidavits from other people with first-hand information. This might include evidence of a spoken admission of adultery by the respondent.

Other sworn evidence showing that the respondent has set up home with the co-respondent, gone away on holiday or spent time alone late at night is also usually acceptable. It is possible to get evidence of adultery through an inquiry agent who will be paid to watch the couple. Most such agents are instructed through solicitors.

Unreasonable behaviour: you will need to give further evidence to substantiate the allegations made in the petition. Again be selective about what you write.

There is a question asking whether the respondent's behaviour has affected your health. A medical report from your doctor or an eye-witness account (which must be sworn in front of a solicitor) of particularly unreasonable behaviour will both be helpful.

Separation: if you have continued to live in the same house because it was impossible or impracticable to maintain separate homes until the divorce was complete, then you will need to show evidence of the 'separateness' of your lives. The less the contact between husband and wife, the more likely is the court to regard you as separated. Unless you can show that the relationship is clearly one of landlord/lady and lodger then you must give evidence that you slept, ate, prepared meals, shopped, cleaned and so on, individually.

7. *The District Judge considers your petition*
Having looked at the papers the District Judge has three options:

- If the District Judge is satisfied that there is sufficient evidence to support the petition, your case will be put on the special procedure list and the District Judge will certify that you are entitled to a divorce decree and any costs claimed.
- If the District Judge is concerned about the contents of the petition, then they will write and ask you for further evidence

or for clarification. Usually this is dealt with by post but you might be asked to attend the court office in person and discuss the points raised with the District Judge.
- If the District Judge has grave doubts about the evidence you've given or the validity of the petition, they will remove your case from the Special Procedure list and direct it to be heard in an open court. Should this happen, you must consult a solicitor at once.

8. Granting of the Decree Nisi

The petitioner and the respondent will be told the date on which the interim decree, the *Decree Nisi*, will be granted. Neither of you needs to attend the court. A copy of the decree will be sent to you. The Decree Nisi is a provisional order and does not dissolve the marriage.

9. Granting of the Decree Absolute

Six weeks after receiving the Decree Nisi the petitioner can apply for the *Decree Absolute*. Until this is granted you remain married. Simply ask the court for the appropriate form, *Notice of Application of the Decree Nisi to be made Absolute*. The form is free; just complete and return it.

The Decree Absolute can be made earlier than six weeks, providing the respondent doesn't object and the petitioner applies for this when the Decree Nisi is granted.

If the petitioner doesn't apply for a Decree Absolute within three months of the date that it was due to be granted, then the respondent can make the application instead.

If the application is made more than a year after the Decree Nisi, then you will also have to give written reasons for the delay when you return the form.

The Decree Absolute is an important document – keep it safe!

DEFENDED DIVORCE

Defending a divorce petition is expensive. Few defended divorces actually come to court. The vast majority are settled outside – usually after a great deal of money is expended – and a decree is granted on an undefended basis. It is highly unlikely that a marriage will be saved by opposing a petition. The only point at issue in a defended divorce is whether the marriage has broken down irretrievably and, if so, on what grounds. Financial matters and arrangements for children are dealt with as separate issues, irrespective of whether the divorce is defended or not.

To defend or not?

Just because the respondent disagrees with the grounds given by the petitioner does not mean that the divorce automatically becomes defended. It may still be possible to have the divorce granted under the Special (undefended) Procedure.

Whether or not the respondent disputes the grounds upon which the petition is based, they may still wish to *cross-pray*, that is petition for divorce on different grounds. If the respondent does this – while not necessarily denying the grounds of the original petition – and the petitioner does not dispute the cross-petition, then the divorce is treated as undefended and dealt with under the Special Procedure.

Although the parties have been separated for two years, the petitioner may decide to base the grounds for divorce on adultery or unreasonable behaviour. The respondent might then deny the allegations and defend in the hope that the petitioner will agree instead to base the petition on two years' separation with consent.

The respondent may feel the marriage has not broken down irretrievably and that the petitioner has been too hasty in going ahead with the divorce. By denying that the breakdown is irretrievable, it is possible to delay the petition. It's worth questioning your motives before doing this.

In adultery cases where the co-respondent denies the adultery, the divorce automatically becomes defended.

The process

1. Respondent files an Answer

On the Acknowledgement of Service form (see above) the respondent indicates whether or not they intend to defend the case. The petitioner gets a copy of the acknowledgement and must keep it in a safe place as it might be needed later.

In addition to the Acknowledgement of Service, the respondent needs to complete another form, the *Answer*. This is where you give your reasons for opposing the petition and you ought to seek the advice of a lawyer before you fill it in. The form must be returned to the court within twenty-nine days. The petitioner is sent a copy of the form.

In the Answer you can either deny that the marriage has broken down irretrievably or deny the grounds given for the divorce and cross-petition – seek divorce on different grounds. In dealing with the allegations made by the petitioner you should indicate whether you deny them totally or whether they contain some element of truth. You may wish to argue that your alleged conduct was justified, and, if so, why.

2. The respondent fails to file an answer

If the respondent indicates on the acknowledgement that they intend to defend the divorce but fails to complete and return an Answer within the required time limit, the case remains undefended. If you (or the co-respondent) then change your mind, you will need to obtain permission from the court in order to defend the case.

3. The case goes to the High Court

Once a case becomes defended it is transferred from the Divorce County Court to the High Court. The hearing will be in open court before a High Court Judge in London or one of the major provincial court centres. If you are a party to a defended divorce you will need professional legal advice.

Before the case is heard in open court, the parties and their legal advisers may be asked to attend a pre-trial review in front of a

District Judge. This provides an opportunity to find out whether the petitioner and respondent can reach an agreement and avoid the unnecessary expense and stress of a defended divorce.

HARDSHIP: SPECIAL PROTECTION FOR RESPONDENTS

If a petitioner files for divorce on the grounds of two years' separation with consent or five years without, the respondent is given special protection. This enables the respondent to stop a divorce being granted without full consideration being given to the financial and other consequences they may suffer.

Five years without consent: preventing a divorce

In order to prevent or delay the divorce, the respondent has to show that as a result of granting a divorce they might suffer either of two consequences:

1. Grave financial hardship: the respondent needs to prove that the hardship will arise from the divorce itself rather than simply the separation or marriage breakdown. The hardship also has to be very serious indeed. Financial hardship might include the loss, for example, to the right to a valuable widow's pension. The court will weigh up whether this loss would be compensated by another gain, perhaps in state benefits.
2. Other grave hardship: this is very difficult to prove. A respondent might feel they will become an outcast in a particular community where divorce is socially unacceptable. However, it's not enough for the respondent to argue that the divorce will cause them personal unhappiness or that they consider it to be morally wrong.

In addition the respondent will have to show: it would be wrong in all circumstances to grant the divorce. Even if the court accepts that the respondent would suffer grave financial or other hardship as a result of the divorce, it still has to be satisfied that taking into account all the factors (such as the interests of any children, the behaviour of both parties, the reasons for the divorce) the divorce would still be wrong.

It is very rare for a divorce to be refused in these cases. However, the court may delay granting the Decree Absolute until it is satisfied that the respondent has been properly provided for (see below).

Delaying the divorce

Whether the petition is on the grounds of two years with consent or five without, the respondent can ask the court to delay granting the divorce until their financial position has been fully reviewed and is satisfactory. Since this is a relatively unusual application to the court, it is wise to seek the advice of a solicitor.

If the court decides that the petitioner should not make any financial provision for the respondent or that proposals for settlement are sufficient then they will grant the final decree. Even if the court is not satisfied about the arrangements, it may still grant the Decree Absolute, if there is a good reason why it should do so.

CHAPTER 15

Married Couples: The Financial Break-up

Separation is not just about leaving your spouse. Part and parcel of splitting up is deciding what to do about your home, your possessions, your financial assets and ensuring you have enough money to live on. This and the following two chapters look at: how you can safeguard your interests; interim measures to tide you over while your divorce goes through – or decide whether divorce is right for you – and long-term solutions.

THE COURTS AND FINANCIAL SETTLEMENTS

The legal system can help in a number of ways to determine what happens to your property and your money. The courts have far-reaching powers to ensure that the entire family is properly provided for after a divorce. How the courts can help you depends on where you are in the separation process. For financial help prior to divorce see page 187. For long-term solutions see page 197.

There are two categories of orders the courts can make:

- *Financial provision orders* which are concerned with income.
- *Property adjustment orders* which are to do with the family's capital assets.

Financial provision orders
There are three types of orders:

1. Maintenance orders

These are orders for periodical payments. Usually one spouse is ordered to pay the other spouse a certain sum each week or month. The amount awarded is designed to cover living expenses. This kind of order will end automatically on the death of either party or on the remarriage of the recipient.

2. Secured periodical payments

This means that some investments are put aside or assets invested in order to produce income to pay one spouse. Usually only a proportion of maintenance is secured. If the maintenance payments end because the receiver remarries or dies, then the assets return to the payer. The payments will not necessarily end when the payer dies.

3. Lump sum payments

One spouse pays the other a more substantial, once and for all, amount. It can, however, be paid in instalments. This 'clean-break' approach, where it's possible to enforce, tends to be favoured by the courts since it does away with the lingering remnants of the divorce procedure.

The courts can also make financial provision orders relating to the needs of children (see page 266).

Property adjustment orders

The court has the power to allocate all your property between you and your spouse as it sees fit. It can order one spouse to transfer the home into the name of the other or sell the house and divide the profits, or allow the partner retaining custody of the children to go on living in the house until the children are adults.

If the family is particularly well off, the court might also allocate some of the property directly to the children. For most families this isn't a realistic proposition.

NOTE: If you disagree with the court's decision, you can appeal against it (see page 204).

CALCULATE YOUR RESOURCES

Before you – or the court – can grapple with 'who gets what' you need to make a list of everything you possess between you, your individual incomes and any assets. It's worth doing the research and the paperwork as far in advance as you can. You'll need to think about:

Your home, your earnings and your assets

Your home
Who owns it, is it in joint names; how much was it bought for; who paid the deposit and what's it worth now; any outstanding mortgage, the type of mortgage and the amount of monthly repayments; the ground rent, service charge and length of the lease for leasehold properties; any substantial improvements you have made to your home, how much they cost and how they were financed; your landlord, amount of rent and any service charges, the type of tenancy and whose name the tenancy agreement is in, if you live in rented property?

  If you have a second home, you'll also need to think about its current value and how and when you acquired it.

Cars
Do you or your spouse own a car, what's its value; do you or your spouse use a company car; who pays for the petrol, insurance, servicing and so on; will either of you need a car in the future; do you own other vehicles such as motorcycle, boat or caravan?

Employment
(Don't worry if you don't know the exact details about your spouse's earning power or fringe benefits.) How much do you each earn (you'll need to produce your last three pay slips if you're an employee, or recent accounts, tax returns and assessments if you're self-employed); do either of you have any fringe benefits such as private medical insurance, subsidised loan or company car; do you incur essential expenses for special equipment or clothing in the

course of your job; what about the cost of child-minding or other care for your children while you work?

Pension
You'll need to supply details of any occupational or other pension scheme to which you belong together with information about any benefits for your widow or widower. The pension company or your personnel officer will be able to give you the necessary information.

Other assets and income
These include joint current and savings accounts, personal current and savings accounts, stocks and shares and unit trusts, life insurance policies, income from investments. You must also include any other valuable property such as jewellery, paintings and antiques, their present value, whether they were inherited or a gift and if not, who purchased them.

Your future financial position

A likely inheritance
Do you expect to inherit money in the foreseeable future or are you likely to gain from a trust?

New partner's finances
If you or your spouse have set up home with someone else, you should write down what you know of the new partner's financial situation.

Other money

Maintenance
Do you make or receive any maintenance payments from a former spouse; do your children receive any maintenance payments; do either of you make or receive other payments to or from someone else?

Benefits
What DSS benefits, if any, are you or your spouse claiming or entitled to claim?

Debts
Make a list of all the money outstanding such as tax arrears, credit card payments, bank overdrafts and other loans; who is responsible for each debt?

Outgoings
You don't need to be exact down to the last penny, but try to be as accurate as you can. Include everything – look back at the budget suggested on page 129. If you don't know how much you spend a week on things like household items, then make a note of everything you buy for, say, a whole month. Remember when you split up and run two households, not all your bills will double. Some, like food or electricity, may be reduced; others such as personal toiletries, divided equally and a few, including school fees or childcare costs, will remain constant.

CONSIDER THE FUTURE

Before you can put forward any proposals about how you divide up your home and your money, you must think about where you will live following the separation and what you will live on. Having spent hours poring over figures, receipts and income and expenditure columns you may find the net results make pretty depressing reading.

The big buck divorce settlements where she gets the Rolls-Royce and the house in the country and he keeps the priceless paintings, the town apartment and a six-figure sum tend on the whole to be confined to the big screen and a small élite. Most people confronted with separation have to make agonising choices and hard compromises. Life, in terms of material comforts, is not necessarily going to be what it was.

Where to live

Thinking about where you might live is not just about balancing
the books. If you have children or you're disabled or have special
needs, you'll have other important considerations. What about the
children's schools, neighbourhood friends, your family? You'll also
need to think about where your job is located, or where you might
find one if you have to start working.

- Consider the financial realities of remaining in your home and
  running it yourself, or selling up and buying elsewhere, or
  moving into rented accommodation. What would be the effects
  of any of these on your spouse?
- If you and your spouse own your own home, try and get a feel
  for the property market. Ask local estate agents to indicate how
  much they might sell your house for; bear in mind that they
  may well hike up the price in order to attract business.
- Work out how much you would have left from the sale of your
  home once you've deducted estate agent's and legal fees and
  the amount of any remaining mortgage. Also calculate the add-
  on cost of buying somewhere new such as conveyancing, Stamp
  Duty and so on plus removal costs, furnishings and decoration.
  This way you'll have a better idea of how much money you
  and your spouse would have available to negotiate with.
- Find out what a smaller house or flat might cost in your area
  or search around for somewhere less expensive.
- Find out whether you can get a mortgage on your own and
  how much it would be. Bear in mind the vast fluctuations in
  interest rates and the instability in the workplace before you
  commit yourself to too great a repayment burden.
- Explore other options such as the rented sector, including council housing. However, don't be too optimistic about the latter.
  Very many councils simply can't cope with the demand for
  housing and some have closed their waiting lists. Even if you
  can prove you are an absolute priority case it doesn't necessarily
  mean you will get a flat or a house: you may end up in bed

and breakfast accommodation or being offered property on a notorious housing estate.

What to live on

Getting divorced isn't cheap. There are legal fees and even if you are on legal aid you may need to repay your fees out of any settlement (see page 54). There are also the costs associated with moving house.

Having calculated your resources carefully you may find on reflection that you cannot realistically realise all your assets. For example, it might be foolhardy to sell a car if one partner was to remain in a rural home; on the other hand you might have to dispose of an expensive vehicle so that both partners could be mobile on less extravagant four wheels. Household goods on the whole have little realisable value and are best divided according to need.

The *one-third rule* has traditionally been used to calculate maintenance between divorcing couples. It is only a starting point and not a hard and fast rule, but useful nevertheless in your initial calculations. Basically, you add up both spouses' incomes. Then you calculate the amount of maintenance the wife would need to be granted in order to make her income up to one-third of the joint earnings. On top of this goes maintenance for any children.

The fundamental flaw in this rule is that it is based on the assumption that the couple began with very little and then slowly over the years amassed more income and assets with the wife staying at home to raise the children while the husband worked. For many divorcing couples this scenario is no longer true.

NEGOTIATING A FINANCIAL SETTLEMENT

The more you can agree between yourselves about your financial and property arrangements, the quicker and cheaper it will be to put them into effect. In negotiating how you will deal with your property and your assets, your single objective must be to achieve a workable financial settlement.

You don't have to conduct the entire negotiation process through a solicitor. It will be far less expensive if you don't. However, even if you and your spouse remain on amicable terms, it's worth each of you seeking the independent advice of a solicitor early on. You can then return later to discuss the merit of any proposals you or your spouse put forward and agree on. Where the relationship is less than harmonious, you will probably want to let your respective solicitors negotiate on your behalf.

Be honest
There's no point you and your spouse attempting to negotiate in the dark. You both need to be absolutely upfront about your financial situations, not only how you stand currently but what you expect, if anything, to change in the near future; for example, if one of you intends to remarry.

Making a proposal
Once you have calculated your resources and thought about your needs for the future (see page 176) you can begin to put forward proposals for a financial settlement. However tempting it might be, there is little to be gained in pitching your opening proposals very low – or very high. All that an unrealistic offer will achieve is to sour the atmosphere and speed you on to the expense of the courts.

Finding a compromise
If you have both considered your positions carefully, there shouldn't be a huge gap in your respective proposals. If there is, you will need to think again. It's likely you know your spouse pretty well, so put yourself in their shoes. Where could you compromise; what would be acceptable to them – and to you? Would bargaining over the car or household goods offset an imbalance in hard cash?

If you reach deadlock, discuss the proposals with your solicitor. They will be able to give an outsider's view and perhaps advise whether one or other of you is in fact being unreasonable.

Reaching agreement

If your negotiations are fruitful, you can ask your solicitors to draw up the terms of your settlement as a *separation agreement* or *deed of separation* (see page 154) and then get the terms of the agreement embodied in a *consent order* by the court (see page 189). If you can't reach a settlement, then you will have to ask the court to do it for you.

SHUTTING THE STABLE DOOR

If there is any danger of your spouse deciding to dispose of the family fortunes in order to reduce their liabilities or provide generous gifts for their new lovers, you need to act fast! Should you find yourself in this situation or with your suspicions aroused, you ought to consult a solicitor immediately.

Securing your home

For many people their home not only provides a roof over their head, it is often their most valuable asset. You need to ensure that your spouse cannot sell it without your consent.

Joint owners

If you own your home jointly and your name appears on the title deeds, then there is no risk of your spouse selling it without your knowledge, short of forging your signature. Your consent and signature will be necessary before the property can be mortgaged, sold or transferred.

Your spouse is the sole owner

If your spouse is the sole owner of the home, then in theory it is possible for them to sell it without you knowing anything about it. There are a number of ways to prevent this from happening depending on whether your home is on registered or unregistered land. If you telephone the Land Registry head office, they will tell you how to contact the District Registry for your area, or your local council or CAB may be able to provide the information.

If your home is on *registered land* you can register what is known as a *caution*. The effect of this is to ensure that a prospective purchaser carrying out routine searches before exchanging contracts on the house will discover you have an interest in the property. Few purchasers would buy a property in these circumstances. Even if they did they would have to let you continue living there until the divorce was granted and maybe for longer.

The purpose and act of registering a caution is much the same for a cohabitee (see page 146) as for a spouse. The major difference is that while a cohabitee enters a caution in order to register their beneficial ownership in the property, spouses register their right of occupation.

If your home is on *unregistered land* then you can register what is known as a *Class 'F' Land Charge* at the Land Charges Department. The fee is minimal.

When you complete the forms, you *must* write down the name of your spouse exactly as it was described on the documents which conveyed – purchased – the property. If you register the name incorrectly, the charge will be ineffective. If you're not sure, register the charge against all possible combinations.

Sarah Maxwell wanted to register a charge on her matrimonial home, of which her husband, David, was the sole owner. Since Sarah didn't know exactly how David had been described on the conveyance of the property, she included on the form all the ways her husband could have been described: David Maxwell, D. Maxwell, David Harry Maxwell, D. H. Maxwell, D. Harry Maxwell, David H. Maxwell.

Securing your money
If you and your spouse have a joint bank or building society account you may run the risk of an unscrupulous partner emptying the coffers without your realising it. To stop this from happening, instruct your bank or building society manager to change the withdrawal arrangements so that cheques will only be accepted if they have been signed by both of you.

In the same way, if you and your partner have a credit or automatic cash card withdrawing from a single account, it's worth the main cardholder stopping the cards. Simply notify the card company and return your card, preferably together with the other user's card. A new card will then be issued to the main cardholder.

Getting help from the court

Providing you can satisfy the court that:

- you have a claim to a share in the family assets or income; and
- your spouse is about to make off with some of the assets in order to defeat your claim,

the court may be able to step in and prevent your spouse from doing so.

The court can issue an injunction stopping your partner from disposing of any of their, or the family's assets. The ultimate penalty for breaching an injunction is imprisonment. Alternatively, the court may order your partner to pay over any personal money to an independent account at the court, or to a bank account in the joint names of both your solicitors.

After the event

The court may be able to put aside any transactions already made by your partner. However, this will depend on the nature of the transaction. If your spouse disposed of any assets to a third person who knew why they were doing it, then the court could put aside the transaction. On the other hand, if the transaction was a sale to someone who knew nothing about your spouse's motives, then the court cannot act.

Jerry Thomas owned a large number of stocks and shares. Unbeknown to his wife, Claire, he put them all into his mistress's name. His mistress knew what he was doing and didn't pay him for them. When Claire applied to the court to take action, they put the transaction aside.

However, Frances Barter, who also owned shares, sold them through her broker before her husband could find out and she happily spent the proceeds. The court could do nothing for Ted Barter since there was no way they could recover the shares.

CHAPTER 16

Short-Term Solutions: Before the Divorce

THE MATRIMONIAL HOME

Whether or not you continue to live in the family home while you go ahead with the divorce will depend on a number of factors. These might include whether you literally 'walk out' of the marriage, or move out to live with someone else, or whether your partner leaves you – and the children. Some couples manage, but rarely without tribulation, to continue to live under the same roof until the Divorce Decree Absolute is granted.

Your rights to occupy your home

Whether you live in a home you own jointly with your spouse or one which is in your spouse's sole name or you live in rented accommodation, you have certain rights of occupation. These are:

- the right not to be evicted without a court order; and, if the court thinks fit,
- the right to return to the home after you've left it;
- the right to exclude the owner from occupying the house for a period of time.

Your right to occupation under these terms will last only until the Decree Absolute is granted. At that point the long-term property solutions (see pages 195–197) come into force. These, however, might continue your right to continue living in your home.

Moving out

If you have any ideas about changing the locks and thereby barring your spouse from entering the house, forget it. A court, if asked, could decide to order you to let your spouse back in – and exclude you, if necessary.

There are pros and cons to moving out of the matrimonial home. On the one hand, it's better to remain there if you want to live there permanently in the long run. On the other, if your spouse insists on remaining too, relations between you might become altogether unbearable at such close quarters. It may be useful to talk this over with your solicitor.

If you or your spouse own your home

If your home is owned by your spouse alone then you should take precautions to prevent the house being sold without your consent, by registering your rights to the property (see page 180).

Ending a joint tenancy

If you and your spouse own any property, it will either be as tenants in common or as joint tenants (see page 68).

If you are joint tenants, you should consider ending this arrangement and, until there is a financial settlement or court order, divide up your respective interests in the property by becoming tenants in common. Your solicitor will be able to advise you whether this would be in your best interests. You can do this at any time by sending a *Notice of Severence* to your partner. This can be in the form of a letter simply stating, *Please accept this letter as notice of my severing the joint tenancy in our property known as* (insert the address of your matrimonial home).

The effect of the notice will be to ensure that if you die, your share of the property will go to your estate and be divided up according to your will or the laws of intestacy.

If you remain joint tenants, then the property would automatically transfer to your surviving spouse on your death.

If you rent your home

Under the Matrimonial Homes Act 1983 both you and your spouse have the right to live in your home so long as you are married – in other words up until the time a divorce is granted. Neither can force the other to leave, even if the tenancy is in only one name. The only exception to this is when one partner becomes violent towards the other (see page 217).

If your spouse walks out on you and the tenancy is in your joint names, then both you and your spouse will remain responsible for the rent. However, you must ensure that the rent is paid regularly, otherwise your landlord will take steps to evict you.

If your spouse walks out and the tenancy is in their name alone, you can offer to pay your landlord the rent. However, they do not have to accept it from you. If you find yourself in this situation, you can ask the court to postpone any eviction hearing until you have sorted out your financial affairs in the divorce settlement.

Remember that whatever your circumstances, your landlord cannot force you out without a court order. If you think your landlord is threatening you, seek advice immediately.

Transferring the tenancy on divorce or separation

If you intend to separate rather than divorce, then obviously you will not need the court's help if you can agree amicably between yourselves who should live in the home. The Matrimonial Homes Act will continue to protect you if the tenancy is in your spouse's name.

If you cannot agree, or you are getting divorced or seeking a judicial separation, you can ask the court to transfer the tenancy into your sole name as part of the divorce or separation proceedings. This applies whether the tenancy is currently a joint one, or in your spouse's name. If you have children the court will usually transfer the tenancy to the spouse who has a residence order.

NOTE: If you want to continue living in your home after the divorce, you must ask the court to transfer the tenancy. If the property is in your spouse's sole name, you will lose your right under the Matrimonial Homes Act to remain in the property after your Decree Absolute, unless you get a court order to transfer the tenancy. In any case once you have an order to transfer, you must ensure it is put into effect.

FINANCIAL HELP

If you are in the process of breaking up, regardless of whether or not you have decided to start, or are in the midst of, divorce proceedings, you may find yourself without money to pay the bills or climbing deeper into debt. Well-intentioned promises to pay regular housekeeping money may have come to nought. The courts can help ensure you have an income to meet your current financial commitments as well as to pay off any bills that have accumulated since you and your spouse separated.

Before divorce proceedings begin

This is also relevant for those people who are unsure whether they want to begin divorce proceedings.

You have two options:

- draw up a *separation agreement*;
- ask the *Magistrates Court* for a *maintenance order*.

Separation agreements

There are three stages in the life of a separation agreement. You can start at stage one or two, and you may find you need go no further.

- Stage one: an informal agreement drawn up by husband and wife.
- Stage two: a formal agreement drawn up by a solicitor which is properly signed and witnessed.
- Stage three: the agreement is embodied in a court order and the separation becomes judicial separation or the agreement

becomes embodied in a court order as part of divorce proceedings.

At its most basic a separation agreement is an informal agreement between spouses about arrangements for property, maintenance and children on their separation. Although you can have a verbal agreement, this isn't really wise. It's easy to dispute how much and how often if you haven't written down what you agreed in the first place.

The best thing to do is to have a separation agreement properly drawn up by a solicitor. You should also make sure that you each take independent advice. The advantage of a properly drawn up agreement is that if you are paying maintenance you will be able to claim tax relief (see page 210).

There are two things you must bear in mind when you make an agreement:

- You cannot prevent one spouse from applying to the court at a later date to review your financial settlement.

Sue and Geoff were trying to draw up a separation agreement. Geoff said to Sue that he would agree to pay her a regular amount of maintenance plus a substantial lump sum on condition she did not go to court in the future. As Geoff's solicitor pointed out, he couldn't put a clause to this effect in the agreement.

- Agreements about arrangements for your children can never be binding.

Varying the agreement

How you vary your agreement will depend on whether or not you can agree about the changes. If you both agree you can alter the terms of the original agreement. You should check with your solicitor whether you need to make a note of the changes in a formal deed. If you disagree you can apply to the court to have the terms of the agreement altered.

Ending a separation agreement
An agreement will come to an end in one of four ways.

- If you both agree to terminate the arrangement. You might in fact have set a time limit when you drew up the agreement.
- One of you breaches the agreement and the other may consider the agreement at an end or goes to court to have the terms of the order enforced.
- You live together again. Whether or not you will have to make a new agreement if you split up for a second time will depend on the terms of the original document.
- One of you dies or remarries. What happens in either of these situations will again depend on the terms of your original agreement.

In addition, the agreement may become a consent order in divorce proceedings (see below).

Separation agreements and divorce proceedings
If you've drawn up a separation agreement which you remain happy with, you can ask to have it endorsed by the court by means of something called a *consent order*. The court will want to see the terms of your agreement and you'll also have to make a very detailed statement about your financial affairs. A form for this is available free from the court office.

Maintenance orders in the Magistrates Court
The Magistrates Court can make orders for periodical maintenance payments and for lump sums up to £500. You will need to show that your partner has deserted you, or behaved in such a way that you cannot reasonably be expected to continue living with them, or that they do not give you enough money for you to maintain yourself and any children.

If you and your spouse have already come to an agreement about maintenance payments, then, providing the court does not think the terms unjust, it will give an order much the same as your agreement. In this case there is no upper limit for the lump sum payments.

Both you and your spouse will have to provide evidence of your respective financial situations at the court hearing. Before making an order, the court will first consider the welfare of any children involved. In addition it will look at each party's earning capacity, their family responsibilities, conduct and any special needs. The court will also take into account the length of the marriage and the previous standard of living.

Since it can take two months or so before your case is heard, you may need to apply to the court for an *interim order*. This will be an immediate payment to enable you to get by in the meanwhile. The order will only last for three months, so you may need to ask to have it extended.

Maintenance orders can be varied if the circumstances of either of you change.

NOTE: It is also possible to get a maintenance order in the County Court. Although it may be able to grant larger sums of money, the process costs more. Unless there are very special reasons, you are unlikely to get legal aid (see page 53) to pursue your case.

During divorce proceedings

Once you have submitted the divorce petition, you can apply for financial relief in the Divorce County Court. It doesn't matter who actually filed for divorce, both the petitioner and the respondent can ask for financial help. If you've already got a Magistrates Court Order (see above) then you don't have to apply again to the Divorce County Court, unless you find you need more money than the Magistrates Court can grant you.

Orders in the Divorce County Court

Although the court can make decisions about who continues living in the matrimonial home and can also stop both spouses from disposing of any family property (see page 182), it cannot offer long-term solutions such as who will own the home, ongoing maintenance and the making over of substantial lump sums to one partner. That can only come into effect when the Decree Absolute is granted.

Since the court's order is temporary and can only last until the divorce decree is made absolute, the order is known as *Maintenance Pending Suit;* in other words, maintenance while the divorce is being decided.

The District Judge may not be able to make an immediate decision about the amount of maintenance to be granted and therefore can make an even more temporary order called *Interim Maintenance Pending Suit.*

You can apply for Maintenance Pending Suit at any time from when the divorce proceedings begin up until the time the divorce is made absolute. At this point any order granted will cease to be paid. If appropriate, the court can backdate any maintenance payments to the time when the divorce petition was filed.

The amount of money you will get will depend on your personal circumstances and that of your partner. You and your spouse will both have to provide a full affidavit of your means: your income, the property you own and any debts.

NOTE: A warning to any spouse who fails to file an affidavit of means: the District Judge will probably make a very high order, forcing the recalcitrant partner to pay up or disclose their financial affairs.

CHAPTER 17

Long-Term Solutions: After the Divorce

Very few couples with fundamental differences about what to do with their property and their money actually make it into court to argue their respective cases. The vast majority are settled long before the case gets to court. However amicably you agree between you how to divide your property and your money, the court will often want to know what you've decided to do and will insist if there are children to be provided for.

Whether you simply want it to embody your separation agreement in a court order (see page 188) or you want it to determine all your affairs for you, the court will follow a number of guiding principles. None the less, there are no magic formulae by which the court calculates 'who gets what'. Each case is decided on its own merits.

Knowing what orders a court can make and how it can divide up your assets and possessions may help you to come to an amicable agreement with your spouse.

THE GUIDING PRINCIPLES

Above everything else, the court must take into account the welfare of any dependent children of the marriage. For more information about children and divorce settlements, see pages 257–266.

The court will take into account all the circumstances of the case and in particular will consider:

- the income and earning capacity of each spouse both now and in the foreseeable future;
- the property and other financial resources of each spouse both

now and in the foreseeable future;
- the financial needs, obligations and responsibilities of each person;
- the length of the marriage and the age of the spouses;
- the standard of living of the family before the marriage breakdown;
- any physical or mental disabilities;
- the contributions each spouse has made, or will make, to the welfare of the family;
- whether either spouse will lose a benefit, such as a widow's pension, as a result of the divorce;
- the conduct of each of the spouses.

What do these mean?

Income and earning capacity

The courts will consider whether either spouse can reasonably be expected to increase their earning capacity. However, they also recognise that a woman approaching retirement who has never worked before is unlikely to find paid employment. Equally, a slightly younger woman without skills may have difficulty finding a well-paid, full-time job which is secure.

In the same way, a young mother looking after her children will not be expected to enter the job market, unless she is already working, in which case the court assumes that she will continue to do so. As the children grow up, the non-employed mother will be expected to find a part-time job followed eventually by full-time work.

The court cannot order a person to take a job. If it thinks someone is avoiding work when they could reasonably be expected to find employment, then the court can deem a husband or wife a level of income. This means it sets a level of income which it believes the spouse could earn and then uses this deemed income in its settlement calculations. This same rule applies if the court thinks that one spouse is deliberately taking a low-paid job or otherwise reducing their income to influence a maintenance claim.

The length of the marriage

No one has quite clarified what constitutes a short or long marriage. It seems that around the four- or five-year mark is thought to be short. However, the court will view a short marriage of a young childless couple differently to that between two people in their late fifties. In the latter case, the wife may have given up secure accommodation, a career or maintenance from a former spouse when she married.

New relationships

If you leave your spouse to live with someone else, then although the effect could be emotionally devastating for your former partner, financially it's very positive.

When one spouse moves in with a new partner it solves the need to find two sets of accommodation. In addition you may well be sharing living expenses with your new cohabitee. However, if by moving in with another partner you take on new liabilities, then the court will take this into consideration when calculating the level of maintenance to be paid or the need for resources.

A new partner cannot be required to contribute towards maintaining their cohabitee's previous spouse and family. Although the court will not necessarily require in-depth details about their earnings and other resources, a new partner may be required to tell the court to what extent they provide for themselves and/or their cohabitee, the ex-spouse.

Pension rights

A factor which the court has to consider is whether one spouse, usually the wife, will lose any rights she would otherwise have been entitled to under an occupational pension scheme. A man who would have benefited under his wife's pension will be treated in the same way as a woman in a similar situation.

Although an ex-wife cannot normally claim any share of a widow's pension, she might be able to claim a dependant's benefit or perhaps part of the scheme's lump sum benefit if appropriate. The court can try to ensure that the wife is compensated for the loss of her pension entitlement, perhaps by increasing her share in the matrimonial home or providing a greater lump sum payment.

In practice, the court is usually concerned with pension rights only where the marriage has been fairly long.

THE MATRIMONIAL HOME

The court's objective is to ensure that both spouses and, more particularly, any dependent children have a roof over their heads after the divorce; and that maintaining that home is financially possible. They also want to ensure that both parties are justly recompensed for their contribution – financial and otherwise – towards acquiring and building the former family home. This is by no means an easy task.

- There may not be sufficient capital from the matrimonial home to enable both parties to acquire a place of their own.
- A spouse remaining in the family home might not have enough income to meet the mortgage repayments or other running costs.
- The court may have no option but to order a somewhat unsatisfactory short-term measure to ensure that the children are provided for.

As a result, divisions in property and hard cash may sometimes appear on the face of it to be unfairly weighted in favour of one spouse. It's always important to consider all the facts of the case together to get a more balanced view.

If you or your spouse own your home

In a short marriage where there are no children, the court will tend to concentrate on the financial contributions made by each spouse and the person who put the most in will usually get the most out. The purely financial input becomes less relevant the longer the marriage has lasted.

The court has a number of options when deciding what to do

with the matrimonial home. It can:

- Sell the property immediately and divide the proceeds between the spouses: the court will be reluctant to do this where the proceeds from the sale will mean that neither party can afford to buy a property and both will have to resort to rented accommodation. The court may also give a larger portion of the proceeds to the spouse who will not be able to get a mortgage to help finance their new home.
- Allocate the house to one spouse and order them to pay the other one a lump sum: this will only really be possible where there is sufficient additional cash or assets to allow the spouse without the house to acquire their own property. Alternatively, the spouse who remains in the matrimonial home may be able to raise an additional mortgage.
- Allocate the house to one spouse and compensate the other: for example, the other spouse may not have to pay any maintenance.
- Postpone the sale of the property for a specified amount of time: delayed sales are usually ordered where there are children involved so that they have a secure home. Once the specified period has elapsed, the property will be sold and the proceeds divided as above.
- Allocate the house to one spouse but give the other spouse the right to part of the proceeds of the sale of the house when it is eventually sold: this might entail a provision that the house is sold if the spouse remaining in it remarries or cohabits.
- One spouse buys the other out: the spouse remaining in the house gives their departing partner a lump sum representing their share in the property. Given the fluctuations in the property market, it's probably worth paying up in the allotted time. If you delay, you may find yourself having to pay out more than originally agreed, simply because the cost of your ex buying a new home has increased.
  If there is likely to be a delay in producing the cash, it may be worth expressing the lump sum payment as a percentage of the

equity of the house rather than as a fixed amount of money.

Mortgages

Mortgages cannot simply be transferred from one spouse to another. The court has no power to order the transfer of a mortgage, only the transfer of the property subject to the mortgage. The mortgage lender will have to agree and unless and until it does so, the person with whom the mortgage was originally agreed will remain liable to pay it.

The mortgage lender must be served with notice of an application to the court for the transfer of ownership. The lender will be concerned to ensure that the new owner can meet the repayments. They have the right to refuse. If necessary you may have to pay off the mortgage and find a new lender.

In some cases where the wife is taking on the mortgage, the lender will ask the former husband to guarantee the repayments. In practice, the wife is likely to get into arrears only if her ex-spouse defaults on the maintenance payments. If you're asked to guarantee payments, check with your solicitor about obtaining an indemnity.

If you have an endowment mortgage (see page 30) you should also make sure that you apply to transfer the beneficial interest in the insurance policy. If you don't, you might find that the spouse who takes on the mortgage may have nothing at the end of the day with which to pay off the mortgage – except the proceeds of the sale of the home. You'll also need to work out what happens to any bonuses that accrue over and above that needed to repay the loan.

If you live in rented accommodation see pages 69–71.

MONEY TO LIVE ON

For information about the kinds of order a court can make see page 172. Also look back over the guiding principles on page 192.

The legal process

Even if you have conducted your own undefended divorce, you would be well advised to consult a solicitor before embarking on a claim for financial relief or a property adjustment order. The details given here are for your general information so that you can familiarise yourself with the procedure. If you've spent time calculating your resources and thinking about your future needs (see page 176) then this needn't be a complete nightmare.

Applications for long-term financial provision or property adjustment orders can be made as soon as divorce proceedings start. However, the court cannot consider finalising the long-term arrangements until after the Decree Nisi is granted. Applications can be made by both husband and wife whether as petitioner or respondent.

1. Beginning your claim

The petitioner needs to complete a form known as a *Notice of intention to proceed with application for ancillary relief made in petition.* The respondent applies by *Notice of application for ancillary relief.* Both forms are free from Divorce Court Offices.

- You will need to complete three copies of the form and return two to the court. Keep one for yourself.
- Play safe and list all the claims you may want to make. You don't need to list specific amounts of money. These will be decided later on, either in negotiations with your spouse and your solicitors or by the court.
- Along with the completed forms you will have to supply an affidavit in support of your application (see below) together with the current court fee.
- It's worth pointing out to your spouse that completing these regulation forms is a run-of-the-mill step in the divorce proceedings. It shouldn't be misconstrued as a means of sabotaging otherwise amicable negotiations between the two of you. The affidavit is in fact an excellent way of setting out your financial situation.

198

2. Completing the affidavit

You can get standard blank forms for affidavits from the Divorce Court Office or from law stationers. Although you don't have to use them, they provide a useful guide to the kind of information you need to supply.

- You must make sure that all the information you give is complete and accurate. Remember, the affidavit is made on oath and false statements constitute perjury.
- Affidavits should be written in the first person and you should avoid hearsay. This means you don't write: *I understand from my husband's cleaning lady that he earns £3,000 a week and his aunt told me that he has six priceless diamonds stashed away in the bank.*

   You must only include information given to you directly: *My husband told me he earns £3,000 a week. In addition he showed me six diamonds of considerable worth which he keeps in the Careful Bank, The High Street, Bullionsville.*
- The affidavit should include details about: your income and your capital; your weekly or monthly outgoings; your assets such as a car, shares and pension policies, any mortgage and insurance policies; information about previous properties owned during the marriage.
- You can also include details about your spouse's financial position. You might want to give details of anything which might 'slip their mind' such as valuable personal belongings or job perks.
- You will also need to attach to the affidavit certain evidence. It's usual to send along three or more of your last pay slips or copies of your most recent sets of accounts if you're self-employed. Each bit of evidence is known as an *exhibit*. They should be numbered to match the order in which they are referred to in your affidavit.

In his affidavit Jerry Collins, a freelance management consultant, gave details of his income over the last two years. He also produced copies of

199

his business accounts. In his affidavit he wrote, 'I produce an exhibit marked JC1 being copies of my business accounts for the last two years.' He then marked the copies of his accounts 'JC1'. He then went on to produce other evidence, the next one being his bank statement; he labelled this 'JC2' and so on.

 - If you are already receiving maintenance on an order from the Magistrates Court (see page 189), you should also attach a copy of the order.

3. *Serving the application*
Once you've completed the application forms and the affidavit, take them along to the court.

 - You will need three copies of the sworn affidavit. The original is lodged with the court, one copy is for you to send to your spouse and one copy is for you to keep.
 - When you hand in your application forms, the court office will *seal* (officially stamp) them and hand one back to you. You then have to send this stamped form, together with a copy of the affidavit, to your spouse within four days.
 - If your spouse fails to show up in court, it will be up to you to prove that you actually sent the documents. For this reason you should send the stamped application and the affidavit by recorded delivery or get a certificate of posting from the Post Office.
 - The application form requires the other spouse to file an affidavit of their means within fourteen days of receiving the Notice of Application.

4. *Unwilling spouses*
If your spouse fails to file an affidavit in response to the application and you think they're not going to get on and do it, don't hang around, ask the court for assistance.

- The court can order your spouse to file an affidavit within a set period.
- You ask to have the order endorsed with a *penal notice* and serve a copy of the order on your spouse yourself, or get your solicitor to do it for you. Your former partner will be then in contempt of court if they fail to comply. The ultimate penalty would be prison.

5. *Responding to your spouse's application*

Once you have a copy of your spouse's affidavit, you should go through it carefully to see whether they have omitted any large assets or other financial resources.

- If you believe there are any discrepancies or you want to respond to the points raised you can file a third affidavit. If you think that some of the allegations are false then you can file another, further affidavit.
- It is quite usual as the case progresses to request, or receive requests for, further information. This is usually done in the form of a questionnaire sent to each party's solicitor.

6. *Preliminary or Directions hearing*

The purpose of this first appointment with the District Judge is so that they can ensure that all the relevant information will be prepared and ready for the full hearing.

- The District Judge can give orders for further information, for documents relevant to one or both applications or, for example, they can request that your home is valued.
- If you want your spouse to be physically present at the full hearing in order to be cross-examined, ask the District Judge to make the necessary order.
- The preliminary hearing may be the appropriate time to ask for Maintenance Pending Suit (see page 190) but the practice will vary from court to court.
- Some courts automatically issue standard directions. You may

want to apply for a preliminary hearing yourself, perhaps to ask for an interim maintenance order. The court clerk will advise you what to do.

7. An informal offer

Once both affidavits have been filed, it's worth sending your spouse an offer to settle.

- You can either head this offer *without prejudice*. This means that its contents cannot be used as evidence in court.
- Or you can head the letter *without prejudice save as to costs;* this is also known as a *Calderbank letter*. If the offer is rejected and the case goes ahead, the judge will be made aware of the terms of the offer, after they make their decision. If the original offer turns out to be more than the amount awarded by the judge, then the person who refused will often be ordered to pay the other spouse's legal costs.

    The idea is that a reasonable offer should persuade the other party to accept the terms, rather than run the risk of incurring extra costs by continuing to a full court hearing. Either way, if you continue the case your legal costs will mount up. Litigation is expensive.

8. The hearing

A hearing will be held only if the parties continue to dispute how they divide up their property after the divorce. This is not something you should attempt without professional legal advice.

- The time you will have to wait for a hearing will depend on how busy the court is but it's likely to be more than three months.
- The case will be held in chambers, that is, in a private room and the hearing will not be open to the public.
- Each spouse will have the opportunity to state their case either personally or through a solicitor. You may be called on to give

oral evidence and you may find yourself cross-examined by the other party.
- If witnesses are called then they will only be allowed in the room to give evidence.

9. *The District Judge's decision*
The District Judge may give the judgement at the hearing. Or if the case is particularly complex they may wait until a later date.

- If the District Judge dismisses a claim for periodical payments (see page 173), then that is final except if you choose to appeal (see below).
- If you cannot be awarded a lump sum immediately because there are insufficient resources available but there's a chance that your spouse might realise a considerable amount of capital in the near future, an application for a lump sum can be put on one side, with the option of applying for it at a later date.
- Always ensure that your legal adviser makes a note of the proceedings and the reasoning behind the District Judge's decision in case there is an appeal.

10. *Costs*
As soon as the District Judge has made the decision you can ask for costs. The District Judge will want to know why you think you should be awarded costs, how much has been incurred and whether there was an informal offer to settle (see above).

- If you are awarded costs on a *standard* basis then you will only get a proportion of the total amount of your legal costs.
- *Indemnity* or total costs will only be awarded in exceptional cases where one party has been obviously vexatious and caused an unnecessary increase in legal fees.
- After the hearing a copy of the order or orders will be sent to you. You should check through them carefully.

11. An appeal

If you think you might want to appeal against the District Judge's decision, discuss the matter over with your solicitor.

- If you decide to go ahead, you will need to file a notice of appeal within five working days.
- If the case proceeds it will go first to the local circuit judge, then to the Court of Appeal and ultimately, although very rarely, to the House of Lords.

12. Registering an order

You can apply for a maintenance order to be registered in your local Magistrates Court. The aim of this is to make enforcement much easier.

- You will have to complete a standard form and pay a small fee. The form is then lodged in the Divorce Court.
- The order is sent to the Magistrates Court and all payments have to be made through the court. The advantage is that the court keeps a record of whether or not the maintenance is being paid.
- If payments are not being made, they can then take action to ensure they are. These might include an *attachment of earnings order* (see below), or seizure and sale of the defaulter's goods or committal to prison for a short period.

ENFORCING COURT ORDERS

The court's decision on your financial affairs may not be the end of the road. All the court orders in the world won't be much use if you can't see the colour of your former spouse's money.

Enforcing lump sum or property adjustment orders

There are two ways to enforce an unpaid lump sum:

1. You can either start bankruptcy proceedings, which may prove fruitless.

2. Or the court can order the defaulter to sell property such as a house or shares in order to raise the money to pay the lump sum. This is usually done at the time the order is first made.

If your ex-spouse fails to comply with an adjustment order, then the court can carry out the relevant conveyancing procedure itself. It would be sensible to get the help of a solicitor if either of these situations arises.

Enforcing maintenance orders
Getting a court order for maintenance is one thing. Ensuring that your ex-spouse pays it regularly may be quite another. If you find yourself short on payments, then it's important to act quickly before the arrears pile up. It's likely the court will not be willing to enforce arrears more than a year old. The court has a number of ways to make reluctant ex-spouses pay up. However, none of them is absolutely foolproof.

Unless the order for maintenance was registered in the Magistrates Court (see above), your application for enforcement has to be made in the Divorce County Court in which the order was made.

Ways of enforcing a court order
There are three main methods of enforcement through the Divorce Court.

1. A warrant of execution
This is an order of the County Court for the bailiff to seize sufficient of the defaulting payer's goods which when sold will raise enough money to pay off the arrears. The only problem is that second-hand household goods rarely raise very much money at auction. However, the threat of seizure is usually enough to get the defaulter to pay up.

To get a warrant issued, you will need to swear an affidavit confirming the amount of the arrears. You will also need to complete the relevant court forms and provide a copy of the original order. There is a fee which is based on a small amount of pence per £

outstanding with a minimum and a maximum fee. However, this is not returnable if there are no saleable goods.

2. *An attachment of earnings order*

The defaulter's employer deducts regular weekly or monthly amounts from their pay packet and sends it on to the courts which then pay the employee's former spouse. This method can be very effective if the defaulter is in regular employment. It's of no use where the defaulter is unemployed, doesn't have a regular job or is self-employed.

The application is made in much the same way as for a warrant of execution (see above), but you will also be asked for the name of your former spouse's employers, if you know who they are.

Any order the court makes must not reduce the defaulter's net income below the *protected earnings rate*. This is calculated according to what an individual – and their dependants – would be entitled to under the state benefit, Income Support, plus allowances for mortgage payments or rent and other essential and long-term payments.

3. *A judgement summons for committal to prison*

If you can show that the defaulter has the means to pay maintenance but has refused to do so, then the court can issue a judgement summons. This is a potentially effective way of making a defaulter who cannot have an attachment of earnings order pay up.

Although, in theory, the defaulter can be sent to prison for nonpayment, in practice the threat is usually enough to get them to settle their debts. Since the remedy is so extreme, your application must be completed correctly and you would be well advised to get a solicitor to do it for you.

The disappearing spouse

If your ex-spouse disappears without a trace – and with them your maintenance payments – you may be able to get the DSS to disclose their current address to the court. The DSS may well have this information through your former partner's national insurance record. The court will supply you with the correct form and you should try and give as much information as you can when you complete it.

VARYING COURT ORDERS

Circumstances change, for better or worse, and therefore it is possible to alter the terms of some orders. These include separation agreements. Even if you both decide when you draw up the agreement not to refer it to court, any statement in the agreement preventing one spouse from seeking the court's assistance will be invalid. There are, however, certain types of order that cannot be changed.

Orders that cannot be altered

Neither a lump sum order nor a property adjustment order can be varied. You also cannot go back to the court to obtain another order, or ask for one later if you didn't ask for it in the original application. The same applies to maintenance orders. If an application for maintenance was initially dismissed, you cannot revive it later.

However, if a lump sum is being paid in instalments, you can request that the terms of the payments are varied so that, for example, a greater part of the lump sum is paid earlier. You cannot, though, change the total amount of the lump sum originally awarded. You also cannot vary an order which was expressed as final. A separation agreement put in these terms is likely to be upheld.

Varying an order

The reasons for wanting to vary an order might include:

- a change in financial circumstances of either party, for example, retirement;
- the remarriage or cohabitation of the receiver, in which case the payments might end;

- the remarriage or cohabitation of the payer;
- the disability of death or either spouse;
- changes in the circumstances of the children.

To vary an order you will need to apply to the court in which the original order was made. If this is now inconvenient you can ask for the case to be transferred. You have to complete a standard form and will only need to add an affidavit if your spouse is slow in responding to your application. There is no fee payable if the variation is uncontested.

Remarriage and cohabitation

If you remarry, maintenance payments cease immediately and cannot be revived even if you are later widowed or divorced again. You are not formally obliged to inform your ex-spouse of your new marriage. However, when they find out, they can ask you to repay any money they've given you since you got remarried. If you fail to pay up, they can sue you for the debt.

If you discover that your ex has got remarried just months after the Decree Absolute, having secured thousands of pounds of your money in a lump sum payment, there is usually nothing you can do. In very rare cases, an application to have the order set aside on the grounds of your ex-spouse's failure to disclose their intention to remarry, or on the grounds of fraud, may succeed. Even if you are still paying off the sum in instalments, you will have to continue doing so despite the fact your former spouse is married to a new partner.

If either spouse starts living with someone else there may be grounds to vary an order. However, if you are the payer and you cohabit, your responsibilities to your former spouse and children will take priority over any obligations you may have in your new relationship.

Varying a Magistrates Court order

An order made in the Magistrates Court for maintenance before a divorce will only end if it is superseded by an order in the Divorce

County Court. The magistrate's order can be varied in the same way as Divorce Court orders. The only difference is that, as far as lump sum payments are concerned, although they tend to be made for much smaller amounts – a maximum of £500 – there seems to be no limit to how often you can apply for them.

If you have registered a Divorce Court order in the Magistrates Court you will have to apply to the latter to have the order varied. You must ensure that the magistrates have in front of them up-to-date information about each spouse's financial circumstances. This is because the magistrates will not have before them the details and calculations upon which the Divorce Court District Judge based their decision.

Death

If the recipient dies, the payer immediately stops making any maintenance payments. However, any outstanding instalments of a lump sum become due to the deceased's estate.

If the payer dies, then unless the order was for secured payments (see page 173), maintenance payments will end. The surviving ex-spouse may then apply to the court for financial provision out of the deceased's estate. You should do this as quickly as possible. The only exception would be where the court expressly excluded such a claim in the original order.

Although after a divorce you are unlikely to benefit from a company pension scheme, if your former spouse dies you may apply to the trustees of the scheme for a share of the money. It will be up to the discretion of the trustees to grant your request.

TAX NOTES

A husband can claim the *married couples allowance* only so long as he lives with his wife. You cannot claim the allowance once you separate. However, you continue to be eligible for the allowance for the remainder of the tax year in which you separate.

Maintenance payments

The tax rules for maintenance payments changed in 1988. This book refers only to the new rules. The old rules may apply to you if you began to make or receive maintenance payments before 1988. In this case you should ask your local tax office for their leaflet that explains the old rules.

1. Tax relief only applies to maintenance payments made under a legally binding agreement such as a court order or a separation agreement which has been properly drawn up. Informal or verbal arrangements will probably not be acceptable.
2. To qualify for tax relief, four conditions have to be satisfied:

   - There must be a court order or legally binding agreement (see above).
   - The payments must be to a divorced or separated spouse. Payments to a former cohabitee are not eligible.
   - The spouse receiving the payments must not have remarried.
   - The payments must be for the maintenance of the divorced or separated spouse.

3. The payer will be eligible for tax relief, even if you remarry.
4. However, if the spouse receiving maintenance remarries, then the payer will no longer qualify for tax relief on the payments you make.
5. If you receive maintenance payments then you will not be liable for tax on them, even if you remarry.

Capital gains tax

1. As no CGT is chargeable on your principal home, you won't be liable for CGT if you split up and sell the property.
2. However, problems can arise if one of you buys the other out, or you give your share of the home to your partner as part of the financial settlement. The person moving out of the marital home may find themselves paying CGT if they move into their new home before the old one is sold or transferred.

   If you're disposing of your share of the property, you won't normally have to pay CGT, providing that you don't designate another home as your principal private residence for CGT purposes and the marital property is sold within a couple of years.

If you have children see page 267 for the relevant tax notes.

CHAPTER 18
Domestic Violence

Almost all domestic violence is committed by men against women. Recognising this fact, this chapter has been written from a woman's point of view. However, if you are a man and find yourself confronting similar violent behaviour by a female partner, you should also take immediate action and follow the advice given here.

Domestic violence is insidious. It mostly takes place behind closed doors away from the public gaze. To the outsider there is a semblance of happy family life. For the victim – a terrifying and lonely existence.

Alcohol accounts for a great deal of violence in the home. The model worker, conscientious and diligent at his desk, may become a violent thug at home after a late-night drinking session. The next day he apologises and returns quietly to his office. Only the mental and physical bruising to his family leave any tell-tale signs.

Women often remain silent despite years of abuse. Anxious about their, and their children's, safety, worried that no one will believe them, frightened of the consequences of speaking out, or believing they are the only ones in this situation: for all these reasons, women keep quiet. Many also believe their partner's repeated promises that each violent bout 'will be the last'.

If you find yourself in this situation you are not alone. There are people who can offer you support. The legal system isn't foolproof, but it can give you some protection. You must act quickly to protect yourself and your children.

PROTECT YOURSELF

If you find yourself trapped in your home with a violent partner or your partner threatens to become violent – call the police.

Attitudes amongst the police towards domestic violence are changing. Many police officers now accept the importance of intervening in what were previously often dismissed as 'internal domestic rows'. At the very least they will wait until peace is restored. They may offer to take you to a refuge (see below) but they can only remove the children if they think their safety is being threatened.

Put the evidence on record

If your partner hurts you or your children in any way, even if you think it's just a bruise, go and see your doctor or the casualty department of your local hospital. Make sure you are thoroughly examined and your injuries noted on medical records. These provide invaluable back-up for any future claims you might make about your partner's violence and can be produced in the court as evidence. If you have any witnesses – family, friends, neighbours or colleagues – ask them if they would be willing to make a statement on your behalf.

LEAVING YOUR HOME

The important thing is to get away from your violent partner, even if it is only for a short time, while you sort things out.

Staying with family or close friends may provide an immediate answer for a safe haven. It's always worth asking for their help. Although it might not prove a long-term solution, people are often willing to help in an emergency. It's quite likely, though, that your partner will know where to come and look for you, so you may need a more secure and secret, temporary home (see below).

Don't worry that your partner will be able to evict you or claim that you have left the home for good – he can't. However, if you live in rented accommodation never give up your tenancy. If you do, you may find that the council regards you as 'intentionally homeless' and will not be obliged to rehouse you, should you ask it to (see below).

Women's refuges

There are now a couple of hundred refuges throughout the country. The addresses are usually kept secret. Your local police station, CAB or the National Women's Aid Federation will be able to put you in touch with your nearest refuge. If you prefer, Women's Aid may be able to fit you into a refuge some distance from your home.

The refuges, which are usually run by the local council or by independent groups of women, offer temporary accommodation to women and their children who have suffered violence. Refuges vary greatly. Most are underfunded and are rarely luxurious; you may have to put up with a mattress on the floor if they are really crowded. Refuges tend to be busy places with little privacy and you may find them difficult to adapt to after an ordinary family home.

The refuge will give you the chance to get advice on where to find a good solicitor, how to claim benefits and how to apply to the council for housing. The professional workers will be able to guide you through the legal and bureaucratic maze. Most importantly refuges offer the chance to talk to other women who have been through a similar experience. Your local refuge can also be a valuable source of advice and support even if you decide not to stay there.

The council

If you have to leave your home because of violence or the threat of violence, and you don't want to return at a later date, you can apply to your council as a *homeless person*. In order to get temporary accommodation you will also have to prove you are in *priority need*.

Although the treatment you receive could vary greatly from council to council, under the *Housing Act 1985 Part III* they all have a duty to help women who have suffered or are under the threat of violence from the person they share their home with. In addition there is a Code of Guidance which tells the council how they should interpret the Act (see below).

You do not have to apply to your local council. All councils have a duty to look at every application. Wherever you choose to go, you should get in contact with the *homeless persons unit* or the *emergency housing office*. All councils have a twenty-four-hour emergency service. Your local police station will tell you how to contact it.

The council does not have to provide permanent accommodation for people who have made themselves *intentionally homeless*. This means anyone who has either done something, or failed to do something, which resulted in them becoming homeless. The Code of Guidance states: *A battered woman who has fled the home should never be regarded as having become homeless intentionally because it clearly would not be reasonable for her to remain.*

The council must accept that you are in priority need if:

- you have children under sixteen, or under nineteen in full-time education;
- you are pregnant;
- you are over sixty;
- you are 'vulnerable'. This can include registered disabled, mentally ill or handicapped people or those approaching retirement age and in poor health.

If any of these apply to you, you should take along evidence when you apply to the council.

If the council accepts you are homeless and in priority need it has a duty to find you somewhere to go immediately. In addition, if it has *reason to believe you may be homeless* it also has to provide a temporary place for you to stay until it finishes its inquiries. These might include council hostels, bed and breakfast hotels and short-life housing schemes. The accommodation it offers you is unlikely to be particularly attractive.

One of the most useful provisions of the Act is that councils have to give you their decision in writing. If you don't like that decision, you can challenge it. Ask for a *Section 64 Notice* and get your local CAB or advice centre to help you complete it.

NOTE: Non-British citizens who came to Britain to marry their husband or who have special conditions attached to their stay, for example that they should not have recourse to public funds (state benefits), should get expert advice before they approach the council. The Joint Council for the Welfare of Immigrants will be able to help you. Your application for housing may affect your right to stay in this country.

USING THE LAW TO PROTECT YOU: INJUNCTIONS

An injunction is a court order designed to stop your partner from threatening or attacking you or your children. There are two kinds of injunction:

- a *non-molestation order* which is to stop him abusing you;
- an *ouster order* which bars your partner from all or part of your home.

Although you can apply for an injunction yourself by going direct to the County Court, you are probably better off seeking the advice of a solicitor. If you are in conflict with your partner then their financial position is disregarded by the legal aid board. So if you have no money or very little of your own, ask whether you qualify for aid.

You can obtain an injunction at any time of the day, including after normal working hours and at weekends. If you haven't already got a solicitor, ask your local police station to put you in touch with the Duty Judge or magistrate. Do be persistent, you are quite within your rights to ask for their number.

Non-molestation orders
Molestation covers a fairly wide range of behaviour including harassment and mental cruelty as well as actual physical violence. You don't have to prove that violence has taken place to obtain an order. The court simply has to be satisfied that looking at the details of the case – your circumstances, your partner's past actions – it is reasonable to grant you an injunction.

The injunction can include orders to your partner:

- Not to molest, assault or harass you or your children. This means anything that disturbs your normal routine such as physical attacks, threats of violence and verbal abuse.
- Not to allow his friends, relatives or any other person to molest, assault or harass you or your children and to restrain them from doing so.
- Not to damage, destroy or remove any of your property from the home.

The court can also make arrangements for the children if there have been particular problems.

Ouster orders

On the whole courts are very reluctant to grant ouster orders since they make the man homeless. Where the man is the sole tenant or owner of the home, the order is likely to have a limited life, usually about three months. This can be extended if necessary and you should ask your solicitor to do so in good time.

In addition to the orders made in the non-molestation order above, an ouster order can also tell your partner:

- To leave the home and not return.
- To keep a certain distance from your home and your workplace, or other places that you visit regularly, perhaps your family's home.
- To let you return to your home. This is usually combined with an order for him to leave.

Since an ouster order is so serious, the court will consider the following points when deciding whether to grant one:

- The nature of your partner's past conduct, including, of course, if he has physically attacked you or your children.
- Your circumstances at home. Whether the accommodation is

adequate for you and your family and where your partner would live if he was ordered to leave.
- How your partner's behaviour is affecting your children. If your children are particularly threatened or upset by your partner, you are more likely to get an ouster order.

If the injunction is sought in the Magistrates Court (see below), the court has more limited powers in what it can order your partner to do. For example it can only make an ouster order where there has been actual physical violence and it cannot forbid your partner to come within a certain distance of your home.

Powers of arrest

If your partner has physically assaulted you and caused you actual bodily harm and there is the likelihood of him being violent in the future, you can ask the court to attach *powers of arrest* to the injunction. This means that if your partner breaks the injunction, the police can arrest him without a warrant.

If you do get a power of arrest – and again some judges may be reluctant to grant one, so be persistent about asking for it – take a copy of the court order to your local police station. If you make them aware of the situation in advance, it may save explanation and time later on should an emergency arise.

A power of arrest means only that the police can arrest your partner, it does not guarantee that they will.

GETTING AN INJUNCTION

Your circumstances – whether or not you are married, have started divorce proceedings or actually live with your partner – will dictate where your solicitors will apply for an injunction. The law provides rather a confusing set of legal options depending on your situation.

If you are married you can get an injunction in the Magistrates Court under the Domestic Proceedings and Magistrates Court Act 1978 where it's also known as a *personal protection order*. Or you can obtain it in the County Court under the Domestic Violence and

Matrimonial Proceedings Act 1976 regardless of whether you are married or not.

If you are already divorced and your ex-husband is threatening you, you can take action against him in the County Court for assault and/or for trespass.

Once you get to court – and this tends to be done in a matter of days, if not the same day (see below) – your case will be heard in private. You will have had to make an affidavit, a sworn statement, about your situation, giving details of your partner's behaviour and stating why you want an injunction. If you do not want your husband to know your current address, you should ask the court to keep it secret.

You may be asked to give additional oral evidence. Once the magistrate or judge has weighed up the case they will decide whether or not to grant an injunction, which type of injunction and what specific orders it should contain.

Getting an injunction in a hurry

You can get an injunction within a matter of hours and you can go to court *without telling your partner*. This is known as an *ex parte order*. If you are successful, the court will serve the injunction together with the other court proceedings on your partner. They will also fix a return date, usually within a week, for your partner to come and put his side of the case. You are likely to be called to the witness box to provide additional evidence, particularly if your partner defends the case. The judge or magistrate has to be satisfied that the injunction is justified.

If the court decides that an injunction is inappropriate they may request that your partner gives an *undertaking* – a promise to the court – not to molest or harass you. Although this means your partner avoids having a court order made against him, breaking the terms of the undertaking can invoke just as severe a penalty as breaking the terms of a court order.

Making the injunction work

Injunctions are only pieces of paper – they are not infallible. If your partner threatens or abuses you again, or in any way breaches the orders spelt out in the injunction, call the police. He may find himself arrested, charged with assault and fined or imprisoned.

You should also contact your solicitor as soon as you notify the police. If you were granted only a non-molestation order, this may be the opportunity to ask for an ouster order.

Whatever you do, if you have an ouster order don't be persuaded to let your partner back into your home. As soon as you do that, you invalidate the injunction. If the situation deteriorates again, and, unfortunately, it most often does, you may find the court very unwilling to grant a second order.

RAPE WITHIN MARRIAGE

In a historic judgment in the Autumn of 1991, the House of Lords confirmed that a man could be guilty of raping his wife; this overturned more than three centuries of legal opinion. Up to this time, the law on rape in marriage was based on the views of Chief Justice Hale, who died in 1676 and who wrote, 'in marriage (the wife) hath given up her body to her husband' and therefore he could not be guilty of raping her.

If your husband has forcibly had sexual intercourse with you against your will, he may now be prosecuted for rape. You should seek the advice of a lawyer.

CHAPTER 19

When a Partner Dies

Part Two: Everyday Legal and Financial Basics looked at the legal and financial formalities when someone dies. In particular: making a will, the Intestacy Rules and the Inheritance Act. To refresh your mind about the essentials look back over pages 72–77.

This chapter tells you:

- how you can provide for your family by making a will;
- what happens to your home and property if your partner dies;
- what happens if your partner dies without making any, or sufficient, provision for you.

On the whole, the law makes a distinction between married and unmarried status when it deals with matters relating to death. In order to address these differences the position of cohabitees and married couples are dealt with under separate headings.

For information relating to children after a parent's death see pages 246–248.

WHEN YOUR COHABITEE DIES

This book has already highlighted how, with little automatic protection from the law, cohabitees are in a very vulnerable position. This is especially true if one partner dies. If you can take time off from your job, domestic responsibilities and your amorous inclinations to consider only two things – then think about your home and your will! If you don't make a will then there is absolutely no guarantee that your partner will be provided for after your death. What's more, you may find that your lifelong companion is not only ousted financially but also physically and emotionally from the rituals of

221

your funeral and the administration of your estate.

Another Cautionary Tale

Jack and Sylvia had lived together for thirty-five years. Jack had been married before he met Sylvia but he had separated from his wife, Pam. Neither Jack not Pam had ever initiated divorce proceedings so, legally, Jack remained married to Pam.

As time went on, Jack and Sylvia recognised that other people assumed they were married. Jack was too embarrassed to follow through the divorce and so reveal the truth that he and Sylvia were simply living together.

Jack became ill and Sylvia started to worry about the future because she knew the house was in Jack's sole name and that he hadn't made a will. All the same, she didn't want to bother him with it while he was so sick. Not long afterwards Jack died.

Since Jack was an only child and his parents had both been dead for years, his whole estate went to his estranged wife, Pam. Not only that, but Pam made all the funeral arrangements, with little regard to Sylvia's feelings.

As the sole beneficiary of Jack's estate, Pam was also appointed to administer it. This meant that she was responsible for going through all Jack's belongings and private papers. Obviously, over the years Jack and Sylvia had accumulated many things such as furniture, pictures and books and many of their savings they had built up together. Consequently, in going through her husband's affairs, Pam intruded on Sylvia's. Eventually, Sylvia was forced to go to her solicitor to battle to protect her interests.

Why make a will?

There are a number of sound reasons:

- You can ensure that your partner has a roof over their head when you die. If you are going to bequeath your home, or a share in your home, to someone else, then you can set a time limit on when your home can be sold, so that your partner is not thrown out on to the street before you're even in your coffin.

- You can ensure that your partner has money to live on. You can also bequeath to your partner the contents of your home, so that other beneficiaries don't leave your partner living in an empty shell.
- You can specify which of the items in your home, if any, belong to you alone, so that your partner is not left to argue about what is theirs and what was brought jointly. You may have already done this in a cohabitation contract.
- You can give an outright gift of a valuable possession such as a car directly to your partner. If you bought the car under an HP agreement, make sure you specify who will pay off the outstanding debt.
- You can specify how you want to be buried and who should be responsible for making the funeral arrangements.
- You can appoint your partner as the executor of your will, thereby staving off any possible interference from an un-accepting family or a revengeful spouse.
- You can also make provision for any children of the relationship (see Part Five: Parents and Children).

Somewhere to live after your partner dies

One of your primary considerations, should you or your partner die, will be whether the surviving partner has a secure, permanent home. Your security will depend on whether you have a legal stake in your home, the provisions made in the deceased partner's will and any potential claim by other members of the deceased's family.

Home owners

Even if you legally own your home, you may not have absolute security to remain in it when your partner dies.

You both owned your home

If you were joint tenants, then your partner's half will pass automati-cally to you whether or not they made a will. If you were tenants in common, then your partner's share of the property will pass to whoever is the beneficiary under their will, or according to the Intestacy Rules where there is no will. If their share passes to you under the will, then you will own the whole property. Although you might inherit or acquire your partner's share of your home, your right to retain that share might still be challenged by a family member or dependant of your partner.

Your partner's share passes to someone else
If your partner's share passes to someone else, then it is likely that the beneficiary will want to realise their interest in the property. This means that you will have to buy them out or that the property will have to be sold. If you need to sell, then how quickly this will have to be done will depend on whether your partner specified any time delay in their will, or how accommodating the beneficiary is. Ultimately the court can decide what is a reasonable time within which to sell the property.

Even if your partner's share of your home passes to someone else and it's necessary to sell the property, then providing you were financially dependent on your partner, you may be able to make a claim under the Inheritance Act to go on living in the house (see page 227).

You are the sole owner
Your legal position will not be affected unless one of three things occurred:

- You previously made a deed entitling your partner to a share of the property: if this happened, you were either joint tenants or tenants in common in which case see above.
- Your partner provided part of the purchase price of the property or made substantial improvements to it: if you are the main beneficiary of your partner's will, then this shouldn't be a problem. However, if others benefit from your partner's estate, then they may argue that your partner, and therefore they, are entitled to a share in your home. If the case goes to

court and the judge decides in their favour, then you may have to sell the property.

- If the property originally belonged to your partner but they gave it to you as a gift within six years of their death: the court may disregard your ownership of the home if someone makes a claim against your partner's estate under the Inheritance Act. This is to stop people from disinheriting their estranged spouse by disposing of their fortune on their death bed.

  The court may also set aside the gift if your partner's estate is not sufficient to pay off their debts. This is particularly true if the gift was made as a means of your partner avoiding their debts.

Your partner was the sole owner

Your partner may have made a will leaving the property to you outright. If not, then it will go to the beneficiaries of their will or, where there isn't a will, to the people entitled under the Intestacy Rules.

However, if your partner doesn't leave their home to you, then you may still be able to make a claim. The position is the reverse of the situation where you are the sole owner. In other words, you may be able to prove an interest in the property if:

- your partner made a deed acknowledging that you have a share;
- you can prove that you made a financial contribution to the purchase or improvement of the property and that it was your joint intention that you should acquire a share;
- you make a successful claim under the Inheritance Act.

Other considerations

If the property was bought with the help of a mortgage which is still valid, then whether or not you need to keep up the repayments after your partner's death will depend on a number of factors.

You will not need to continue the payments if:

- You had a joint mortgage with a linked life policy which paid out on your partner's death. Or your partner had some other type of insurance policy that paid on their death, in which case you should seek advice from whoever is dealing with your partner's estate.

- The same points apply if the mortgage was solely in your partner's name. If the mortgage was not covered by an insurance policy then the payments become a debt of the estate and whoever inherits your partner's home will have to pay them, unless stated otherwise.

You *will* need to pay if:

- The mortgage repayments are not covered by an insurance policy and you are responsible or inherit the property, or you continue to be the sole owner.

You should also notify your insurers of any changes to the ownership of the property.

Rented Homes
This applies equally to spouses and cohabitees.

If you were married or living together as man and wife, then the tenancy will continue in your name if you are the sole or joint tenant. The position is more complicated if the tenancy was in your partner's name alone.

- Your exact rights to take over the tenancy will depend on what type of tenancy agreement it is. If you have a protected, secured or assured tenancy, then it will probably transfer automatically to you.
- However, immediately before your partner died, you must have been occupying the property and it must have been your only, or your main, home.
- The automatic transfer might not apply if, amongst other things, your partner acquired the tenancy under a court order,

for example as part of a divorce settlement, or on the death of someone else.

- If you have a protected or assured tenancy, other members of your partner's family may also be entitled to succeed to the tenancy. In practice this is only likely to happen if your relationship is complicated in some way. For example, if you cohabited with someone who was still married or if there is conflict between the surviving spouse and the adult children who live at home.
- If there is a dispute about a protected or assured tenancy and you cannot reach any agreement, then the County Court will decide for you.
- If there is a dispute about a secured tenancy, then your landlord will decide for you.

Savings and other assets

Any accounts or investments in your partner's sole name will form part of their estate. However, if they're in your joint names and do not pass to you outright, there may be problems. Unless it is very obvious who made the contributions and how you intended the money to be divided, you may find the accounts frozen until this can be determined.

The same applies to household items. It can be incredibly difficult to establish what belonged to which partner after someone dies, particularly where items were bought together or given as gifts. Again, this is a potential disaster area that can be avoided by being spelt out in a will.

When your partner doesn't provide for you

The Inheritance Act enables dependants who have been cut out of an estate, either because they were not provided for under a will or because they are not blood relatives who can inherit under the Intestacy Rules, to make a claim on that estate. You can also make a claim if you think that the provision made for you is insufficient.

But a word of caution. Making a claim can be time-consuming, drawn out and expensive. The rules about who can apply and how they can apply are stringent. Do not be misled into thinking that just because you have lived with your partner for thirty years you are entitled to make a claim or that even if you are successful, you will get a substantial sum.

Are you eligible to make an application?
The Inheritance Act lists who can make an application (see page 76); the final category of eligible applicants is intended to include cohabitees. The wording of the Act is critical in determining whether or not you are eligible to apply. It says: *any person . . . who immediately before the death of the deceased was being maintained, either wholly or partly, by the deceased.* What does this mean?

Immediately before the death: this does not literally mean that you have to have been living together up until the moment of death. If your partner died in hospital or in care, then your claim won't automatically be disallowed. You need to show that it was your basic intention to remain together for the rest of your lives.

Being maintained: this isn't as straightforward as it sounds. Essentially, so long as you were not splitting all your living costs fifty-fifty or you were providing domestic and other care beyond traditional 'housewife' duties your application will probably be acceptable. What the court will be trying to weigh up is whether the maintenance your partner provided for you in terms of a roof over your head and the money to pay the bills and provide sustenance outweighed any contribution, financial or otherwise, that you provided.

The irony is that the more deserving the case, for example where someone provides total nursing care for their partner in return for board and lodging, the less likely that their application will be allowed.

In addition you also have to prove that your deceased partner assumed responsibility for your maintenance. If your partner simply suggested that you live together as a matter of convenience but did nothing to suggest that they took responsibility for your welfare, then the court might disallow the application.

NOTE: You do not have to prove that your partner intended to make provision for you after their death.

How much will you get?
For a start you will only be able to make a claim for *reasonable* financial provision, that is, enough to pay your bills and maintain your existing lifestyle. Although awards are made only for maintenance, this could take the form of a property transfer or settlement, or a lump sum. However, you might not get anything at all even if your application is acceptable.

The court has to balance a number of factors when deciding an award. It will look at the extent and basis upon which your partner assumed responsibility for you and the length of time they maintained you. In addition the court will also examine the needs of other beneficiaries and the deceased's obligations towards them.

Finally, there is only so much money in the pot – there simply may not be enough to go round and someone else might just take priority.

If you are in dispute with your partner's spouse, you should read the notes on pages 231–232. As a cohabitee your position is, once again, far more vulnerable.

WHEN YOUR SPOUSE DIES

The situation is much more straightforward for married couples and less of the minefield faced by cohabitees. However, if you are in the process of getting divorced, you should beware: your estranged partner may benefit under your will if you die before the final divorce decree. For all the reasons outlined in the introductory section of the book, you would be wise to make a will, particularly if you have children.

There are a couple of points you ought to bear in mind if you're married or ever have been.

– Any will you make before you marry is revoked on your

marriage. If you remarry, then any previous will is no longer valid.
- You cannot disinherit a spouse under your will. Spouses have an automatic claim to be maintained by their partner's estate. A spouse whose deceased partner fails to provide for them sufficiently or at all will have a claim under the Inheritance Act.

Your home

If you and your spouse owned your own home, or your home was in your spouse's name, then you should have no problems in remaining in your home regardless of whether or not your partner made a will.

If for some reason your spouse left the home to somebody else you could challenge this under the Inheritance Act. Attempts to oust you from your home under the Inheritance Act are unlikely to be successful. If you find yourself challenged, seek the advice of a solicitor immediately. The same applies if you are challenged by your partner's creditors.

If you are left the house you may have a problem if you have a mortgage which is not paid off through a linked life or other insurance policy. If you cannot afford to pay the mortgage yourself, you may have no other option but to sell up. This also might be true if you can no longer afford to run your home once you're on your own.

Rented homes
See page 226.

Savings and other assets

The amount of money you inherit will depend on the terms of the will or, where there is no will, the Intestacy Rules. If you think your spouse has made insufficient provision for you – and over-compensated other people – then you can challenge their will under the Inheritance Act. The same applies if you think the Intestacy Rules have dealt unfairly with you.

Make sure that you claim any pensions or money from life insurance policies to which you might be entitled.

DIVORCED OR DIVORCING SPOUSES

If you marry, make a will and then the marriage is subsequently dissolved, then any bequests to your spouse or instructions that they act as your executor will be treated as if they never existed.

If your spouse dies without making a will then you are entitled to inherit all or part of their estate under the Intestacy Rules. This applies even if you are divorcing and have been granted a Decree Nisi but are awaiting a Divorce Decree Absolute. For this reason you should review your will early on in the divorce procedure and if you don't have a will – draft one!

If you are quite happy for your former spouse to inherit your estate on the terms of your original will, regardless of the divorce, then you should make this plain, otherwise your wishes will be disregarded when the final divorce comes through.

LEGAL SPOUSES, EX-SPOUSES AND THE INHERITANCE ACT

Spouses are in a stronger position than cohabitees in making an application under the Inheritance Act. However, not all spouses will have their application allowed.

Former spouses

If you are divorced from your partner and have subsequently re-married, then you are not entitled to apply for a share in your ex-spouse's estate.

If you are divorced and have not remarried, then your application may be disallowed if you have been properly provided for by the divorce settlement. You can't get two bites at the cherry. Applications by former spouses are rarely successful and, like cohabitees, the award is limited to maintenance.

A claim might be eligible if, for example, you divorced a long time ago with your spouse continuing to maintain you and on their death you discover they have amassed substantial capital. However, the fact that they got richer after you left is not enough reason for a claim.

Legal spouses

This means the person who was legally married to the person at the time they died. Although the court will look at all the circumstances of the case when deciding what award to make to a spouse, the amount of the award is not limited to maintenance. The court is instructed to consider what would have been appropriate in a divorce settlement, had there been one. A judicially separated spouse can apply under this heading but their claim is limited to maintenance.

TAX NOTES

1. When someone dies they are treated as if they have given away all their property. Therefore their estate attracts inheritance tax. IHT is a particularly sticky area of tax law. If you are in any doubt about what you should do either planning in advance for your own demise, or as the Personal Representative administering someone else's estate, ask your solicitor for advice.
2. Death will also affect the tax position of the surviving spouse.
3. If the wife dies, the husband can continue to claim the married couples allowance for the rest of the tax year in which she dies.
4. If the husband dies, then his widow can claim:

   - any of her late husband's married couples allowance for the tax year in which he dies, which cannot be set against his income;
   - the *widow's bereavement allowance* for the tax year of her husband's death and the following tax year, unless she remarries.

If you have children, then there are other allowances that you may be entitled to: see page 267.

PART FIVE:
Parents and Children

CHAPTER 20

The Law and Children

This part of the book looks at the rights and responsibilities of parents and their children. Unlike the preceding parts, Getting Together and Breaking Up, the following chapters do not deal with the position of cohabitees and married couples under separate headings. Much of the information is relevant to all parents, whatever your marital status. However, much of this section deals with issues that arise when the traditional concept of the family is challenged in some way, for example where the parents are unmarried, or separate, or a parent dies.

If you're unmarried, or you're about to remarry or enter a relationship where your partner already has children, you should read all the chapters in Part Five.

If you are an unmarried father, you should be aware that you do not have any automatic rights to the care and upbringing of your child.

THE LEGAL POSITION AND THE COURTS

The law relating to children has undergone something of a radical spring-clean recently. In the autumn of 1991 The Children Act 1989 came into force. Its aim was to provide a clear, consistent and comprehensible code of law which did away with the previous conflicting legislation which had been amassed over the decades.

New Act changes familiar terms

The new Act changed some familiar terms. *Parental rights and duties* are now referred to as *parental responsibility*. The old *access orders* become *contact orders* and *residence orders* replace orders for *legal custody* and *custodianship*. This book uses the new terms.

Since the Act is so new, it is only possible to present the bare bones of the legislation. It will be some years before cases coming before the courts give a clearer indication of how the Act will be interpreted.

Disputes

In dealing with disputes over children, the court's primary consideration remains the same: the welfare of the child above everything else. The Act directs the courts to have particular regard to the wishes of the child – even very young children – their emotional, physical and educational needs, any potential or actual harm they may or do suffer and the capabilities of a parent or other person to meet their needs.

The court is also directed only to make an order if it considers that to do so would be better than not making any order at all.

LEGITIMATE OR NOT?

To a great extent the social stigma associated with illegitimacy has gone. With increasing numbers of children brought up by lone parents, the question about whether their parents were or were not married when they were born becomes irrelevant and the distinction between legitimate and illegitimate begins to blur.

However, the law does distinguish between the two. It is noticeable, though, that the new Children Act now refers to the marital status of the parents rather than the birth status of the child in an attempt to avoid labelling children.

As far as the law is concerned, children are legitimate if they are conceived or born while their parents are married. Children are legitimate if:

- Their parents were married at the time of their conception but divorce before they are born.

Sharon Lewis was born in September. In August her parents were granted their Divorce Decree Absolute. Since her parents were married at the time she was conceived, Sharon is legitimate. Only her mother automatically has parental responsibility.

- Their parents were cohabiting at the time of conception but marry before they are born.

Barry Mayhew's parents were cohabiting when he was conceived. However, three months before he was born, they got married and so Barry is legitimate. Both parents have parental responsibility.

- Even though children are born out of wedlock they can still achieve legitimate status later on (see below).
- The law presumes that any child of a married woman is the child of that woman and her husband – until proved otherwise.
- Children who are born during a marriage which is subsequently annulled (see page 157) are legitimate.
- If a marriage is void, for example, because it is bigamous (see page 108), then the children of the 'marriage' are legitimate providing that at least one of the parents believed the marriage to be valid at the time of the marriage or of conception.
- A child who was born illegitimate and is then adopted will be regarded as the legitimate child of its adoptive parents.

LEGITIMATION

Although children are born illegitimate they may, at a later date, be made legitimate. This is known as *legitimation*. There are three ways to legitimate a child:

1. The parents subsequently marry: this applies even if you were married to someone else at the time child was born. You should re-register the child's birth as though it had been born legitimate. The father will need to attend the registration to confirm his paternity, unless he was originally registered as the father or ordered to make maintenance payments to the mother.

2. The child is adopted jointly by the mother and her husband (who is not the father of the child).
3. The child is adopted by the mother alone: this is only possible if the father is dead or missing, or there is some good reason to exclude him from the child's future.

A legitimated child has almost exactly the same rights as if it had been born legitimate. However, the complex rules on inheritance and property rights do make some differences. For example, where the right to inherit depends on the relative seniority of the children, the legitimated child ranks as if it had been born on the date of legitimation. You cannot legitimate a child simply by putting their father's name on the birth certificate.

PROVING PATERNITY

It is possible to prove by DNA testing whether a man is the father of a particular child. Tests can be done privately or by order of the court.

- DNA testing is very expensive but it is usually covered by legal aid. However, even if you're not eligible for legal aid, you may recover your costs if you win the case.
- The Home Office keeps information about companies which the courts use to do DNA testing and who will also carry out private tests. Your doctor may also have the details.
- A court cannot order someone to undergo a test, although if they refuse to do so, the court is likely to presume the man is the father. The court will also be very wary about making a child take a test, if it thought it was not in its best interests.
- Traditional blood testing is used less and less since it can only prove absolutely that the man was not the father of the child.

CHAPTER 21

After the Birth of a Baby: The Formalities

REGISTERING THE BIRTH

Every child born in this country must be registered within six weeks of its birth. To do this you will need to go to the registry in the sub-district where the baby was born. The hospital or local town hall will tell you where to go. Alternatively addresses of the sub-district offices can be found in a telephone directory under 'Registration of Births, Deaths and Marriages'. Check the opening hours before you go along.

Some hospitals have an arrangement with the local Registrar where they come in on certain days to register new births.

If you move away from the district in which the baby was born before you're able to register the birth, you don't need to go back there to do it. Simply go along to any Registrar. You will need to complete a declaration which will then be sent back to the appropriate sub-district office.

Married parents

Normally the mother or father register the birth. If neither is able to do this, then a *qualified informant* can register it instead. This might be someone who was present at the birth, or the occupier of the house or other place where the birth took place.

Certain details must be entered into the register. These include: the date and place of birth; the names and sex of the child; the name and surname of the mother at the time of birth, as well as her maiden name and, if different, the name in which she married the father. The Registrar will also want to know the name, birthplace and occupation of the father. The mother can also enter her occupation.

Unmarried parents
The unmarried father is under no obligation to register the birth of his child and has no independent right to have his name entered on the register.

The mother cannot enter the name of the father unless:

- They both agree and both sign the register.
- The mother or father can produce two sworn statements: one from her stating that he is the father of her child and one from him acknowledging that he is the father.
- Either the mother or father requests his name to be entered and produces a copy of a relevant court order, such as an order stating the father has acquired parental responsibility.

If the last option is taken up and the child is over sixteen, then the written consent of the child to registration is also needed.

BIRTH CERTIFICATES

There is no fee for registering the birth. You will receive a free shortened version of the entry in the register: the birth certificate. The certificate does not disclose the names of the parents – and therefore the legitimacy of the child. A full copy of the entry in the register and further short certificates can be bought from the District Registrar or obtained at a later date, from the General Register Office.

Re-registration of the birth
Parents who marry after their child is born and decide to *legitimate* it (see page 237) can re-register the birth, so long as they do it within three months of their marriage. Ask the Registrar of the sub-district in which the child was born for the appropriate form. You will have to produce the original birth certificate as well as a copy

of your marriage certificate. One parent will then have to go to that Registrar, or if you've moved, your local Registrar, and make the necessary declaration. A new birth certificate is then issued.

THE CHILD'S NAME

It is customary for a legitimate child or the child of unmarried parents to take the surname of the father. However, there is no requirement to do this.

Most parents will have chosen the child's name by the time they register the birth. You must still register the child, even if you haven't finally decided what to call it. Names can be entered, or changed, within twelve months of the registration.

Once a year has elapsed there is no way you can change the entry on the birth certificate unless you can prove that the child was called by the new name during the original twelve-month period. Forms of proof might include a baptism certificate, medical registration card, savings account and so on.

You cannot unilaterally decide to change your child's name without the consent of your spouse. In exceptional cases the court will order that the other parent's consent is not necessary.

In most cases it will not be possible to change a child's name even after a divorce unless the child is adopted by the parent and their new partner.

CHAPTER 22
Parental Responsibility

Since children cannot look after themselves, the law places this responsibility on their parents or other designated adult. However, the law also assumes that parents will relinquish some of their decision-making powers as their children develop into mature and capable adults.

PARENTAL DUTIES

Although there is no legislation listing the rights and duties of a parent, current law and practice suggests what is expected and what is acceptable. Parents have enormous control over their children: what they eat, how they dress, who they play with, where they learn. However, if parents fail to adhere to a reasonable standard of care, then the law will step in.

- Anyone caring for a child, whether or not they are the parent, is expected to maintain that child. If they don't do so adequately then that child may be removed from their care. Although in this context *parental responsibilities* refers to the powers parents have to bring up their children, the law expects other carers such as step-parents or unmarried fathers without responsibility to adhere to the same responsibilities and duties.
- The law does not lay down any guidelines about discipline but any parent who acts unreasonably and inflicts excessive punishment on a child may be prosecuted.
- Children under sixteen cannot normally undertake medical treatment without their parent's consent. However, recent cases suggest that the courts are willing to restrict parental control.

In one well-publicised case, there was a dispute between a mother and her local health authority over the supply of contraceptives to a child under sixteen. The court ruled that providing the girl understood the doctor's advice, she couldn't be made to inform her parents. Since she was likely to continue having unprotected intercourse, it was in her best interests to be prescribed contraceptives even though her parents did not give their consent.

In other cases where, for example, parents have refused to consent to medical treatments for their children because of religious beliefs, the court has overruled them.

- Parents can choose whether to bring their children up in a particular religion but, in the same way, the court may intervene if those beliefs harm the child.
- Parents have the right to decide how their children are educated. However, once again that right is limited by the fact that education is compulsory in this country.

WHOSE RESPONSIBILITY?

If the parents of the child were married to each other at the time of the child's birth, or the child is subsequently legitimated (see page 237), then they both have parental responsibility. Where the parents are unmarried, parental responsibility for the child rests solely with the mother. The father does not have any automatic rights to assume parental responsibility.

Other people can acquire parental responsibility, for example, by getting a residence order (see page 259) or through guardianship (see page 245) or adoption (see pages 249–253). It's also possible for parental responsibility to be delegated to someone else such as a nanny or a school. However, many, but not all, of these forms of parental responsibility are only temporary.

As a parent, you can never give up your parental responsibilities, even if other people acquire them as well. Parental responsibility will only be lost if the child is adopted. If a child is taken into care, parents will still retain their parental responsibilities, albeit in a somewhat restricted form.

THE UNMARRIED FATHER AND PARENTAL RESPONSIBILITY

Although as an unmarried father you have no automatic right to parental responsibility, you can acquire responsibility equal to that of the mother. There are two immediate ways of doing this, regardless of whether or not you are living with the mother.

- Providing you both agree, you can make a *parental responsibility agreement*. This should be drawn up in the proper form with the advice of your solicitor.
- You can apply directly to the court. This is only likely to happen if the mother resists your attempt to acquire parental responsibility through a mutual agreement.

The court is unlikely to make an order if it becomes clear that the application was prompted by an existing dispute about raising the child. The court is also likely to be reluctant if the mother strongly opposes the application, unless there are exceptional circumstances. Neither of these measures takes away from the mother her parental responsibility.

While both parents, or the father alone, can apply to the court for an order for parental responsibility, once it's been granted it can't simply be terminated without going back to the court.

An unmarried father's parental responsibility, unlike that of a married father, can be ended by the child or another person who has parental responsibility applying to the court. The responsibility will end in any case once the child reaches eighteen or is adopted.

Unmarried fathers can also acquire parental responsibility if the mother makes the father her child's guardian after her death (see pages 245 and 246). Fathers can also apply to adopt their child after the mother's death.

CHAPTER 23
When a Parent Dies

It's vital that anyone with children looks to the future and makes a will. Because it's a painful subject, many parents avoid the issue of who will bring up their children if they die. It may be something you've discussed informally. But, like many other family-related matters, you should commit your wishes to paper. This ought to be in a signed and witnessed statement, a deed or a will.

APPOINTING GUARDIANS

In your will you can appoint what is known as a *testamentary guardian*. This is the person, or people, who you wish to look after and bring up your children until they reach eighteen. Guardians are rarely called upon to take up their duties. And in most cases where they are, this is done very informally. You are not required to go through any court procedure. The only time you might have any recourse to the courts is if someone challenges the position of the guardian or if there is some disagreement about the way the child should be brought up.

If neither parent appoints a guardian, then it is up to the courts to appoint one instead. If there is no one willing to act, then the children must be taken into local authority care.

Anyone with parental responsibility can appoint a guardian. That is: the mother, the married father or the unmarried father providing he has acquired parental responsibility (see page 244). In addition adoptive parents and people already acting as guardians can appoint guardians of their own.

Although guardians acquire parental responsibility, they do not get absolute responsibility. Guardianship can be challenged in the courts and if thought appropriate, parental responsibility and the care of the child may be withdrawn and the guardian replaced.

In some cases the child might not live with the guardian because they are already living with someone who has a residence order. In these circumstances the appointed guardian cooperates with that person in the upbringing of the child.

It's always best to check that a guardian is willing to be appointed. However, should the guardian be required to take up their duties, they can refuse to act, but they must decide quickly. Once you become a guardian, you cannot relinquish your duties.

If you change your mind about who you want to act as a guardian, then you must record your decision in writing or destroy your original statement.

Each parent does not have to appoint the same guardians, although it's probably better if you do. Should the parents, having appointed different guardians, then both die, the guardians would bring the child up jointly. Any disputes would be settled by the court.

WHAT HAPPENS WHEN PARENTS DIE

Married parents die

1. *The mother or father dies*: the survivor looks after the children and the guardian appointed by the deceased parent is irrelevant.*
2. *The surviving parent dies*: both guardians act jointly or the court appoints a guardian.

Unmarried parents die

1. *The mother dies*: the unmarried father looks after the child providing:

   – he has acquired parental responsibility;*
   – he has been appointed guardian in the mother's will.

   If he has not acquired parental responsibility, the unmarried father can apply to become the child's guardian or adopt the child.
2. *The father dies*: the mother continues to look after the child.*

3. *The father with parental responsibility and a residence order dies:* his appointed guardian looks after the child.
4. *The father dies and has no parental responsibility*: his appointed guardian is irrelevant.

Separated or divorced parents die
1. *The parent with a residence order dies*: their appointed guardian looks after the child.
2. *The parent who does not have a residence order for their child dies*: their appointed guardian is ignored and the surviving parent continues to look after the child.*

*In these cases the right of the parent to look after the child cannot be challenged in court.

As you can see, the issue of guardians is not so simple. If you are worried about appointing guardians for your children, or you want to challenge an existing guardianship, you should take specialist legal advice.

PROVIDING FOR YOUR CHILDREN IN YOUR WILL

If you have children from a number of relationships, then you might want to make different provisions for each of them. This may be particularly true if there's a great variation in their ages. If you make a will leaving all, or part of your estate simply to your 'children', then your estate will be divided up equally amongst them regardless. If you want to differentiate, then you must name each child and list their entitlement separately.

Fred Thompson and Lorraine Bull had two young children aged five and seven. Fred had been married previously and had three sons who were now grown up with children of their own.

Fred had always said that he would make sure that the two youngest were provided for and that since his older children could manage for themselves, there would be more to go round for Lorraine's kids.

When Fred died suddenly, Lorraine discovered that he hadn't specified which of his children would inherit his estate and consequently the property was divided equally between all five.

If you have young children from a second or third relationship and you want to make provision for them, then make sure you name them in your will. You can always change the terms of the will later on if you find yourself still alive and kicking while they've grown up to become self-made millionaires!

If you have step-children or children who have been legitimated, then once again ensure that you refer to them by name.

Stephie Morris had three sons. Anthony, an adopted son who was twenty-five, and Josh, twenty-three, and Nigel, nineteen, both of whom were her natural sons. In her will she left her house to her 'eldest son'.

Stephie had intended that Anthony should inherit the house; instead it went to Josh. Why?

Inheritance depends on seniority. Adopted children, like legitimated children, depend for their seniority ranking on the date they were adopted or legitimated and not the day they were born. Anthony was officially adopted after Josh was born. Since Stephie made no reference to leaving her home to 'her son, Anthony', the house went to her second eldest son, Josh, who for inheritance purposes had the most senior rank.

Children and the Inheritance Act

Under the Inheritance Act, children can make a claim if they have not been provided for at all, or if they feel the provision is inadequate. The courts will not look favourably upon a claim from a self-supporting adult child.

Children, who are neither natural nor adopted children, can also make a claim if they believe that the deceased treated them as part of the family and assumed some sort of financial responsibility for them.

For information on wills, the Intestacy Rules and the Inheritance Act see pages 72–77.

CHAPTER 24

Becoming the Legal Parent: Adoption

Adoption is often perceived as the legal privilege of childless couples and orphans. In fact, adoption as a legal process has far wider uses. For step-parents and unmarried parents in certain circumstances, adoption is a means of legitimating a child and acquiring parental responsibilities.

Once an adoption order is made, the legal status and rights of the natural parent are transferred to the adopter. Unlike other non-parental relationships such as guardianship, adoption is final, irrevocable and for life. As with any other legal procedure involving children, the child's welfare is of paramount importance. The adoption process is strictly regulated. Except in certain circumstances children can only be adopted through a recognised adoption agency where both prospective adopter and adoptee undergo rigorous investigation.

There are only a few instances where a child can be adopted without the intervention of an adoption agency. These include:

- where the child is adopted by a parent or step-parent;
- where the adopter is a relative of the child;
- where the adopter is the child's unmarried father.

WHO CAN APPLY FOR ADOPTION?

There are two groups of people who might apply to adopt a child: people who are unrelated to the child and those who are directly related, usually parents.

Unrelated adopters

Traditionally only married couples, usually under thirty-five, have been considered for adoption. However, with fewer babies available to be adopted and more homes needed for older children and those with special needs, attitudes have changed.

- You have to be over twenty-one and domiciled in Britain to be able to adopt a child.
- Only one of a cohabiting couple may normally apply.
- While you are under no legal obligation to tell your adoptive child about their background, it is unlikely that an adoption agency would accept anyone who intended to keep the truth from the child.

Related adopters

There are many instances where a parent might want to adopt their child, for example in order to legitimate its birth or to enable a step-parent to become a joint legal parent.

Parent and step-parent

A parent, whether or not they were married when they had their child, may later marry or remarry and wish to adopt their child with their new spouse. In these cases, the court will be particularly concerned about whether the child has any relationship or recall of its other parent. This will usually be a father. The court will be extremely reluctant to interfere with that relationship.

The over twenty-one rule does not apply. Providing the step-parent is at least twenty-one, the natural parent of the child needs only to be over eighteen.

Mother or unmarried father

Where either the mother or the unmarried father is the sole applicant the court will not make an adoption order unless it is satisfied that the other parent cannot be found or there is some reason to exclude them from parenthood.

Following the death of the child's mother, an unmarried father can apply to the court to adopt his child. The adoption order will mean that he takes on all parental responsibilities and will also mean the child becomes legitimate.

Unmarried couples
Unmarried couples will not be able jointly to adopt their child. Adoption orders in favour of joint applicants are only possible where the applicants are married to each other, for example parent and step-parent.

THE CHILD

A child cannot be adopted until it is at least nineteen weeks old. An adoption cannot be made unless the child has lived with the prospective adopter.

In the case of foster parents, the child must be at least a year old, and have lived with them throughout the preceding twelve months.

Freeing a child for adoption
Before an adoption order can be made, the child must be freed for adoption. This means that the court has to be satisfied that the parent, or guardian, agrees that the child can be adopted and understands what that means. Adoption agencies usually apply to the court for the child to be freed for adoption before placing the child with prospective adopters.

Any agreement given by a mother before the child is six weeks old is invalid.

Where the child is legitimate and both parents are alive, then both must give their agreement.

Although an unmarried father does not have to give his agreement unless he has a residence order (see page 259), his views will be taken into account if he has been in regular contact with the child.

The court may dispense with the agreement of the parent or guardian if:

– they cannot be found;

- they are incapable of giving their consent;
- they have neglected or mistreated the child;
- the court considers they are unreasonably withholding agreement.

THE ADOPTION PROCESS

Where the adoption is not being carried out through a specialist agency the adopters must give at least three months' written notice to their local authority so that the necessary investigations can be carried out.

1. You will need to file an official application in the County Court. Adoption applications can also be made through the Magistrates Court and the High Court. Although you can file for adoption as soon as the child starts living with you, the adoption hearing cannot take place for at least thirteen weeks.
2. The court will fix a date for the hearing and notify the natural parents and the local authority. In special circumstances, for example where the adoption is contested, the court may appoint a *guardian ad litem*, an official who acts on behalf of the child.
3. Adoption hearings take place in private. The court will only make an adoption order if it feels it's in the best interests of the child. On rare occasions the court may make an *interim adoption order* which lasts for two years, after which you will need to apply again. Alternatively the court may decide to place the child in care or may refuse to make an adoption order.
4. Once the adoption order is made, a copy of it will be sent to the Registrar General. The order will contain all the details about the child, including its original name, its natural parents and its new name.

The adopted child is no different from any other child in the family. The only time it may make a difference is where entitlement to an inheritance depends on the seniority of the children involved. In this case, the child's 'date of birth' will be equal to their date of adoption.

STOPPING AN ADOPTION

Once you have freed your child for adoption, there is no going back: you have relinquished all your rights as its parent. However, there may be cases where one parent disapproves of the other's intention to put their child up for adoption. Since it is usually the mother of the child who agrees to or initiates the adoption, it will be the father who may wish to stop the process and object to the adoption going ahead.

The father of the child will need to apply to the courts for a residence order, giving him custody of the child. However, it is not enough simply to say that you don't think it's in the child's interests for it to be adopted. You will also have to prove that it would be in the child's best interests to be in the custody of the father.

CHAPTER 25

When the Court Becomes Parent: Wardship

Wardship is a very old procedure by which the High Court acquires legal custody of the child. This doesn't mean that they have day-to-day care but they do take all the major decisions about the child's welfare. Wardship is only used in very serious cases and where there is an emergency.

WHY MAKE A CHILD A WARD OF COURT?

The most usual cases are where the child has been snatched or there is a fear it might be abducted.

Sally and Abdul's relationship has been going through a very rough patch. Abdul keeps threatening to take their son back to his family in Saudi Arabia. Sally is terrified that he'll carry out his threat and she'll have little chance of seeing her son again. She applies to have her son made a ward of court.

There is a major dispute over the way a child is cared for by a parent or someone with parental responsibility.

Nicky Marlow and Graham Taylor have a baby son, Sam. Sam is ill and it has been suggested that he have a blood transfusion. Because of her religious beliefs, Nicky is refusing medical assistance. Even though he hasn't acquired parental rights, Graham files an application to have Sam made a ward of court.

A local authority can also apply to have a child made a ward of court where, for example, a parent consents to a medical procedure like sterilisation, which a social worker opposes. By making the child a ward of court, the court can then decide whether or not the operation is in the child's best interests.

Wardship can also be used to prevent the child from an undesirable association, for example where the parents disapprove of a girlfriend or boyfriend.

The procedure
The point about wardship is that it takes effect immediately. Once you have filed the application form and paid the court fee to the High Court, the child automatically becomes a ward of court. Anyone connected with the child can make an application, including the child. Initially the wardship will only remain in place for twenty-one days, so once you've filed the original application form, you will need to follow this up with a request for a hearing.

The effect of making a child a ward of court is that no decisions about the child's upbringing can be made without the court's permission. This includes: moving home; living with someone else; going abroad, even for a day trip; medical treatment, other than routine visits to a doctor or dentist; adoption or changing the child's name.

NOTE: If you want to make a child a ward of court, you should seek the advice of a solicitor, especially if there's an emergency.

THE LOCAL AUTHORITY: TAKING A CHILD INTO CARE

Local authorities have wide-reaching powers, through the courts, to take on responsibility for a child. There are three types of situations where a child might be taken into care.

– Where the parents cannot cope, or cannot be found.
– Where the child has committed some offence or got into trouble. The courts may recommend that a child be taken into

care, even against the parents' wishes.
- Where there's an emergency, for example the child has been neglected, abused or abandoned.

The law and regulations relating to care proceedings are complex. It is beyond the scope of this book to tackle them. If you need more advice on your rights regarding a child in care you should contact a specialist legal adviser or agency.

CHAPTER 26
When Parents Split Up

The vast majority of parents facing a breakdown in their relationship will inevitably put the care of their children as their number one priority.

Despite some people's perceptions, separation or divorce is not solely about the break-up of an adult relationship: the effects on children can be equally unsettling, if not devastating. It's important to keep this in mind should you be tempted to argue over the future welfare of your children. A child, even a very young one, can quickly sense upset and disagreement in the family. This is not to suggest that you should 'stay together for the sake of the children' but that you should do all you can to maintain some stability for your children throughout the separation process.

NOT IN FRONT OF THE CHILDREN

Disagreements between partners will be inevitable, whether they take the form of a quiet exchange of words or a blazing row. Try to be assertive in your negotiations (see pages 8–13) but ensure that any fights you have are in private.

- Don't make the children pawns in your negotiations. It may make you feel better but it certainly won't do a lot for them.
- Don't try to 'get the children on your side' by engendering hatred and name-calling against your former partner. If you use your children against their other parent, the court may well take a dim view of your attitude.
- Involve them in the decision-making. This may not mean that they actually sit round the table with you, especially if they're very young, but do seek their agreement to any arrangements.

- If you find yourself cast in the 'mean parent' role either because you have day-to-day care while the other parent gets to do all the 'treats', or because you're on a limited budget, try to shrug off any hurtful comments and seek the advice of a support organisation (see Part Six: Useful Addresses).
- When you come to discuss arrangements be flexible, put the children first. If you agree quite amicably that one parent should look after the child during the week and the other at weekends, bear in mind that there may be school events or invitations from school friends at the weekend. It would be a pity if the child missed out on important school and social contacts just because both adults had come to a tidy arrangement about where their child should spend its time.

THE OPTIONS

Even if you have a child under sixteen, or under eighteen in full-time education, or a child with special needs, you will not necessarily have to involve the court in deciding future care arrangements.

Cohabitees, and married parents who do not wish to divorce

You can make an arrangement between yourselves, either informally or in a document drawn up by a solicitor, stating who will care for the children, the status of the non-caring parent, and what provision, if any, will be made for maintenance. You will only resort to the court if the agreement is breached in some way and you cannot resolve the issue between yourselves.

Unmarried parents, particularly if they don't live together or share the care of the children, might draw up a similar agreement about maintenance in any event.

Married parents who are divorcing

The court will want to be satisfied about what you intend to do with your children before granting a Decree Absolute. If you can agree between yourselves about what happens, then the court may simply approve your agreement.

Whatever your marital status, if you cannot agree about what happens to your children when you separate, then the court will decide for you.

NOTE: If you have any dispute over arrangements for the care and provision for your children, you should seek the advice of a solicitor.

THE ORDERS A COURT CAN MAKE

There are three main types of orders a court can make:

- *Residence orders*: stating with whom the child shall live.
- *Contact orders*: stating the child's right to access to another named person.
- *Orders for maintenance*: the comments below are not directly relevant: see separate note on page 266.

The prevailing view seems to be that courts are reluctant to make orders in uncontested cases, since they might in fact serve to alienate one or other of the parents, and in the long run be detrimental to the welfare of the child.

Residence and contact orders can be made in favour of people other than the parents. Whichever order a court may decide to make, it can impose certain restrictions and make special conditions as it sees fit according to the circumstances of the case.

Residence orders

Residence orders replace the old notion of custody and are intended to be much more flexible. Unless the court orders otherwise, for example where a child is mentally or physically handicapped, residence, like contact, orders will end when the child reaches sixteen.

- When you are granted a residence order you automatically get parental responsibility – if you don't already have it – which lasts for as long as the residence order is in force.
- There are certain restrictions on what you can and cannot do.

Unless you are the parent or guardian of the child, you will not be able to free them for adoption, appoint a guardian, change its name or take it out of the country for more than one month.

- Unmarried fathers applying for a residence order will automatically be granted a parental responsibility order if they are successful. The order granting parental responsibility cannot be ended while the residence order is still in force.
- The granting of a residence order to one parent or to someone other than the parents will not remove parental responsibility from either of the natural parents.
- The courts can make a residence order in favour of two people, enabling the child to live with both parents. However, there may be a reluctance to do this if it results in the child constantly chopping and changing its home.
- Both residence orders and contact orders will cease to have effect if the parents live together continuously for six months or more.

Contact orders

A contact order replaces the previous concept of access. The new wording is intended to emphasise that this is about the child's right to contact with its parents and not the parents' right to access to their child. A contact order requires the person with whom the child is living to allow the child to have contact with the person named in the order. The person named in the contact order is not compelled to have contact with the child.

Other orders

You may also come across two other kinds of orders.

- A *prohibited steps order:* prevents the person who has care of the child from doing certain specified things, like taking the child out of the country. This order should not be confused with wardship (see pages 254–255).
- A *specific issue order:* as its name suggests is an order that

addresses a specific problem or dispute which might arise in connection with parental responsibility.

WHO CAN APPLY?

The law lays down who can apply for residence and contact orders. These include:

- The parent of a child, whether married or unmarried or step-parent or former step-parent.
- The child's guardian.
- Anyone with whom the child has lived for at least three years. This doesn't have to be the three years immediately preceding the application so long as it's not more than five years before.
- Anyone who applies with the consent of those who have existing parental responsibility for the child.

The court may also give other people leave to apply for an order in special circumstances.

HOW DOES THE COURT REACH A DECISION?

There are no hard and fast rules about how judges decide who cares for a child when a relationship breaks up. As always, the bottom line remains what is best for the child. Every case is different but there are certain common factors that a court will take into consideration when making a decision.

- The need for stability: the court will be keen to ensure that the child experiences as little upheaval as possible. For this reason, the parent who currently looks after the child will often be at an advantage, especially if the child appears happy and settled.
- Quality of care: neither mother or father has a greater claim than the other to care for the child. As a general rule, very young children stay with their mother. Amongst older children, girls tend to remain with their mother and boys with their

261

father. However, courts are reluctant to split siblings, so if there's a very young child, the mother might be granted a residence order for all the children.

- Where parents work, the court will want to be satisfied that the person applying for the residence order has made adequate child care arrangements. They will tend to favour those arrangements where the child will be looked after by someone they already know.
- Material comforts: although the material benefits offered by each parent will be considered, they are highly unlikely to be the deciding factor. The court is much more concerned about the day-to-day care of the child than whether they will live in an inner city or high rise or a detached villa in the suburbs. As a rider to this, if you are getting divorced, then don't forget the courts will take into account your needs as the child's carer when making a financial settlement.
- The parents' behaviour: the court is not interested in which parent, if any, caused the break up, unless it had or has a direct effect on the welfare of the child.

Barbara and Paul have three children. Two years ago, Barbara started having an affair with another man. They were very discreet about their relationship and would only meet at Barbara's house while the kids were at school. This fact alone does not make Barbara unsuitable to have the continued care of her children.

However, say that after Barbara's husband Paul had left her, she began to go out four or five nights a week leaving her children in the care of a baby-sitter. Each night she would bring home a different man and the kids would frequently wake up to find a stranger sharing their mother's bed. In this case, the court may well consider Barbara's behaviour crucial to its decision.

The court will also look at each parent's attitude towards the other. They will be particularly concerned that the parent who is granted a residence order enables the child to maintain a good relationship with their other parent.

- Welfare reports: if the court has asked for a welfare report, then its contents will carry great weight.
- The child's view: the new Act encourages the court to take the view of the child into account. However, some judges may continue to be concerned that a child has been primed by one or other of its parents to reply in a certain way.

THE PROCESS

Divorce – where parents agree
If you and your partner come to a mutual agreement about the future care of your children, then the decision about what happens to them can be made as a general part of the divorce proceedings, providing that the divorce itself is uncontested (see page 161).

When you complete the divorce petition, you should also complete a *Statement as to Arrangements for Children*. This is a standard form available from the court office which asks for details about your children and proposals for their care after the divorce. The respondent has the right to reply to the proposals in much the same way as replying to the divorce petition itself.

You will automatically be given a hearing date for a *Children's Appointment*. The hearing will always be before a judge and will be held in private. Providing there is no dispute, which there shouldn't be at this point, you do not need a solicitor. You will probably be asked for more information about the statements you have made.

In most cases the judge will give their unqualified approval to the arrangements. You will then get a copy of the official order enabling you to apply for the Decree Nisi to be made absolute (see page 167).

On the other hand the judge may not feel able to give their unqualified approval. This might be for a variety of reasons, for example:

- they need more information;
- they feel that you have not resolved some of the issues;

- they think it's necessary to sort out some particular problems, such as housing, first.

In this case the judge has a number of options:

- they may ask you to return for another appointment, to give you time to deal with any outstanding matters.
- they could refer the case to the court welfare officer to investigate and report on.
- they can put off making the decision until a particular issue is resolved. This is quite often to do with future property arrangements.

In a very limited number of cases a judge will permit you to go ahead and finalise the divorce, even though the court isn't satisfied with the arrangements for your children.

NOTE: If you run into problems and the court does not agree with your proposals or you start to disagree, you should seek legal advice immediately. This is particularly urgent if the child is living with your partner and you want it to live with you in the long run. The court is unlikely to want to disrupt an established routine.

Where parents disagree
Like all other disputes, failure to agree about the future care of your children will become entangled and expensive. Courts are likely to refer you to a conciliation service, or you may wish to take their advice independently.

Married parents
Your solicitor will advise you about making an appointment for a hearing and when this should be done.
Before the hearing you will probably each need to swear an affidavit setting out your proposals for your children's care. Since your solicitor will not be familiar with your individual family's

needs, you must volunteer all the information you think might be relevant. You'll need to tell your solicitor about any friends, relatives or other people who may be willing to act as witnesses.

The court will always ask for an independent report from the court's welfare officer. They will want to interview both you and your partner and anyone else who might be involved in looking after the child, as well as the children themselves.

The actual hearing will be before a judge and will be heard in private. It is rare that children will be called as witnesses, although the judge may request to see them alone in a private room.

Once you have the court's decision, always check with your solicitor that other matters which arise as a consequence of that decision are also sorted out. For example if a residence order is granted, you want to make sure that you and your partner agree about future contact with the child.

Unmarried and non-divorcing married parents

Similar steps to obtain residence and contact orders can be taken through the Magistrates Court, the County Court and the High Court. Again, you would be advised to seek professional legal help.

CHALLENGING THE COURT'S DECISION

The court's decision is intended to be long term but it is not irreversible. Just because you are dissatisfied with the judgement, you cannot simply return to the court a few weeks later and ask to have the case reopened. However, if for some reason you become seriously concerned about the way the child is being brought up or you feel the other parent is denying the child the right to maintain contact with you, then the court might be prepared to reconsider the existing orders. Unless both parties agree that the orders should be altered, the court may be extremely reluctant to act.

FINANCIAL PROVISION FOR CHILDREN

Both married and unmarried parents can apply to the courts for maintenance and other financial orders for their children in much the same way as married partners can apply for financial help for themselves. Information about financial provision can be found on pages 172–173. However, there are a number of points that are directly relevant to requests for provision for children.

General
- Maintenance and other orders for financial relief can be made payable to the parent or other person with a residence order or to the child directly.
- Periodical payment orders can only be made to a child under eighteen, unless there are special circumstances, and will not initially extend beyond the child's seventeenth birthday in any case.
- An order for periodical or secured payments will cease if the parent making the payment and the parent receiving the payment live together for more than six months.

Unmarried parents
- Although unmarried parents cannot claim maintenance for themselves, they can claim for their children.
- Unmarried parents can only make a claim against their partner for the children of that relationship. You cannot make a claim against your partner for a child of a former relationship.

Married parents
- Married parents are responsible for any child in their care including stepchildren and adopted children but not foster children. The court will always consider whether there is someone else, such as a previous spouse, who could be considered liable to make financial provision for a child.

TAX NOTES

1. If you have a child under sixteen or under eighteen in full-time education, you can claim the *additional personal allowance* (APA) providing one of the following applies:

   - you are a single or cohabiting parent;
   - you are separated or divorced and have responsibility for bringing up your child;
   - you are widowed and have responsibility for bringing up your child.

2. If you are cohabiting parents then you can only claim one APA between you.
3. If you are a cohabitee and split up, then providing the child still lives with you, you can continue to claim the APA. If your child lives for some of the time with you and the rest with your former partner, then you can divide the APA between you according to the amount of time the child spends with each of you. If you cannot agree how to divide the allowance then the Inland Revenue Appeal Commissioners will decide for you.
4. If a spouse dies, then the surviving spouse may be able to claim the APA if their children still live with them.

Maintenance

Please see general comments on page 209.

1. If you pay maintenance to children directly, even if they are under twenty-one, you will not get tax relief on the maintenance payments.
2. If you pay maintenance for your children to your former spouse, then you are entitled to tax relief on that payment, providing you satisfy the other general rules.
3. Payments to your former cohabitee for the benefit of your child will not attract tax relief.
4. If you receive maintenance payments then you will not be taxed on them.

Remarriage

1. If the husband is claiming the additional personal allowance (APA) for his children in the year he remarries, he must choose whether to continue with the APA or to take a proportion of the married couples allowance. You cannot take both.
2. Where the wife claimed the APA for her children immediately before her remarriage, she can continue to claim the allowance for the rest of the tax year.
3. In the tax year following the remarriage, neither husband or wife can continue to claim the APA for children. Instead the husband must claim the married couples allowance.

NOTE: THE CHILD SUPPORT ACT 1991

The Child Support Act was passed by Parliament in July 1991. The government expects to bring the Act into force in phases so that its provisions are fully operational by mid-1993. The Act will radically affect the calculation and enforcement of maintenance for children throughout the United Kingdom.

The Act, when it's put into practice, will do two things. The first is to standardise the basis on which child maintenance is calculated, and the second is to establish a Child Support Agency. The Agency will provide specialist services tracing absent parents, investigating means, assessing maintenance levels and collecting and enforcing payments.

Once the relevant provisions of the Act are in force, maintenance will be calculated by the Child Support Agency in accordance with a 'formula'. The formula takes four things into account:

- the amount needed to support the child in question
- the combined disposable incomes of the parents,
- the proportion of the combined disposable income which should go towards maintaining the child
- the minimum income the absent parent needs to maintain themself.

There is little scope for discretion in calculating the amount of child maintenance payable.

Although parents will be able to conclude maintenance agreements – and even embody them in a consent order – it will not be possible to stop a parent applying to the Child Support Agency for child maintenance to be calculated in accordance with the formula. If the Child Support Agency assesses maintenance, the amount the Agency assesses overrules any amounts previously agreed.

Once the Act is in force, maintenance for children will generally be assessed by the Child Support Agency, and not by the courts. Any parent will be able to apply to the Child Support Agency to assess the amount of maintenance an absent parent ought to pay for the benefit of his or her children. In Scotland, but not elsewhere, a child may apply for maintenance. The Agency will take primary responsibility for the collection and enforcement of child maintenance.

Where a parent with care of a child is receiving state benefits, the Department of Social Security can require the parent to apply to the Child Support Agency to assess maintenance and recover it from the absent parent. If the parent caring for the child refuses to co-operate, their state benefits may be reduced. This provision will have a significant impact on single mothers, whose state benefit will be at risk if they do not reveal to the Child Support Agency the name of the father of their child. There are exceptions to this disclosure requirement in cases where the mother or her child would be at risk.

PART SIX:

Useful Addresses

How to Use This Section

Many of the organisations listed in the following pages have already been mentioned in the book. Others have been included to provide an additional source of information and advice.

Organisations do change addresses and telephone numbers, occasionally they fold or may merge with another similar body. If you find a number unobtainable or the telephone is answered by a different organisation or business *don't give up*. Ask the new occupants if there is a forwarding address or telephone number for the organisation you're seeking or call Directory Enquiries.

If you can't trace a particular group, contact one of the other organisations listed here and see if they can supply you with a number or address.

This list is by no means complete and there are numerous other research bodies, self-help groups and campaigning organisations that might be useful to you. Use this resource section as a starting point. Even if you think one organisation might not be right, call them in any case – if they can't help you, they'll no doubt recommend someone who can.

NOTE: Those organisations marked with an asterisk (*) have additional local and regional offices which can be found by looking in your telephone directory.

GENERAL ADVICE AGENCIES

NATIONAL ASSOCIATION OF CITIZENS ADVICE
BUREAUX*
115 PENTONVILLE ROAD
LONDON
N1 9LZ
071 833 2181

SCOTTISH ASSOCIATION OF CITIZENS ADVICE
BUREAUX*
26 GEORGE SQUARE

EDINBURGH
EH8 9LD
031 667 0156/7/8

NORTHERN IRELAND ASSOCIATION OF CITIZENS
ADVICE BUREAUX*
11 UPPER CRESCENT
BELFAST
BT7 1NT
0232 231120

GENERAL INFORMATION ON SELF-HELP & VOLUNTARY ORGANISATIONS

NATIONAL COUNCIL FOR VOLUNTARY
ORGANISATIONS
26 BEDFORD SQUARE
LONDON
WC1B 3HU
071 636 4066

NATIONAL FEDERATION OF SELF-HELP
ORGANISATIONS
150 TOWNMEAD ROAD
LONDON
SW6 2RA
071 731 8440
Will put you in touch with African, Caribbean and Asian groups
around the country.

ABDUCTION

REUNITE – NATIONAL COUNCIL FOR ABDUCTED
CHILDREN
POB 158
LONDON
N4
071 404 8356
Offers support and legal advice to parents who fear their child may
be abducted, or who has been abducted.

ADOPTION AND FOSTERING

BRITISH AGENCIES FOR ADOPTION & FOSTERING
11 SOUTHWARK STREET
LONDON
SE1 1RQ
071 407 8800

NATIONAL FOSTER CARE ASSOCIATION
FRANCIS HOUSE
FRANCIS STREET
LONDON
SW1P 1DE
071 828 6266
Provides support, counselling and legal advice for prospective and
current foster parents and for children in care.

NATIONAL FOSTER CARE ASSOCIATION (SCOTLAND)
25–27 ELM BANK STREET
GLASGOW
G2 4PB
041 248 5566

STEPFAMILY (NATIONAL STEPFAMILY ASSOCIATION)
72 WILLESDEN LANE
LONDON
NW6 7TA
071 372 0844
071 372 0846 – Counselling service
Support and advice for all stepfamilies – parents, grandparents,
children and their siblings.

CHILDREN & YOUNG PEOPLE

CHILDLINE (for children in trouble or danger)
0800 1111 Free

NATIONAL SOCIETY FOR THE PREVENTION OF
CRUELTY TO CHILDREN*
67 SAFFRON HILL
LONDON
EC1N 8RS
071 242 1626
0800 800 500 (24-hour helpline)

BRITISH YOUTH COUNCIL
57 CHALTON STREET
LONDON
NW1 1HU
071 387 7559
An umbrella organisation for young people's clubs and groups throughout the country.

CONCILIATION

THE NATIONAL FAMILY CONCILIATION COUNCIL
SHAFTSBURY CENTRE
PERCY STREET
SWINDON
WILTSHIRE
SN2 2AZ
0793 514055
NFCC will put you in touch with conciliation services in your area.

FAMILIES NEED FATHERS
BM FAMILIES
LONDON
WC1N 3XX
081 886 0970 (Helpline)

MOTHERS APART FROM THEIR CHILDREN
BM PROBLEMS
LONDON
WC1N 3XX

COUNSELLING

BRITISH ASSOCIATION OF COUNSELLING
1 REGENT PLACE
RUGBY
CV21 2PJ
0788 578328

INSTITUTE OF FAMILY THERAPY
43 NEW CAVENDISH STREET
LONDON
W1M 7RG
071 035 1651

SAMARITANS*
46 MARSHALL STREET
LONDON
W1
071 734 2800
0753 532713 (Helpline)

RELATE (formerly THE MARRIAGE GUIDANCE
COUNCIL)*
HERBERT GRAY COLLEGE
LITTLE CHURCH STREET
RUGBY
CV21 3AP
0788 73241

JEWISH MARRIAGE COUNCIL
23 RAVENSHURST AVENUE
LONDON
NW4 4EE
081 203 6311
081 203 6211 (Crisis Line – 'Miyad')

CATHOLIC MARRIAGE ADVISORY COUNCIL
1 BLYTH MEWS
BROOK GREEN
LONDON
W14 0HW
071 371 1341

NATIONAL ASSOCIATION OF YOUNG PEOPLE'S
COUNSELLING AND ADVISORY SERVICES (NAYPCAS)
MAGAZINE BUSINESS CENTRE
11 NEWMARKET STREET
LEICESTER
LE1 5SS
0533 558763
They will put you in touch with a local youth counselling service.

DISABILITY

DISABILITY ALLIANCE
25 DENMARK STREET

LONDON
WC2H 8NJ
071 240 0806

See also National Council for Voluntary Organisations

DRUGS & ADDICTIONS

Illegal Drugs
STANDING CONFERENCE ON DRUG ABUSE (SCODA)
1–4 HATTON PLACE
HATTON GARDEN
LONDON
EC1N 8ND
071 430 2342
Will put you in touch with services in your area for people with
drug problems.

NARCOTICS ANONYMOUS
POB 1980
LONDON
N19 3LS
071 351 6066
071 351 6794 (Helpline)

FAMILIES ANONYMOUS
ROOM 8
650 HOLLOWAY ROAD
LONDON
N19 3NU
071 281 8889
Provides information and support for families and friends of drug
users.

Alcohol
ALCOHOLICS ANONYMOUS*
POB 1
STONEBOW HOUSE
STONEBOW
YORK
YO1 2NJ
0904 644026/7/8/9

AL ANON
61 GREAT DOVER STREET
LONDON
SE1 4YF
071 403 0888
Provides information and support for families and friends of alcoholics. Will give information on local groups.

Smoking
QUIT
102 GLOUCESTER PLACE
LONDON
W1H 3DA
071 487 2858
071 487 3000 (Smokers' Quitline)

FUNERALS & THE BEREAVED

NATIONAL ASSOCIATION OF FUNERAL DIRECTORS
618 WARWICK ROAD
SOLIHULL
WEST MIDLANDS
B91 1AA
021 711 1343

NATIONAL ASSOCIATION OF MASTER MASONS
CROWN BUILDINGS
HIGH STREET
AYLESBURY
BUCKS
HP20 1SL
0296 434750

CRUSE – BEREAVEMENT CARE
126 SHEEN ROAD
RICHMOND
SURREY
TW9 1UR
081 940 4818

See also Age Concern and Help The Aged

HOMES

HM LAND REGISTRY – LAND CHARGES DEPARTMENT
BURNGATE WAY
PLYMOUTH
PL5 3LP
0752 779831

HM LAND REGISTRY
LINCOLN'S INN FIELDS
LONDON
WC2A 3PH
071 405 3488

NATIONAL ASSOCIATION OF ESTATE AGENTS
ARBON HOUSE
21 JURY STREET
WARWICK
CV34 4EH
0926 496800

ROYAL INSTITUTE OF CHARTERED SURVEYORS
12 GREAT GEORGE STREET
LONDON
SW1P 3AD
071 222 7000

NATIONAL FEDERATION OF HOUSING ASSOCIATIONS
175 GRAYS INN ROAD
LONDON
WC1X 8UE
071 287 6571

SHELTER (NATIONAL CAMPAIGN FOR THE HOMELESS)
88 OLD STREET
LONDON
EC1V 9HU
071 253 0202

LONDON HOUSING AID CENTRE (SHAC)
189A OLD BROMPTON ROAD
LONDON
SW5 0AR
071 373 7276
071 373 7841

IMMIGRATION & REFUGEES

THE BRITISH REFUGEE COUNCIL
BONDWAY HOUSE
3–9 BONDWAY
LONDON
SW8 1S
071 582 6922

JOINT COUNCIL FOR THE WELFARE OF IMMIGRANTS
(JCWI)
115 OLD STREET
LONDON
EC1V 9JR
071 251 8706

UNITED KINGDOM IMMIGRANTS ADVISORY SERVICE
(UKIAS)
190 GREAT DOVER STREET
LONDON
SE1 4YB
071 357 6917

THE LEGAL SYSTEM

THE LAW SOCIETY (FOR ENGLAND & WALES)
133 CHANCERY LANE
LONDON
WC2 1PL
071 242 1222

THE LAW SOCIETY (FOR SCOTLAND)
26–27 DRUMSHEUGH GARDENS
EDINBURGH
EH3 7YR
031 226 7411

THE LAW SOCIETY (FOR NORTHERN IRELAND)
LAW SOCIETY HOUSE
90–106 VICTORIA STREET
BELFAST
BT1 3JZ
0232 231614

ROYAL COURTS OF JUSTICE (NORTHERN IRELAND)

CHICHESTER STREET
BELFAST
BT1 3JZ
0232 235111

SOLICITORS COMPLAINTS BUREAU
PORTLAND HOUSE
STAG PLACE
LONDON
SW1E 5BL
071 834 2288

THE BAR COUNCIL
11 SOUTH SQUARE
GRAYS INN
LONDON
WC1R 5EL
071 242 0082

DEAN OF FACULTY OF ADVOCATES (SCOTLAND)
ADVOCATES LIBRARY
PARLIAMENT HOUSE
EDINBURGH
EH1 1RF
031 226 5071

THE LEGAL AID BOARD*
NEWSPAPER HOUSE
8–16 GREAT NEW STREET
LONDON
EC4A 3BN

THE LEGAL AID BOARD (SCOTLAND)
44 DRUMSHEUGH GARDENS
EDINBURGH
EH3 7FW
031 226 7061

LEGAL AID (NORTHERN IRELAND)
THE LAW SOCIETY
BEDFORD HOUSE
16–22 BEDFORD STREET
BELFAST
BT2 7FL

CHILDREN'S LEGAL CENTRE

20 COMPTON TERRACE
LONDON
N1 2UN
071 359 6251

SOLICITORS' FAMILY LAW ASSOCIATION
POB 302
KESTON
KENT
BR2 6EZ
0689 850227

FAMILY LAW BAR ASSOCIATION
4 PAPER BUILDINGS
TEMPLE
LONDON
EC4Y 7EX
071 583 0497

RIGHTS OF WOMEN (ROW)
52–54 FEATHERSTONE STREET
LONDON
EC1Y 8RT
071 251 6577

LESBIANS & HOMOSEXUALS

GAY BEREAVEMENT PROJECT
C/O UNITARIAN ROOMS
HOOP LANE
LONDON
NW11 8BS
081 455 8894
Offers telephone counselling, information on wills, support on the death of a partner.

GAY & LESBIAN SWITCHBOARD
BM SWITCHBOARD
LONDON
WC1
071 837 7324 (24 hour help & information)

LESBIAN LINE
BM BOX 1514
LONDON

WC1
071 251 6911

GAY LEGAL ADVICE (GLAD)
071 253 2043

LESBIAN CUSTODY PROJECT
RIGHTS OF WOMEN
52–54 FEATHERSTONE STREET
LONDON
EC1Y 8RT
071 251 6576

MONEY

BANKING INFORMATION SERVICE
10 LOMBARD STREET
LONDON
EC3V 9AP
071 583 1395

THE BUILDING SOCIETIES ASSOCIATION
3 SAVILE ROW
LONDON
W1X 1AF
071 437 0655

BRITISH INSURERS & INVESTMENT BROKERS
ASSOCIATION (BIIBA)
BIIBA HOUSE
BEVIS MARKS
LONDON
EC3 7NT
071 623 9043

SECURITIES & INVESTMENT BOARD (SIB)
2–14 BUNHILL ROW
LONDON
EC1Y 8SR
071 929 3652
SIB keep a Central Register of all authorised investment businesses
and will be able to tell you whether your adviser is independent.

FINANCIAL INTERMEDIARIES, MANAGERS AND
BROKERS REGULATORY ASSOCIATION (FIMBRA)

HERSTMERE HOUSE
HERSTMERE ROAD
LONDON
EC14 4AB
071 583 8860

LIFE ASSURANCE & UNIT TRUST REGULATORY
ASSOCIATION (LAUTRO)
CENTRE POINT
103 NEW OXFORD STREET
LONDON
WC1
071 379 0444

ASSOCIATION OF BRITISH INSURERS
51 GRESHAM STREET
LONDON
EC2V 7HV
071 600 3333

OLDER PEOPLE

AGE CONCERN (ENGLAND)*
ASTRAL HOUSE
1268 LONDON ROAD
LONDON
SW16 4ER
081 679 8000

HELP THE AGED*
ST JAMES WALK
LONDON
EC1R 0BE
071 253 0253
0800 289 404 – Helpline

Carers
CARERS NATIONAL ASSOCIATION
21–23 NEW ROAD
CHATHAM
KENT
ME4 40J
0634 813981

PARENTHOOD

BRITISH PREGNANCY ADVISORY SERVICE
7 BELGRAVE ROAD
LONDON
SW1 1QB
071 222 0985

FAMILY PLANNING INFORMATION SERVICE
27–35 MORTIMER STREET
LONDON
W1N 7RJ
071 636 7866

ISSUE – THE NATIONAL FERTILITY ASSOCIATION
(formerly NATIONAL ASSOCIATION FOR THE
CHILDLESS)
318 SUMMER LANE
BIRMINGHAM
B19 3RL
021 359 4887
021 359 7359 – Fertility Helpline

NATIONAL CHILDBIRTH TRUST
ALEXANDER HOUSE
OLDHAM TERRACE
LONDON
W3 6NH
081 992 8637

CELLMARK DIAGNOSTICS
BLACKLANDS WAY
ABINGDON BUSINESS PARK
ABINGDON
OXON
OX14 1DY
0235 528609
For DNA testing to determine paternity.

Lone parents
NATIONAL COUNCIL FOR ONE PARENT FAMILIES
255 KENTISH TOWN ROAD
LONDON
NW5 2LX
071 267 1361

SCOTTISH COUNCIL FOR SINGLE PARENTS
13 GAYFIELD SQUARE
EDINBURGH
031 556 3899

GINGERBREAD ASSOCIATION FOR ONE PARENT
FAMILIES
35 WELLINGTON STREET
LONDON
WC2 7BN
071 240 0953

Childcare
NATIONAL CHILDMINDERS ASSOCIATION
8 MASONS HILL
BROMLEY
BR2 9EY
081 464 6164

REGISTRATION OF BIRTHS, DEATHS & MARRIAGES*

REGISTRAR GENERAL OF BIRTHS, DEATHS &
MARRIAGES
ST CATHERINES HOUSE
10 KINGSWAY
LONDON
WC2
071 242 0262

REGISTRAR GENERAL
OPCS ADOPTION CENTRE
SMEDLEY HYDRO
TRAFALGAR ROAD
BIRKDALE
SOUTHPORT
MERSEYSIDE
PR8 2HH
0704 69824
For information about birth certificates of adopted children.

RELIGIOUS ORGANISATIONS

COUNCIL OF CHURCHES FOR BRITAIN & IRELAND
35 LOWER MARSH
LONDON
SE1 7RL
071 620 4444

GENERAL SYNOD OF THE CHURCH OF ENGLAND
CHURCH HOUSE
LONDON
SE19 3NZ
071 222 9011

REGISTRAR OF THE COURT OF FACULTIES
FACULTY OFFICE
DEAN'S YARD
1 THE SANCTUARY
WESTMINSTER
LONDON
SW1
071 222 5381

BRITISH HUMANIST ASSOCIATION
14 LAMBS CONDUIT PASSAGE
LONDON
WC1R 4RH
071 430 0900

THE BOARD OF DEPUTIES OF BRITISH JEWS
WOBURN HOUSE
UPPER WOBURN PLACE
LONDON
WC1
071 387 3952
071 387 4044 (Central Enquiry Desk)

RELIGIOUS SOCIETY OF FRIENDS (QUAKERS)
FRIENDS HOUSE
173 EUSTON ROAD
LONDON
NW1 2BJ
071 387 3601

UNION OF MUSLIM ORGANISATIONS
109 CAMPDEN HILL ROAD

LONDON
W8 7TL
071 221 6608
071 229 0538 (Answerphone)

TAX

INLAND REVENUE*
PUBLIC ENQUIRY OFFICE
SOMERSET HOUSE
STRAND
LONDON
WC2R 1LB
071 438 6420

WOMEN IN DANGER

The following organisations will provide temporary refuge for women and their children suffering mental and physical harassment.

NATIONAL WOMEN'S AID FEDERATION
POB 391
BRISTOL
BS99 7WS
0272 633494
0272 633542 – Helpline
061 236 6540 – Helpline for women in the North

LONDON WOMEN'S AID
52 FEATHERSTONE STREET
LONDON
EC1Y 8RT
071 251 6537

SCOTTISH WOMEN'S AID
13–19 NORTH BANK STREET
EDINBURGH
EH1 2LP
031 225 8011

WELSH WOMEN'S AID
38–48 CRWYS ROAD
CARDIFF
CF2 4NN
0222 390874

RAPE CRISIS CENTRE★
LRCC POB 69
LONDON
WC1X 9NJ
071 278 3956 (24 hours)
071 837 1600

JEWISH WOMEN'S AID ORGANISATION
0532 695885

Extra Notes: For people living in Scotland and Northern Ireland

Laws in Scotland are different to those in England and Wales. Although there are also some differences in the laws in Northern Ireland many of them are very similar to those in England and Wales. This section outlines some of the *principal differences* and indicates areas of the law where there are substantial variations.

These additional notes are intended to complement the information given in the preceding pages. They are intended only as a general guide. You should always seek the help of a qualified lawyer or advice worker who is an expert in the relevant law and practice.

LEGAL AND FINANCIAL BASICS

Taking Legal Advice

Scotland
* Scotland has a separate Legal Aid Board from England and Wales, and a separate, though similar, legal aid system.

* The Scottish equivalent of the Green Form Scheme is known as the Pink Form Scheme.

* The Law Society of Scotland does not arbitrate on fees. If you are not satisfied with the fee your solicitor has charged, you may ask the Auditor of Court (an independent official) to review or tax it.

* The Law Society of Scotland handles complaints about the conduct of Scottish solicitors. There is no separate complaints bureau. If your complaint cannot be easily resolved, it will be considered by the Complaints Committee. In cases of inadequate professional service (for example, poor or shoddy work), the Society can order the solicitor to reduce or refund his fees, rectify mistakes, or pay for

another solicitor to rectify mistakes. In serious cases the Complaints Committee will refer the complaint to the Scottish Disciplinary Tribunal, which has power to strike solicitors off the Roll of Solicitors.

* The Law Society of Scotland will not deal with allegations of negligence (other than in cases of inadequate professional service – shoddy work). However, they do maintain a list of 'troubleshooters', which is similar to the negligence panel.

* In Scotland, *advocates* perform a role similar to barristers. However they do not practise from chambers and there is no Bar Council. Complaints about the professional misconduct of an advocate should be made to the Dean of the Faculty of Advocates, who is the head of the Scottish Bar.

* The Sheriff Courts are local courts – like County Courts – situated in most towns throughout Scotland. They deal with most family related matters. More complicated cases, and appeals against decisions reached in other courts, are decided by the Court of Session which is based in Edinburgh.

Northern Ireland
* Northern Ireland has a separate Legal Aid Board from England and Wales, and a separate, though similar, legal aid system.

* The Law Society of Northern Ireland handles complaints about the professional conduct of Northern Irish solicitors. There is no separate complaints bureau.

* The Law Society of Northern Ireland will not deal with allegations of negligence. If you have difficulties in finding a solicitor who is prepared to take on a case of negligence against another solicitor, the Law Society of Northern Ireland will help in finding a solicitor to advise you.

* Complaints about fees charged by a solicitor can be sent to the Law Society of Northern Ireland. Alternatively the procedure for *taxing* fees can be obtained from your local County Court office.

* Barristers in Northern Ireland do not practise from chambers. Complaints about barristers should be made to the Bar Council of Northern Ireland at the Royal Courts of Justice, Belfast.

A roof over your head

Scotland

* The Scottish law relating to property ownership is very different. The rules of *equity* are not applied in Scotland, and Scottish law does not distinguish between beneficial ownership and legal title. Although express *written trusts* can be established in Scotland, Scottish law does not recognise *implied trusts*.

* Unless your name appears on the title deeds, the law will not regard you as owning any interest in your home.

* If you want to own a share in your home, your name must either appear on the title deeds – if necessary by amending them – or you must enter into a formal written agreement with the person whose name is on the title deeds.

* Scottish law takes no account of any contribution you may make toward your home, whether in money or in kind, in determining if you have any share in the ownership. Any contributions you make will be regarded as being for your own benefit, or a gift. It may be possible for you to get your financial contributions back, although even this may prove to be very difficult.

(In divorce cases the court will make rulings about financial and property settlements – see below)

* If both your name and the name of your partner appear on the title deeds, you are both co-owners, and will be presumed to each have a 50% share of the property. If you want to own your home in different shares, you must say so in the title deeds. If you die, your share in the home will be distributed according to the terms of your will or the Rules of Intestacy.

* If you want our co-owner to automatically inherit your share of the home when you die, you must expressly say so in the title deeds. This is known as a *survivorship destination*.

* Unlike severing a joint tenancy in England and Wales, one party cannot always terminate a survivorship destination without the consent of the other.

* In Scotland title deeds have always been registered. A new system of registering title to land is gradually being introduced throughout Scotland, which will eventually replace the present system.

Rented property
* As ever, the law relating to rented property is very complicated. It is different in both Northern Ireland and in Scotland. If you have any questions or concerns about your tenancy, you must seek the advice of a local lawyer or an advice agency.

Life after life

Scotland
* A Scottish child aged 12 or over can make a will.

The intestacy rules are different in Scotland.

* What happens if you die and . . .

Your spouse and children survive you
Your spouse receives: the household contents up to a value of £12,000; the home in which they are living at your death if it is worth no more than £65,000 (if it is worth more they receive £65,000 in cash); £21,000 in cash and one-third of the remaining moveable property (that is everything except land and buildings). Your children (or their descendants) receive: everything else (money for young children is usually paid to their parents for investment until the child reaches 18).

Your spouse survives you but there are no children
Your spouse receives: the household contents up to a value of £12,000; the home in which they are living at your death if it is worth no more than £65,000 (if it is worth more they receive £65,000 in cash); £35,000 in cash and one-half of the remaining moveable property (that is everything except land and buildings). Your brothers, sisters, their descendants and your parents receive: everything else. Complex rules apply to apportion the remainder of your estate. Half-brothers and sisters can only inherit if there are no full-brothers or sisters or descendants of them.

Your spouse survives you, but there are no children, parents, sisters or descendants of any of them
Your spouse inherits your whole estate.

Your spouse dies before you
If you have children, your estate goes to them or their descendants. If you have no children, complex rules apply to apportion the

remainder of your estate between your brothers, sisters, their descendants and your parents. Half-brothers and sisters can only inherit if there are no full-brothers or sisters or descendants of them. If you do not leave any of these relatives, your estate goes to your grandparents and their descendants (uncles, aunts, cousins etc.), then to great grandparents and their descendants (great uncles, great aunts, second cousins etc.) and so on until some relative is found.

* There is no equivalent to the Inheritance Act in Scotland. However, you cannot completely exclude a spouse or children from sharing in your estate after you die, no matter what your will says.

A surviving spouse is always entitled to at least one-third of your moveable property (that is everything excluding land and buildings). This proportion increases to one-half if you leave no descendants. Similarly, your children are always entitled to at least one-third of your moveable property (one-half if you have no surviving spouse). These rights which are known as *legal rights* are automatic, and cannot be taken away in your will. Executors are required to take account of them without the need for court proceedings.

If you make provision in your will for your spouse and children, they have the choice of taking their legal rights under the intestacy rules, or taking the legacy left in the will. They must choose between them, they cannot have both.

* In Scotland a will is not automatically revoked by marriage.

* A cohabiting partner cannot usually challenge the terms of a will or inherit under the intestacy rules. Rarely, a cohabiting partner might be able to establish a marriage by cohabitation with habit and repute (see below), in which case they would be entitled to the rights of a spouse under the intestacy rules.

* The people who administer an estate on intestacy are called *executors-dative*. Before executors and executors-dative are allowed to carry out the terms of your estate, they must have their authority confirmed by the local Sheriff Court.

GETTING TOGETHER

Cohabitation

Scotland
A form of 'common law' marriage still exists in Scotland. This is known as *marriage by cohabitation with habit and repute*. This means

you must have the reputation of being a married couple – your friends and neighbours must believe that you are married – and you must both be free to marry each other. In addition you will have to have spent a substantial part of your life together in Scotland. As most co-habiting couples make no secret of their unmarried status, they can never become married by cohabitation with habit and repute. Couples who are married by cohabitation with habit and repute have the same rights and duties as any other married couple.

Your home
Without a written agreement, or without your name appearing on the title deeds, you cannot acquire any interest in your home. The rules governing co-ownership are different in Scotland (see above).

Your belongings
Generally, items that you buy are yours, no matter whether they are bought out of joint money, or even your partner's money. Only if the item was bought on behalf of your partner, can he or she claim it. If the item was bought using your partner's money, he or she can claim back from you the money that you spent.

* There is an important exception to this rule where the ownership of the item is recorded on a certificate, for example for shares or investments. Only those whose name appears on the certificate are the owners – unless there is some later written agreement amending the ownership.

Marriage

Scotland
* No parental consent is required for children under 18 to get married.

* To marry in Scotland, you must each complete a *Marriage Notice* and send it to the Registrar for the district in which the marriage is to take place. The notice must be submitted *at least* 15 days before the wedding, but in practice they should be submitted four weeks before the wedding (six weeks if either of you were previously married). If you are having a religious ceremony you should talk to the person who will perform the wedding before you complete the Marriage Notice.

* If you are having a religious marriage then one of you must go personally to the Registrar's office prior to the wedding to collect the *Marriage Schedule*. This must be given to the person performing the marriage. Immediately after the ceremony, the Marriage Schedule must be signed by the bride and groom, the person performing the marriage and by the two witnesses. It must then be returned to the Registrar, who will register the marriage.

* If you are having a civil wedding, the Registrar will not issue a Marriage Schedule, but will have it at the marriage ceremony ready for signature. You will still need to go to see the Registrar shortly before the wedding to finalise arrangements.

BREAKING UP

Cohabitees
For the main points see 'Getting Together' above.

Married couples

Scotland
There is no minimum period you have to wait before starting divorce proceedings. The grounds for divorce are much the same as in England and Wales.

* However, you cannot base your case on adultery if you have *condoned* the adultery – forgiven your spouse and lived with them for three months or more after you found out – or *connived* at the adultery, which means active encouragement such as wife swapping.

* There is only one single divorce decree which is effective immediately. There is however, a two or three week period allowed for appeal. The time depends on whether the case is heard at the Sheriff Court or the Court of Session.

* In Scottish divorces the petitioner is known as the *pursuer* and the respondent as the *defender*.

* There are two types of divorce procedure. The *simplified procedure*, usually called the D-I-Y divorce, and the *ordinary procedure*. You can use the first where, amongst other things, the divorce is uncontested: you don't have children, there are no arguments about money and you are basing the divorce on the fact that you haven't lived

together for two years (with consent) or five years (without consent).

* Standard forms are available from CABs. The form will have to be sworn before a notary public or Justice of the Peace. Most solicitors in Scotland are also notaries public.

* If you cannot get a D-I-Y divorce then you will have no option but to use the ordinary procedure. You would be well advised to get a solicitor to act for you. The procedure is similar to that in England and Wales with sworn statements by each party.

* Financial and property settlements follow much the same pattern as in England and Wales. The same comments about avoiding costly disputes in court apply.

* If you find your ex-spouse is not keeping up with maintenance payments (or *ailment*) there are a number of steps you can take to recover the arrears. These include: *earnings arrestment* whereby your ex spouse's employer deducts the arrears from their salary; *arrestment of a bank or building society account* which freezes money in your ex-spouses account enabling you to apply through the courts for the bank or building society to pay you; *poinding and sale of goods* which means the sheriff officer goes to your ex-spouse's home or business and makes a list of their goods. The court can order these goods to be auctioned to pay the arrears. The ultimate penalty is imprisonment.

* However, none of these measures – except perhaps the threat of a repeat performance – will get you your maintenance regularly. The only option you have is if your ex-spouse is in regular work is a *current maintenance arrestment* which works more or less like an attachment of earnings order.

* After your divorce you should review your will. This is because wills are not automatically revoked on divorce or cancelled by a subsequent remarriage. Although you cannot claim anything from your ex-spouse's estate if they die without a will or leave you nothing, you are entitled to anything left to you under a will.

Northern Ireland
The law in Northern Ireland in matrimonial proceedings is almost identical to that in England and Wales. There are however a number of differences.

* A divorce petition cannot be filed until two years after the marriage.

* There is no special procedure divorces. You must attend the court in person and give your evidence to the judge.

DOMESTIC VIOLENCE

Scotland

If your partner is violent you can get a court order, called an *interdict*, prohibiting them from assaulting, molesting or threatening you. As soon as you have lodged your application form with the court, you can apply for an *interim interdict* which is usually granted at once and will give you immediate protection – even if your partner hasn't been given notice.

* A *matrimonial interdict* – which despite its name is available to both spouses and cohabitees, can have powers of arrest attached to it. However to apply for this type of interdict, you must either own your home with your partner or have been granted occupancy rights in it. It's possible to apply for occupancy rights at the same time as you apply for an interdict.

* If you are the sole owner or tenant of your home, you can ask your partner to leave. If they refuse you can eject them and change the locks.

* If you own your home jointly or your partner owns the home, you can ask for an *exclusion order*. You will only be granted such an order if you can show it is necessary in order to protect you and your children from behaviour – actual or threatened – which has or may harm you mentally or physically. However, this procedure can take time even if you apply for an *interim exclusion order*.

DEATH

For the main points see 'Life After Life' above.

CHILDREN

Scotland

* In Scotland the birth of a child must be registered within 21 days.

* In general equivalent provisions exist in Scottish law to the statu-

tory provisions relating to children in England. However there are exceptions and differences. These are particularly important in relation to court procedure, wardship, and local authority care.

* Children in Scotland who are under 16, with few exceptions, cannot enter into any legally binding transactions, their parents enter into the transaction on their behalf. Once a child reaches 16, he is entitled to enter into legally binding transactions himself. However the courts have powers to set aside transactions entered into by a child aged between 16 and 18, where the transaction would cause substantial prejudice to the child. Children under 16 can themselves consent to medical treatment, if the doctor attending the child is satisfied that the child is capable of understanding the nature and consequences of the treatment.

* An unmarried father cannot acquire parental rights and responsibilities by agreement with the mother. An unmarried father can however apply to the court to be granted parental rights, to be exercised either solely or jointly with the mother.

* Children have rights to inherit on the death of their parents, see the notes to Part 1 above.

* You can enter into a written agreement with your partner or spouse to provide ailment (maintenance) for your child. Such an agreement can be registered in the Books of Council and Sessions, which enables it to be enforced without the need to go to court. The court has powers to amend such an agreement if circumstances change.

* Parents (whether or not they are married) are jointly liable to maintain their child. The court only has powers to make orders for ailment, it cannot order lump-sum payments or settlements of property. However it can require small additional payments to be made to cover once-off expenses. Orders for ailment usually last until the child reaches eighteen, though they can be extended until the child reaches 25 if he or she is still in full-time education.

Index

ABWOR, *see* Assistance By Way Of Representation
access order, *see* contact orders
Acknowledgement of Service, in divorce 164, 165, 168–9
adoption 243, 249–53
  adopters 249–51
  freeing child for 251–2
  of illegitimate child 237–8, 250
  procedure 252–1
  stopping 253
adultery, as grounds for divorce 158–9, 160, 162, 164, 165–6, 168
Affidavit to Dispense with Service, in divorce 164–5
Affidavit of Evidence, in divorce 165–6
affidavits 65
age, and marriage 110–11
anger, expressing 12–13
annual percentage rate of charge (APR) 29
annuity 38
annulment of marriage 111–12, 154, 156, 157, 237
Answer, in divorce 169
APR, *see* Annual Percentage Rate of charge
assertiveness 8–13, 257
assets, protection when marriage breaks up 182–3
Assistance By Way of Representation (ABWOR) 53
attachment of earnings order 204, 205–6

bailiff, court 164, 205
banks
  credit cards 26
  credit facilities 25–6
  as executor 73
  savings accounts 35
banns, and marriage 81, 114
Bar Council 60
barristers 48–9
  complaints against 60

behaviour, unreasonable, as grounds for divorce 158, 159, 160, 163, 166
beneficial ownership, *see* home ownership
beneficiary, under a will 73, 74–5, 224–5
benefits, state, and divorce 176
bigamy 109–10
birth
  certificate 240–1
  registering 239–41
body language
  and assertiveness 10
  and listening 5
budgeting 32, 128–9
building societies
  credit facilities 25
  savings accounts 35

CAB, *see* Citizens Advice Bureaux
Calderbank letter 202
Capital Gains Tax (CGT) 45–6,
  and cohabitees 104
  and marriage 134–5
  and divorce 210–11
car, ownership at divorce 174
CGT, *see* Capital Gains Tax
charge cards 26
children
  and death of parent 74–5, 223, 245–8
  and divorce procedure 161, 162, 173, 192, 258, 263–5
  and domestic violence 213, 217, 218
  financial provision for 256, 266
  and parental separation 257–68
  and remarriage 138
  taking into care 255–6
  wardship 254–6
  see also adoption; birth; guardianship; legitimacy; legitimation; parental responsibility; unmarried fathers; tax; wardship
Children Act 1989 235–6, 263
Children's Appointment, in divorce proceedings 263

301